TEACH YOURSELF
MACHINE PIECING & QUILTING

TEACH YOURSELF
MACHINE PIECING & QUILTING

DEBRA WAGNER

Chilton Book Company
Radnor, Pennsylvania

All quilts made with Cotton Classic batt, courtesy of Fairfield Processing

Photographs by Lee Lindeman

Designed by Anthony Jacobson
Manufactured in the United States of America

Library of Congress Cataloging in Publication Data

Wagner, Debra.
    Teach yourself machine piecing and quilting / Debra Wagner.
        p. cm. — (Contemporary quilting)
    Includes bibliographical references and index.
    ISBN 0-8019-8190-5 — ISBN 0-8019-8189-1 (pbk.)
    1. Patchwork—Patterns. 2. Machine quilting. I. Title.
  II. Series.
  TT835.W332   1992
  746.46—dc20   91-58292
                                                      CIP

1 2 3 4 5 6 7 8 9 0   1 0 9 8 7 6 5 4 3 2

OTHER BOOKS AVAILABLE FROM CHILTON
Robbie Fanning, Series Editor

Contemporary Quilting Series

Contemporary Quilting Techniques, by Pat Cairns

Fast Patch, by Anita Hallock

Fourteen Easy Baby Quilts, by Margaret Dittman

Machine-Quilted Jackets, Vests, and Coats, by Nancy Moore

The Quilter's Guide to Rotary Cutting, by Donna Poster

Scrap Quilts Using Fast Patch, by Anita Hallock

Speed-Cut Quilts, by Donna Poster

Creative Machine Arts Series

The Button Lover's Book, by Marilyn Green

Claire Shaeffer's Fabric Sewing Guide

The Complete Book of Machine Embroidery, by Robbie and Tony Fanning

Creative Nurseries Illustrated, by Debra Terry and Juli Plooster

Creative Serging Illustrated, by Pati Palmer, Gail Brown, and Sue Green

Distinctive Serger Gifts and Crafts, by Naomi Baker and Tammy Young

The Fabric Lover's Scrapbook, by Margaret Dittman

Friendship Quilts by Hand and Machine, by Carolyn Vosburg Hall

Innovative Serging, by Gail Brown and Tammy Young

Innovative Sewing, by Gail Brown and Tammy Young

Owner's Guide to Sewing Machines, Sergers, and Knitting Machines, by Gale Grigg Hazen

Petite Pizzazz, by Barb Griffin

Putting on the Glitz, by Sandra L. Hatch and Ann Boyce

Sew, Serge, Press, by Jan Saunders

Sewing and Collecting Vintage Fashions, by Eileen MacIntosh

Simply Serge Any Fabric, by Naomi Baker and Tammy Young

Twenty Easy Machine-Made Rugs, by Jackie Dodson

Know Your Sewing Machine Series, by Jackie Dodson

Know Your Bernina, second edition

Know Your Brother, with Jane Warnick

Know Your Elna, with Carol Ahles

Know Your New Home, with Judi Cull and Vicki Lyn Hastings

Know Your Pfaff, with Audrey Griese

Know Your Sewing Machine

Know Your Singer

Know Your Viking, with Jan Saunders

Know Your White, with Jan Saunders

Know Your Serger Series, by Tammy Young and Naomi Baker

Know Your baby lock

Know Your Pfaff Hobbylock

Know Your White Superlock

Teach Yourself to Sew Better Series, by Jan Saunders

A Step-by-Step Guide to Your Bernina

A Step-by-Step Guide to Your New Home

A Step-by-Step Guide to Your Sewing Machine

A Step-by-Step Guide to Your Viking

Contents

Foreword

Color photos in books or magazines, no matter the skill of the photographer and printer, are never going to do justice to well-made quilts. I had seen and admired Deb Wagner's machine-pieced and machine-quilted quilts in various publications. But when the actual quilts arrived here for photography, we all gasped. They were fantastic! The choice of color and fabric, the precision and fineness of the piecing, the proportions, and most of all, the intricate machine quilting all proclaimed "Here is a master quiltmaker."

Then as I read the manuscript, I found myself muttering "Clever!" over and over. Deb covers feed dogs with template plastic; she makes her own spray starch and heats it in the microwave; she gathers by zigzagging over dental floss; she pieces with the open-toed foot, so she can see; and on and on.

Deb's "Ohio Bride's Quilt" not only won first place in its category at the American Quilt Society's annual show, but was voted Viewers' Choice. Yet this is a woman who can say, "Everyone else's work always looks perfect, while my work is *never* perfect."

Her approach to quiltmaking is original and ingenious. And best of all, it's all in this book for you.

ROBBIE FANNING
Series editor

Are you interested in a quarterly newsletter about creative uses of the sewing machine, serger, and knitting machine? Write to The Creative Machine-s, PO Box 2634, Menlo Park, CA 94026.

TEACH YOURSELF
MACHINE PIECING & QUILTING

Introduction

Welcome to *Teach Yourself Machine Piecing and Quilting*. This workbook is designed for the quilter who is interested in expanding his or her machine skills, as well as his or her quilting skills. Machine piecing and quilting is more than transferring hand methods to the sewing machine. It is an entirely different approach to quilting. My goal is to introduce you to specific techniques designed to use the machine to best advantage. In the process I will give you the tools to realize the quilts you dream of making.

Take time to skim through the book. Note that the information is presented in three sections: basic materials and instructions (Chapters 1 and 2); quilting and block patterns (Chapters 3 and 4); and project directions (Chapters 5 to 7). Think of this book as your own personal quilting tutor. The projects are designed to allow you to combine your level of expertise and creativity with the amount of time you want to invest. The block patterns are presented in order of difficulty and the project directions are generic. Simply choose the block pattern you like and plug it into the project directions. A beginner might start with a single simple block and make a pillow. An accomplished quilter might proceed to a queen-size quilt made of complex blocks.

Avid machine quilters know what a wonderful tool our sewing machine is. The novice quilter is in for a pleasant surprise. Machine stitching makes quilting fast and accurate, without sacrificing quality or creativity. We no longer think of making a quilt in terms of months or years of labor-intensive hand stitching. With the help of our machines, heirloom quilts can be completed in a matter of weeks—*completed* being the key word.

The sewing machine, along with modern cutting and marking tools, has drastically changed quilt making, enabling busy people to carry the tradition of quilting into the 21st century.

CHAPTER 1

Getting Organized

The finished product can only be as good as the material and equipment used to create it. Buy the best that you can afford.

Equipment

SEWING MACHINE

The sewing machine is the indispensable tool in machine piecing and quilting. To be a good quilter doesn't require an expensive machine or extensive experience in sewing. You need a dependable machine that sews a good-quality straight stitch on regular sewing or darning.

Take a moment to find your presser feet and instruction book and go step-by-step through the accessories and features. You may want to check with your machine dealership about the availability of optional accessories. The Resource List in the back of the book can also help you obtain the correct equipment, and the Bibliography lists some good books.

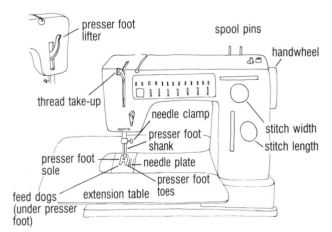

Fig. 1.1 Parts of a sewing machine

Regular presser foot. The regular presser foot is the basic foot that comes with all machines. It has a zigzag needle hole opening and sometimes is called a zigzag foot. The edge of the presser foot is often used as a guide for $\frac{1}{4}''$ seams, although the foot may not be a true $\frac{1}{4}''$.

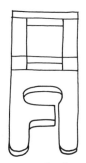

Fig. 1.2 Regular presser foot

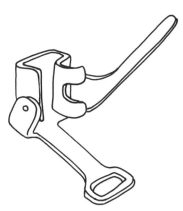

Fig. 1.4 Darning foot

Straight stitch foot. The straight stitch foot is a very narrow foot, with a small needle hole opening. This foot is rarely a standard accessory with newer machines. The straight stitch foot is recommended for accurate $\frac{1}{4}''$ seam allowances when piecing. The width of the right toe of the straight stitch foot can vary from $\frac{1}{8}''$ to over $\frac{1}{4}''$. I use the narrowest straight stitch foot and find it wonderful for stitching curves.

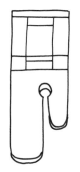

Fig. 1.3 Straight stitch foot

Darning foot. The darning foot is perhaps the most distinctive foot in the accessory box. It can be made of metal or transparent plastic. It is a small oval or square foot with a spring or an arm that can hook on the needle clamp. Originally designed to mend small holes or tears, this is the most-used foot in machine quilting. To quilt, lower or cover the feed dogs. Each machine is slightly different, so refer to your instruction book to set up your machine for darning.

Not all machines have darning capability. Generic darning feet are available for most machines, but inactivating the feed dogs requires creative accessory making. To make a cover for the feed dogs, use template plastic and a vinyl tape—not masking tape or invisible tape—but a tape like electrician's tape. In the center of a 2″ square of template plastic, cut a hole the size and shape of the opening in the needle plate. To cover the feed dogs, line up the needle hole in the plastic with the needle hole on the needle plate. Securely tape the plastic to the bed of the machine. To stop the motion of the feed dogs, turn the stitch length to 0 or the shortest stitch length on your machine. Remove the tape from the machine when not in use. Frequent taping to the machine can leave adhesive residue on the needle plate. To remove the residue, use WD 40 spray lubricant and a soft cloth. Spray the tacky area and wipe dry.

A small number of machines do not have a darning foot and will not accept a generic foot. The instruction book may suggest you use the regular foot with loosened pressure on the foot, or that you use a hoop and no foot at all. In general, mastery of machine quilting requires a darning foot. Machine quilting can be done a number of ways, but without the proper equipment, the beginner will be working under a severe disadvantage.

These machine owners face a dilemma: having to buy a new machine to gain the darning capability without knowing if they will like machine quilting. To try quilting on a nondarning machine, there is a makeshift alternative.

Embroidery springs or spring-wrapped needles may be substituted for a darning foot. Both use a small spring around the needle to hold the fabric in place as the stitch is formed. Skipped stitches can be a problem with these methods. To stop skipped stitches, use a 7″ to 12″ wooden or plastic hoop (see the Resource List for mail-order sources). The hoop should be about $\frac{3}{8}$″ wide, narrow enough to fit under the needle when it is raised to its highest point. Traditional quilting hoops are about 1″ to $1\frac{1}{4}$″ wide and are unsuitable for machine work. To place the quilt in the hoop, place the *outer ring* on a sturdy table top. Place the quilt right side up over the ring. Pop the *inner ring* over the quilt.

Open darning foot. A variation of the basic metal darning foot, the open darning foot is designed for free-hand embroidery and quilting. A small portion of the front of the foot has been removed for better visibility. It changes the foot from a closed circle to a C shape. This is my favorite foot. It is offered as an optional foot for my brand of machine.

Fig. 1.5 Open darning foot

But not all machines have this foot available. You can adapt the regular darning foot by filing or cutting away a small section of the foot. I suggest you purchase a second, metal darning foot. Cut or file away a small section of the foot directly in front of the needle. (I used a file from my dad's tool box.) Remove about $\frac{3}{16}$″. Think of the foot as an O shape. Change the foot to a C shape, not a U shape. Removing too much of the foot will cause skipped stitches. If you don't want to do this yourself, take the foot to a scissors sharpener.

Open-toe or no-bridge foot. The name *open-toe* or *no-bridge* applies to a number of presser feet. They can be a modified regular presser foot, an embroidery foot, or even a buttonhole foot. They may be available as a specific optional foot for some brands of machines or as a generic foot for any machine (see the Resource List). Either way, they have comparable features. Designed for appliqué, satin stitching, or intricate sewing, the portion of the foot directly in front of the needle has been removed to give an unobstructed view of the stitch. This foot makes accurate piecing a breeze. I use it for 90 percent of my piecing and strongly recommend it to my classes (the rest of the time I use the straight stitch foot). It is the most important machine accessory you can purchase. The open access to the needle allows the matching pin to remain in place, until the moment the needle secures the match. On some machines, the design of the foot occasionally may cause skipped stitches. The problem stems from the reduced surface space of the foot, which lessens the pressure or hold on the fabric. Therefore, the fabric can move with the needle, preventing stitch formation. Changing the needle size one number larger or smaller usually solves the problem, as does starching the fabric heavily. Some people like to use a single-hole needle plate, but I don't use one.

Fig. 1.6 Open-toe or no-bridge foot

Walking or even-feed foot. This foot smoothly feeds the multiple layers of quilt when doing machine-guided quilting. The foot provides a set of feed dogs on top of the fabric that synchronizes with the lower feed dogs, keeping the quilt flat and unpuck-

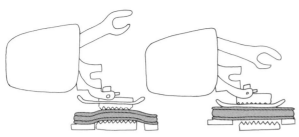

Fig. 1.7 The walking foot is synchronized with the feed dogs

ered. On some machine brands the feature is built in and doesn't require a special presser foot. Generic feet will fit many machines but may not match the feeding system. To insure proper feed, buy the foot designed for your brand and model machine.

Quilting and seam guides. Quilting guides and seam guides have been used for decades and are a standard accessory on many machines. Even treadle machines have these simple devices in the attachment box. Both guides insure perfect seam allowances and are frequently used by beginner sewers. Although they work differently, both guides increase the accuracy and speed of piecing. The quilting guide is attached to the presser foot, while the seam guide is attached to the bed of the machine.

The quilting guide usually has a small bar about 2″ long with a metal runner attached to one end. The bar fits into the back of a presser foot and is held in place

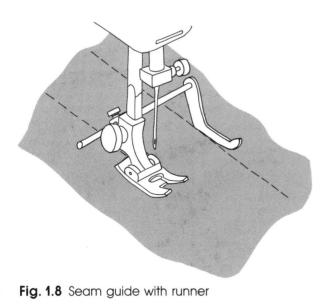

Fig. 1.8 Seam guide with runner

by a screw. The runner is adjusted to mark the seam allowance and is guided along the edge of the fabric.

The seam guide can be a narrow strip of metal attached with a screw to the machine near the presser foot or a magnetized strip placed on the machine bed. The guide is adjusted to match the seam allowance, and the edge of the fabric is guided against the edge of the guide. The magnetized guide may interfere with computerized machine functions. Check the instruction book or with an authorized dealer before using a magnetized guide with a computerized machine.

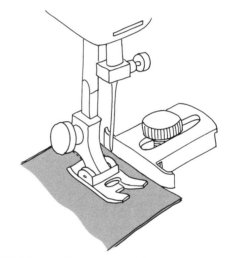

Fig. 1.9 Magnetic seam guide

Extension table for free-arm machines. This table of metal or plastic fits the free arm, increasing the working surface. Unless your machine is in a cabinet, this accessory is an absolute requirement for the serious machine quilter.

Needles. Sharp or universal point size 12 (80) is used for piecing, size 14 (90) for quilting.

Needle stop down and auto knot. Needle down and auto knot frequently are found on new machines. These features are not necessary to quilting but are a pleasure to use. Needle down means that the needle will always stop in the fabric. It is used when pivoting or redistributing fabric. Auto knot secures the threads with a touch of a button. Auto knot should not be confused with the reverse button. In auto knot, the machine feeds the fabric forward, taking very tiny straight stitches that inconspicuously knot the threads. Auto knot can be programmed into most computer machines. On my machine I can program the type of knot I want for what I am sewing.

Problem Solving

No matter how adept the sewer, occasionally things go wrong with the machine. Luckily, many problems are simple-to-solve glitches. This checklist will help you correct and prevent the most common problems.

Start by rethreading both the top and bobbin. Make sure you have both the needle and presser foot at their highest positions. Forgetting to raise the presser foot is a common mistake with the darning foot. The top tension dial won't accept the thread when the presser foot is lowered. As a result, the stitching may loop on the back or jam the machine. In general, if there are thread loops on the bottom side of the stitch, the top thread is causing the problem. Usually it is misthreaded. Check the threading before adjusting the upper thread tension.

Treat your machine to a new needle. Choose the needle suitable for your fabric and thread and check your instruction book for the proper way to insert the needle into the clamp. Skipped stitches often are caused by putting the needle in the machine incorrectly, or by using an incorrect size needle for the material.

Clean the bobbin area frequently. Use a small brush to dislodge the lint and threads. Some machines require regular oiling to keep them running quietly and smoothly. Check your machine's instruction book, and oil only the specified areas.

Hold on to both thread tails when you start to sew. This prevents thread snarls at the beginning of seams and stops the machine from eating small fabric pieces.

Last but not least, have regular maintenance on your machine by a qualified repairer—this means at least yearly.

PRESSING EQUIPMENT

Steam or dry iron. Keep your iron clean. Warm water and a terry cloth will remove starch build-up. To remove fusible interfacing or scorching, use a commercial iron cleaner.

Ironing board. I use and recommend a firm pressing surface. My ironing board pad is a cotton blend, much like a mattress pad. Foam pads are great for pressing clothing but are too soft for pressing the seam wells from tiny pieces. Choose a cotton cover. Metallic or silicone-coated covers are not absorbent. Spray starch puddles on the surface of the cover and sticks to the iron. A build-up of spray starch or fusibles can ruin an ironing board cover and the iron. The cotton cover works well, as it is easy to remove and wash. It also absorbs excess starch and keeps the iron clean. I make all the covers for my ironing boards. They are easy and inexpensive to make, and best of all, they are custom-fitted to the board. I use a purchased cover or a commercial pattern as a basic pattern and add width or length as needed to get an ample fit. Use a good-quality 100 percent cotton muslin and double-fold bias tape. Stitch double-fold bias tape around the cover to enclose the raw edges and to form the casing for a cable cord drawstring.

Spray starch. I use spray starch on all the fabrics I use for machine-made quilts. You can use ready-mixed starch in aerosol cans or nonaerosol bottles or mix your own using liquid starch and a plant mister. To make spray starch mix one part starch with one part warm water. If your mister should clog, remove the starch and water mixture and heat in your microwave before refilling. The warm liquid will clear away any solidified starch in the mister. My favorite plant mister is the sophisticated type available at garden-supply stores. This large spray bottle holds two pints of liquid and works much like a tire pump. Pumping the plunger on the top of the sprayer forces air into the mister and produces a pressurized spray. A touch of a button activates the spray. This mister sprays as well as an aerosol can and is much better for the environment.

CUTTING, MEASURING, AND MARKING TOOLS

Fabric Markers

Choose a marker that is accurate and easy to see. It must be able to withstand abrasion and yet be easy to remove from the finished project. Any marker that brushes off from contact with your hand or other fabric is not suitable for machine quilting. Upon completion of the project all marks should be rinsed out with plain tepid water, then washed in tepid water and mild soap. Detergents may set some markers, so use mild dishwashing soap or soaps designed for quilts.

For quilting use bold, highly visible markers, like blue washout, or chalk pencils. Fine-line markers like colored or lead pencils are perfect for piecing but are too light to see for quilting. Keep in mind that the presser foot obscures portions of the line and that most machine quilters sew at a moderate speed. The line needs to jump off the fabric to reduce eye strain and aggravation.

I use blue washout markers, an assortment of chalk markers, and assorted size #0.5 lead pencils: 2B, HB, and 2H. Always test markers before using them. Do not expose marked fabric to heat or intense light. Remove the marks from the fabric as soon as possible.

A word about blue washout markers: I've used blue washouts for years and buy them by the dozens. I've never had problems with my markers but have heard enough horror stories to know that there can be problems. I always follow an exact procedure when I use these markers. First I spray starch the fabric. Then I mark the quilting design. I keep the quilt away from heat and intense light, especially sunlight. Most important, I mist the completed areas with plain water as I work. When I finish

quilting for the day, I use a plant mister filled with distilled water to remove the marks in the completed areas. A light mist makes the marking move. When the quilt dries, the marks may reappear, but they will be completely gone when I wash the quilt. I suspect the marker chemicals bond to the starch and wash away with the starch.

Scissors vs. Rotary Cutter

Scissors. Scissors and shears should be sharp without catches. Make sure your scissors cut straight. Old, damaged, or inexpensive scissors may pull to the right or left. This pull makes cutting a straight edge difficult and causes fatigue in your cutting hand. Choosing a comfortable scissors or shears is like buying a pair of shoes. Sometimes it takes some looking around to find the right fit.

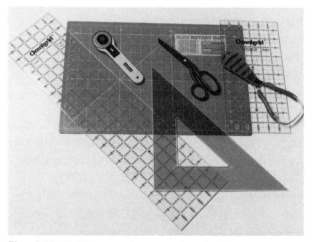

Fig. 1.10 Cutting and measuring tools

I use spring-band scissors. Originally designed for those who find cutting with scissors difficult or painful, these wonderful scissors are great for anyone who does frequent hand cutting. The handles don't have thumb or finger loops. To use, grip the scissors with your entire hand; a light squeeze cuts the fabric. The handles and blades spring back open, without use of thumb or fingers. No more blisters! (See the Resource List for sources.)

Rotary cutter. A cross between a pizza cutter and a razor blade, these superaccurate cutters come in two sizes. I use the 2″ size, but either size works great. When buying a cutter choose one that has a safety shield to protect both the blade and you. Replace nipped or dull blades.

Rotary mat. This is a special plastic mat designed for use with a rotary cutter. It self heals and is not damaged by the cutter, plus it protects the cutter and the table top. Mats are available in a wide variety of sizes, but I prefer the 18″ × 24″ mat.

Rulers for the rotary cutter. There is an astonishing array of $\frac{1}{8}$″ thick Plexiglas rulers designed for use with the rotary cutter. Choose a ruler with clear, easy-to-read markings that are visible on both light and dark fabrics. It should be marked in inches, quarter inches, and eighth inches. The marks should be easy to tell apart; you don't want to mix up $2\frac{1}{4}$″ and 2″. I prefer rulers that have the markings in a grid on the ruler, so that the inches are marked on both the length and width of the ruler. Buy the best ruler you can find. Inexpensive rulers are often inaccurate. An inch on one edge of the ruler may not be the same size as an inch on another edge. Rulers are an important investment, and good rulers result in good piecing.

I recommend three basic sizes for the beginner: 6″ × 12″, 6″ × 24″, and a 12″ 45-degree triangle. Be warned: your ruler collection will grow in direct proportion to your quilting skills.

Template Supplies

Templates are made of paper or plastic and are used to draw or cut out individual pieces of a block. I frequently use plastic templates because they are accurate and reusable. To make a template use clear, easy-to-cut plastic like the specially designed template plastic or x-ray plastic. Trace the pattern to the plastic using a fine-line permanent marker. Cut out the template with paper scissors. To prevent the interior lines from rubbing off, cover the template with invisible (clear cellophane) tape.

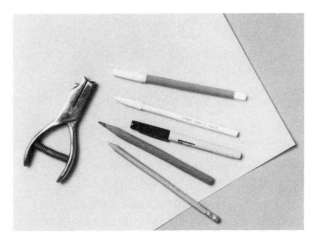

Fig. 1.11 Template supplies and markers

Mark the corners where the two seam lines intersect. Use a $\frac{1}{16}$″ punch (see Resource List) to mark corners and matching dots. A large hand-sewing needle may be substituted for the punch. To make a neat small hole heat the needle briefly over a candle flame before putting it to the plastic. The size of the hole is $\frac{1}{16}$″ because an $\frac{1}{8}$″ hole is too large to be accurate.

Paper templates are used in combination with Plexiglas rulers for quick cutting methods with the rotary cutter. They are also suitable for unusual or single-cut shapes. The paper template is never traced around but is used as a cutting guide.

Pins

Both safety pins and straight pins are used in machine quilt making. Straight pins are used in piecing and binding. They should be long, thin, and sharp, with a large plastic or glass head. Safety pins are used to baste the quilt layers together for machine quilting. Size #1 nickel or brass pins are the commonly used size. Brass pins don't rust and are easy to close but are not especially sharp. Nickel pins are much sharper but are harder to close and can rust if the quilt gets damp or if the pins are left in the quilt for a long time. To baste, the pins should be at 4″ intervals over the entire quilt top, with extras along the edges. That means about 500 pins for an 81″ × 96″ quilt.

Materials

FABRICS

Medium-weight, closely woven, 100 percent cotton fabrics are the best choice for beginning quilting. Cotton fabrics are easy to press, starch, cut, and sew. Traditional cotton fabrics are muslin, calico, gingham, and broadcloth.

Don't be too concerned about fabric names. They can be confusing, because the common usages rarely match the true meaning of the word. Many fabric names have colorful histories or localized names with little meaning for the novice quilter. Here are some fabrics you might find when you go shopping. The descriptions do not necessarily match the correct textile definitions, but they should help you understand the clerk and be an informed consumer. Remember, the fabric name doesn't tell you the fiber content. All of these fabrics can be made of 100 percent cotton or a cotton/polyester blend. Look for 100 percent cotton fabrics.

Muslin. Usually refers to a plain white or unbleached fabric. It also can be any plain-colored fabric. Muslin comes in a wide range of qualities. Wrinkle-free finish is available on some muslins. A good-quality muslin should not be transparent. It should have body and a smooth finish not affected by washing. Inferior fabrics have a low thread count. You can use starch to give the fabric the body and appearance of the more expensive fabrics, but this added filler can make the fabric more susceptible to tears and bearding. When washed, inexpensive muslin is soft and badly wrinkled with skewed grainlines. Quality muslin retains its body, and the wrinkles press out easily.

Calico. A broad term used to describe midweight printed cotton fabrics. Usually the prints are small overall designs. Like muslin, calicos should be firmly woven. The price of printed fabric is determined by both the thread count and the number of colors used in the print. A single color on a white or natural background is much easier and less expensive to print than intricate and delicately shaded designs. Good prints are well registered with clear colors.

Gingham. A woven plaid fabric. It can be of traditional single color with white or it may be multicolored. Woven checks or plaids are identical on the right and wrong sides. Printed plaids are one-sided. The wrong side of the fabric is lighter or plain-colored. An advantage of woven plaids is that the grain lines can be straightened. If a plaid is printed off the grain or bowed, there is no way to correct it.

Broadcloth. Usually refers to solid-colored midweight fabrics but can also mean a printed fabric, with "broadcloth" referring to its weight and thread count.

Chintz. A cotton fabric with a finish that makes it look like satin. The glaze can be used on plain or printed fabrics and can vary from a soft sheen to a high gloss.

With all the choices in colors and prints, finding the fabric you want can be overwhelming. A few simple hints may help make the process easier.

Buy high-quality fabrics. Poor fabrics are not worth your time and energy.

Look at other quilts for ideas. Study quilts that really appeal to you. Do they have a common color? Do they have small prints or large? Do they use plain fabrics? Are they dark or bright? Bold or subtle? You can also tap the skill of commercial artists by studying wallpapers, fabric prints, and even greeting cards. Designers make their living using color. From them you can learn which colors to use in your own project.

Ask for help at your local quilting store. Clerks work with fabric combinations every day and can help you find the one that is right for you.

Plan ahead. Prints conceal stitching errors while plain colors accentuate the

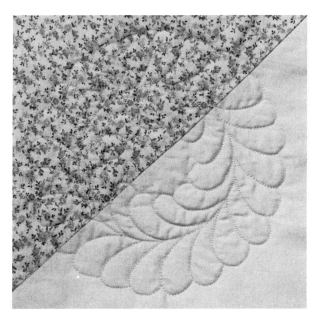

Fig. 1.12 Print conceals stitching line

THREADS

Two types of thread are used in quilting: the sewing thread used for piecing and the quilting thread used to stitch the layers of the quilt together.

Fig. 1.13 Assorted threads, pins, and needles

quilting. If you're unsure of your quilting skill, stick to prints.

Limit the fabric to two or three colors. This can make things easier. If you're really having problems, think monochromatic. Choose a color you like—say, blue. Use any shade of blue, from almost white to the deepest navy. Of course, you can always toss in a neutral, like white, off-white, or black.

Rely on the fabric company. This is my favorite way to choose fabric. Fabrics are designed in color and style groups. Choosing all the pieces from the same group ensures a successful color combination. Or start with a distinct multicolored print. Choose solids and small prints to coordinate with the colors in the print.

Use prints creatively. Mixing large and small prints, floral and geometric designs, can add interest even to monochromatic schemes.

Choose what you like. Quilting is supposed to be fun, a way of self-expression—not a competition. Don't listen to your best friend, your mother-in-law, or the local quilting "expert." If you don't like it, don't buy it. Your opinion is the only one that counts!

For piecing use a fine, strong thread. The finer the thread, the more accurate the piecing and the less conspicuous the knots. One hundred percent cotton machine-embroidery thread, size 50, is a good choice (see Resource List). Cotton thread has proven longevity and matches the cotton fabrics for both care and strength. One hundred percent polyester sewing thread or cotton-wrapped polyester thread are alternatives.

Choose a neutral color thread for piecing—white for light colors, pastels, or white fabrics. Off-white or winter white is suitable for all light-colored fabrics except white. Surprisingly, off-white thread can show through a white seam. Grey or beige thread is used for medium to dark fabrics.

The choice of machine-quilting thread is limited only by your imagination and needle size. There are metallics, rayons, pearl cotton, and many more exciting possibilities. For the beginner it is best to stay on the sedate side. For all the projects in this book I've used the two basic types of machine-quilting thread: *nylon invisible thread* or *machine-embroidery threads* like those used in piecing. Your choice depends upon a number of factors: the type of quilt you want to do, its color, its intended use, and your quilting skills.

Nylon invisible thread is a monofilament thread, much like fine fishing line. This thread is available in a number of different sizes, but only the finest thread should be used for machine quilting. Buy invisible thread at your fabric or quilt store (or see the Resource List) to ensure you are using the right weight. Invisible thread comes in two colors: clear for light colors and smoke for dark colors. Invisible thread, as the name implies, is impossible to see on most fabrics. It is the perfect choice for multicolored quilts or colorful prints. I often use invisible thread, but it does have some drawbacks. Like its cousin, fishing line, invisible thread may be hard to knot securely. Although transparent, it is a smooth and shiny thread that glints or sparkles on the quilt. Invisible thread is made from nylon and is very strong, so the nylon thread may cut the weaker cotton fabric. Last, but not least, nylon fiber is extremely susceptible to sunlight, which breaks down the fiber. It may take decades, but the thread will eventually deteriorate.

What does all this mean? Don't throw away your invisible thread, but use it with discretion. Invisible thread is invaluable for machine quilting. Use it for quilts having many colors or high color contrasts. It is the perfect choice for quilts that are used regularly.

Invisible thread comes on cones, like serger thread, or on a cardboard tube. Neither spool type can be used on vertical spool pins. To use invisible thread you will need a thread stand or cone holder. Use invisible thread in the needle and cotton or polyester thread in the bobbin.

Cotton machine embroidery thread, sizes 30 or 50, are available in a large selection of colors. Embroidery thread has a soft sheen and is very lightweight and pliable. It is easy to sew with and knots securely. Cotton thread matches cotton fabric regarding both care and strength, and it has proven longevity. Cotton thread is the perfect choice for densely quilted designs, like stipple or tiny motifs. Choose cotton threads for quilts with heavy quilting or on

heirloom quilts meant to be handed down for generations. Cotton thread will help keep your work as beautiful 100 years from now as it is today. Its one drawback is that it is colored and may show on some areas of the quilt. Mismatched threads and fabrics accentuate the quilting. Unless you are a skilled quilter, match the thread and fabric color as exactly as possible.

An easy solution to choosing a quilting thread is to use both threads. Use cotton machine embroidery thread whenever possible, and invisible nylon thread when necessary.

BATTING

Batting is the layer that gives the quilt its loft and warmth. It can be made of wool, cotton, polyester, silk, or blends of fibers. Polyester, cotton, and cotton/polyester blends are readily available. Batting is available in sizes that correspond to bed sizes, from 45″ × 60″ for a baby quilt up to 120″ × 120″ for a king-sized quilt.

Fig. 1.14 Different types and weights of batting

Polyester batting is made of 100 percent polyester fibers. Short lengths of polyester fibers are bonded together to form a fluffy blanket. Bonding stops the fibers from shifting when the quilt is used or washed. Polyester batting is sold by loft.

Loft refers to the thickness of the fiber blanket. *Traditional* or *low-loft* batting is thin batting, while *high loft* or *extra thick* batting is thick batting. The loft may also be numbered; the higher the number, the thicker the batting. Because of the bonding process, polyester batting doesn't require much quilting to hold it in place. Your quilting lines should be 4″ to 6″ apart. Dense quilting is not recommended on polyester batting. The quilt loses its softness and drapability, and the loft will flatten.

One-hundred-percent cotton batting has been a quilting mainstay for generations. Most 19th-century quilts have cotton batting. Quilts with cotton batting have a soft yet stable hand, much like a blanket has. Cotton fiber breathes; it is warm in the winter and cool in the summer. Its one drawback is that it cannot be bonded. To prevent the fibers from shifting when the quilt is used, the quilting lines must be very close together, $\frac{1}{2}$″ to 2″.

Cotton/polyester-blend batting is made from 80 percent cotton and 20 percent polyester. Polyester is used to bond the batting and prevent the cotton from shifting. This batting has the look and feel of antique cotton quilts but requires less quilting. It should be quilted every 1″ to 3″ but may be quilted closer without sacrificing its soft hand.

When choosing a batting consider two things: First, how much quilting do you want to do? Polyester batting require less stitching, while cotton or cotton-blend batting is better for dense quilting. Second, how skilled are you at quilting? The thicker the batting, the harder it is to handle. Beginners should stay with low-loft polyester or cotton-blend batting.

CHAPTER 2

Basic Quilting Instructions

Fabric Preparation

PREWASHING

All fabrics should be washed before they are used. Washing removes chemicals, like formaldehyde, used in finishing the fabric. It will also shrink the fabric and remove any excess dyes.

Cotton fabrics should be machine washed in tepid water with a mild soap. Use a mild dishwashing soap or a soap specially designed for quilts. Soap made for wools or silks may discolor cotton fabrics. Wool and silk are animal fibers, while cotton is a plant fiber. Wash like colors together and machine dry on a medium setting.

It is important that the water temperature be tepid, neither cold nor hot. A little basic chemistry explains why. Warm water holds more solids in solution than cold water. It's like making instant tea: when you make iced tea with cold water, there is always a little of the mix that you can't stir into the water, so it sits on the bottom of the glass. When you make instant iced tea in warm water, all the mix dissolves and stays dissolved, even after the tea is chilled. Think of the chemicals and dyes on your fabric as tea.

When you wash fabrics, the excess dyes and chemicals are carried away with the water. If the water is cold, it can't hold as much of the dyes, so they may settle back onto the fabric. Hot water can strip out the color. Tepid water holds the dye without damaging the fabric.

Also check for colorfastness when you prewash your fabric. Three things can happen: The fabric may fade and change color, the excess dye may tint the wash water, or the excess dye can bleed onto adjoining fabrics.

Stitch together 4″ squares of the quilt fabrics. Wash by hand or machine. Blot with a terry towel and let the samples air dry. There should be no bleeding of color from one piece to another. The key is, does one fabric color another? I have fabrics that consistently tint the water every time I wash them. The fabric fades slightly, but never bleeds onto another piece. Rewash and machine dry any piece that doesn't prove color fast. Repeat the test. If the fabric dye is still unstable, do not use that fabric.

CHECKING AND STRAIGHTENING GRAIN

Woven fabric is made of two sets of threads, called the warp and weft. The warp threads are parallel to the selvage and form the lengthwise grain. The weft threads are perpendicular to the selvage and are called the crosswise grain. In a perfect world the warp and weft threads cross at 90-degree angles; however, this rarely happens. Unless the fabric is badly off grain, most quilters don't try to correct this problem. Straightening the fabric across the grain can waste as much as an eighth of a yard of fabric. Slight variations in the grainline will not affect the finished quilt. Seams and quilting lines will stabilize any imperfections caused by off-grain cuts.

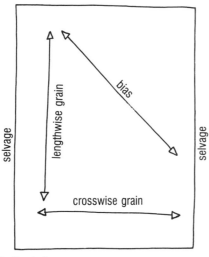

Fig. 2.1 Grainlines

When working with printed stripes for borders or specific pieces in a block, cut *following the design, not the grainline*. Prints do not follow the grainline.

To straighten a badly skewed grainline, tear the fabric or pull a thread to find the crosswise grainline. Pull on opposite corners (Fig. 2.2). The warp and weft threads will shift to straighten the grain. The only time straightening the grainline may be important is on woven plaids or stripes. If the warp or weft is bowed or skewed, the plaid or stripe will be crooked. To cut blocks as nearly perfect as possible, you must straighten the grain and cut each block by hand. Better yet, take a tip from antique quilts and don't worry about grain-perfect plaids.

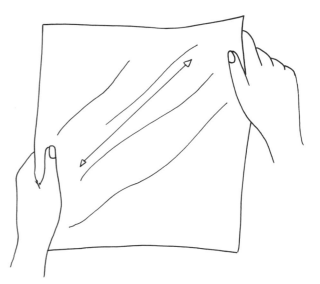

Fig. 2.2 Straightening the grain

PRESSING AND STARCHING

Press the fabric before using. Spray starch all the fabrics to go into your quilt to give them a crisp finish. The finish makes the fabrics easier to cut and sew. It also acts like a stain guard, making marker lines easier to remove.

To spray starch, press a single layer of fabric. Do not press in folds. Lightly mist the fabric; it should be damp to the touch. Press dry with an iron set at cotton. Repeat this process twice on each side of the fabric. Starch flaking usually is caused by too much liquid starch on the fabric. Stop flaking by using a lighter application of ready-mixed starch, or, if you've mixed your own spray starch, add water to the solution. I don't worry about flaking unless it is scorching the iron. The excess starch won't hurt anything and will be brushed away long before the quilt is stitched.

How much to starch the fabric depends on what you are making. A light to medium coat of starch is adequate for most quilting projects. Intricate piecing needs to be heavily starched.

Let me digress. Some sewing machine dealers and repair people use a type of cotton fabric called demo fabric when demonstrating their machines. This fabric is white or pastel and heavily starched. They use it because it shows the stitches to their best advantage. The starch stops the fabric from puckering and keeps the fabric edges from being pulled into the needle hole opening.

Use that information when you piece. Starched fabrics stitch better, and never again will your sewing machine eat the fine points on pieces. Starch also makes cutting and marking easier and more accurate. The fabric can't bubble in front of a marker or slide away from the rotary cutter.

Remember, this is machine piecing for machine quilting. Starch makes hand quilting difficult, if not impossible, but your machine performs better with starched fabrics.

Cutting Methods

Two basic methods are used to cut the pieces for blocks: hand cutting and rotary cutting. A working knowledge of both methods is necessary.

Hand cutting uses a plastic or paper pattern to mark the individual pieces, which are hand drawn and scissor cut. This method can be tedious and time consuming. Although rotary cutting has replaced much of traditional hand cutting, templates are still valuable for intricate or curved piecing.

Rotary cutting excels for straight cuts and large pieces. It is a fast and accurate way to cut simple shapes and good for cutting borders and bindings. Pieces are cut as they are measured, eliminating the need to mark each individual piece. Rotary cutting

often is combined with strip piecing. Fabric strips are sewn together and recut, making dozens of pieces with only a few cuts.

A third more advanced method of cutting combines rotary-cut strips with paper templates. Integrating techniques uses the best of both methods, offering speed and accuracy.

MAKING AND USING TEMPLATES

Determine the seam allowances. All templates used for machine piecing need a uniform seam allowance. One-quarter inch is the common size. When working with patterns with premarked seam allowances, check the $\frac{1}{4}''$ seam allowance against your machine's $\frac{1}{4}''$. They can vary enough to affect accuracy. If there are no seam allowances on the pattern, you must add your own. Use graph paper or a ruler for the straight edges. Curved edges pose more of a problem. A compass works on simple shapes but is difficult to use on complex pieces.

An easier way to add seam allowances to a pattern is to use the edge of your presser foot as the standard measure. This customized seam allowance works great on curved pieces. It also can eliminate the problem of finding a true $\frac{1}{4}''$ seam allowance on your machine.

To add a customized seam allowance to your patterns. Accurately trace the pattern to plain paper. Pieces should be spaced about 1″ apart. Leaving $\frac{1}{2}''$ margins, cut out

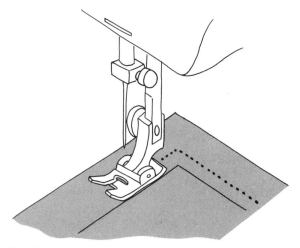

Fig. 2.3 Straight stitch to add customized seam

the pieces. With the pattern to the right of the foot, line up the pattern edge with the foot edge. Unthread your machine and straight stitch around the pattern. The needle will leave a row of holes to mark the seam allowance. Use a pencil or fine marker to connect the dots.

To make plastic templates. Accurately trace the pattern to the template plastic or X-ray film. Use a fine-line permanent marker and draw carefully. Mark the stitching lines as well as the cutting lines. Cut out the template with paper scissors. Cut the line off. This compensates for the width of the pencil line when you mark the template on the fabric. Punch the corners with a $\frac{1}{16}''$ punch, using the seam lines as crosshairs. Also punch any matching dots. Label the template with the pattern name and grainline. If space allows, you might want to indicate color or the number needed for the quilt. To prevent the label from wearing off, cover the writing with invisible tape.

To make a paper template. Accurately trace the pattern on typing paper. Label the template with the pattern name and grainline, and note the right side of the template. Many pieces are not reversible, so it is important to know which is the right side. If space allows, indicate color or the number of pieces needed for the block. Cut out the template with paper scissors.

To trace the plastic template onto the fabric. Place the template right side down, on the wrong side of the fabric. Line up the straight of grain with either the crosswise or lengthwise grainline. Draw the templates as close together as possible. Adjacent pieces should share a cutting line. Most shapes can be fitted together so there is no fabric waste. Trace around the template with a fine-line marker. Mark each corner dot and matching dot. The dots are not necessary on large pieces, only for intricate piecing. Cut out each piece, cutting on the line. Stack the pieces.

USING A ROTARY CUTTER

Straight Strips

A straight strip cut on the crosswise grain of the fabric is the basic cut.

Fold the fabric in half, lining up the selvages. The cut or torn edges of the fabric may not line up. Fold the fabric in half a second time. Line up the selvage edges with the first fold. The first cut straightens the fabric edge and is perpendicular to the fold.

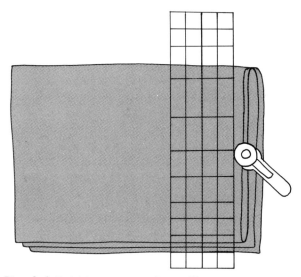

Fig. 2.4 Fold to prepare for cutting

For the first cut. Place the fabric to your left on the rotary mat. Place your 6″ × 24″ ruler on top of the fabric, lining up the fold of the fabric with the horizontal lines on the ruler. Cut away about $\frac{1}{2}''$ of fabric. Hold the ruler in place with your left hand, pressing down to keep it from slipping. Open the safety shield on the cutter. Guide the rotary cutter along the ruler edge. Use firm pressure, and push the cutter away from you to make a neat cut. Always cut beyond the fabric edges to insure a complete cut. Be very careful as the blade is extremely sharp. At the completion of every cut, close the safety shield.

Fig. 2.5 Cutting strips with a rotary cutter

Rotate the fabric and mat so the fabric is on your right side. Place the ruler on the fabric to the correct width. Line up the cut edge with the vertical lines and the fold edge with the horizontal lines. Make the second cut. Open the fabric to check if the cuts are straight.

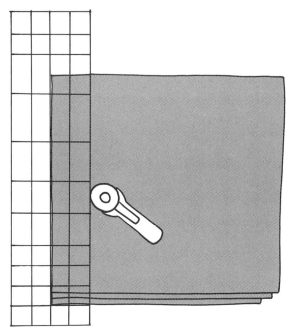

Fig. 2.6 Make the second cut

Continue cutting strips. If the strips are going crooked, straighten the fabric as you did for the first cut.

Fig. 2.7 Incorrectly cut strip

Squares and Triangles

Straight strips can be used as a basis for template-free cutting. Squares and triangles are simple to cut with basic tools. For complex shapes there are myriad rulers and templates to create almost any pattern with your rotary cutter.

To cut squares or rectangles: Cut a straight strip the desired width. Unfold the strip to only two layers of fabric. Line up the cut edges of the strip with the horizontal lines on the ruler. Measure and cut squares or rectangles as you did for the strips.

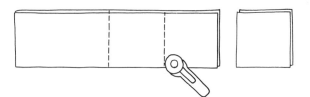

Fig. 2.8 Cutting squares and rectangles

To cut triangles: There are two types of 45-degree triangles. The straight of grain can be parallel to the longest side of the triangle or the grainline can be parallel to the

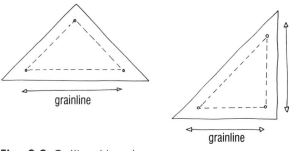

Fig. 2.9 Cutting triangles

two short sides of the triangle. To cut these shapes you need a 45-degree triangle ruler. A paper template taped to the back of the triangle ruler is the cutting guide.

When the straight of grain is on the long side of the triangle, tape the template to the 90-degree angle side of the ruler.

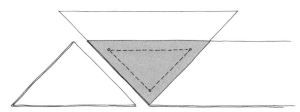

Fig. 2.10 Grain on long side of triangle

Determine the initial strip width by measuring from the long side to the 90-degree angle, including seam allowances.

To cut the triangle, place the ruler/template over the fabric strip, lining up the long edge of the template with a cut edge of the strip. All cuts will be on the bias. Flip the ruler to cut the next triangle. Continue across the strip.

When the straight of grain is on the short side of the triangle, tape the template to the 45-degree angle side of the ruler. Determine the initial strip width by measuring a short edge of the triangle.

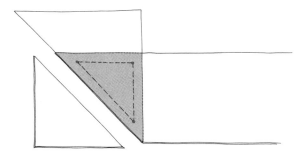

Fig. 2.11 Grain on short side of triangle

To cut the triangle, place the ruler/template over the fabric strip, lining up a short edge of the template with a cut edge of the strip. Flip the triangle to cut the next triangle. Every other cut will be on the bias or straight of the fabric.

Pieces other than squares and triangles can be quickly cut by combining the rotary-cut strip with a plastic or paper template.

This method is extremely effective with a piece that must be hand marked and cut. For example, to cut the diamonds in Dutch Rose (see color pages), rotary cut a strip $1\frac{3}{4}''$ wide. Use the template to draw the piece. Notice that the width of the strip is identical to the width of the piece. You only have to draw one edge and the four matching dots on each piece. Plus, only one edge on each piece will have to be hand cut. That reduces the amount of hand marking and cutting by three-quarters.

COMBINING CUTTING TECHNIQUES

When you cut squares or triangles from straight strips, you are combining template and strip cutting. Take that idea one step farther by adding strip piecing to the sequence. The strips are cut and sewn together to form striped fabric, then cut again to make sets of individual pieces.

This method works well in patterns made of squares or rectangles. Suitable patterns include Nine Patch, Irish Chain, Puss in the Corner, and Four Patch.

I will use a Nine Patch block to explain the technique. Nine Patch contains nine identical squares. Broken down into units, there are three units of three squares. The outer units have the identical sequence: for the sample, dark-light-dark. The center unit is reversed, light-dark-light. Each

Fig. 2.12 Nine-Patch block

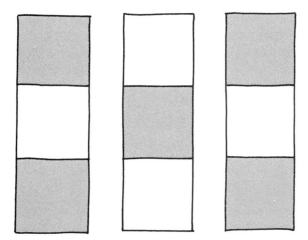

Fig. 2.13 Three units of three squares each

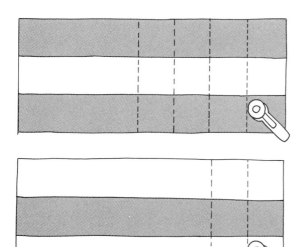

Fig. 2.14 Sew and cut strips into units

square could be cut and sewn individually, but it is faster to sew and cut units. To make the outer units, stitch three long strips together, dark-light-dark. Then cut the strips into the units. To make the center unit, stitch three strips together, light-dark-light, and cut.

Squares and Rectangles

To determine the width of the strips, measure the finished size of the square and add $\frac{1}{2}''$ for seams. A finished block size of $1\frac{1}{2}''$ would require a strip $2''$ wide.

Before sewing the strips, cut all the fabrics to the same width. If the narrowest fabric is 42", tear or cut off the selvage of

wider pieces to make them measure 42" wide.

Cut the strips on the crosswise grain of the fabric and sew them together with a $\frac{1}{4}''$ seam allowance. Use a few pins along the length of the strips. The ends *must* be even to keep the strips straight.

Sewing straight seams is a basic skill in quilting or garment construction. A common experience to beginner sewers is a side seam where the front skirt panel is an inch longer than the back panel. What has gone wrong? Either the sewer's guiding of the fabric or the machine's feed dogs has eased one piece while stretching the other. If that happens to fabric strips, they will be curved. I call it "rainbowing," and no amount of pressing can undo the damage. By pinning and starching and making sure the ends are even, you will not have to rip the seam.

After stitching the strips together, press the seams to the darker fabric, or press the seams open. (There will be a more extensive discussion of pressing techniques in Chapter 4 on piecing.)

Place the stitched strips on the mat. Place the ruler on the fabric to the correct width. Line up the cut edges and seams of the strips with the horizontal line of the ruler. Cut and stack the pieces.

Bias Strips

By cutting bias strips instead of straight strips, any number of two-color pieces can be cut quickly. The secret to knowing when to use bias strips instead of straight is in the pattern. Compare the seam that joins the two pieces to the grain line. If the seam is on the bias, so is the strip. Bias strips result in squares and triangles with edges on the straight of grain. Marsh McCloskey introduced me to this wonderful method of speed cutting. This technique is used in Kansas Trouble in Chapter 4 to make two-color squares.

Every pattern requires different yardages and strip widths, but as an example of the basic method, cut two different colored 11" squares of fabric. Place them right sides together. Cut on the diagonal to form two

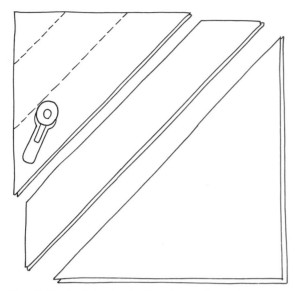

Fig. 2.15 Cut straight strips from bias edge

triangles. To cut four layers at once, stack the two light and two dark triangles, lining up the bias edges (optional step). To cut the strips, measure from the bias edge. Cut as straight strips. Stitch together strips of matching length. Press open seams. (I don't use steam because the pieces are so heavily starched.)

To use bias strips, make a plastic template of the combined pieces. Mark a line on the template indicating the bias seam line. Place the template on the wrong side of the strip with the line on the pattern directly on the seam line. Trace pieces along the seam line. Cut out pieces with scissors. Do not cut into the excess fabric, because it will make another row of pieces. Seam the remaining two pieces of fabric along the bias edge, press open seams, mark, and cut another row of pieces.

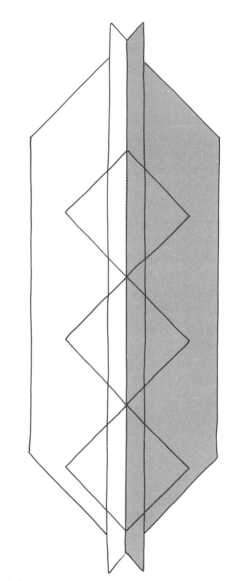

Fig. 2.16 Place template on wrong side of strip

you use. Mark and cut that line with a scissors. The bias cut is too long to be measured with a 24″ ruler and won't fit the cutting mat.

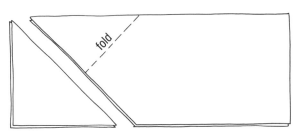

Fig. 2.18 Cut corner on bias line and fold fabric as shown

Now fold the fabric, much as was done with the 44″ width, to make it easy to cut with the rotary cutter. Fold the fabric, lining up the bias edge. The cut is shortened to half the original length. The folded piece looks like a triangle. Fold again, lining up the bias edges. Now the cut is shortened to $\frac{1}{4}$ the original and and can be rotary cut. Line up the ruler as was done for the straight cuts. Refold the fabric as necessary to maintain a usable width.

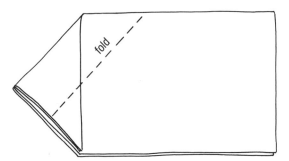

Fig. 2.19 Fold again, lining up the bias edge

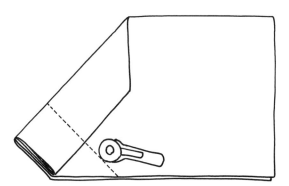

Fig. 2.20 Rotary cut on dashed line

Fig. 2.17 Trace along seam line and cut out pieces

Finding and cutting bias strips on a small square is not too difficult. But the small square doesn't yield very many pieces. On large quilts that require hundreds of pieces, it is more economical to use yardage the full width of the fabric.

To cut a large amount of bias, use the fabric requirements in the pattern. For example, Kansas Trouble calls for $1\frac{3}{4}$ yards for the bias strips needed to make a twin-size quilt. Layer the two fabrics together as you did for the small square. Find the true bias line that crosses a corner. By habit I run the bias line through the upper left hand corner, but it doesn't matter what corner

Piecing Methods

There are two ways to approach piecing: cut and sew perfect $\frac{1}{4}''$ seam allowances, or sew accurate pieces at the expense of perfect seam allowances.

PERFECT SEAM ALLOWANCE

This method is fast and easy. It is the only method to use with strip piecing. It is best for beginners or for patterns with large pieces. The drawback is, this method emphasizes perfect seam allowances rather than perfect pieces.

Stitching a true $\frac{1}{4}''$ seam allowance can be difficult. A straight stitch foot combined with a seam guide gives maximum accuracy. Determine a precise $\frac{1}{4}''$ by using graph paper. Place the paper under the foot with the needle piercing a line. Set the guide exactly $\frac{1}{4}''$ to the right of the needle. Simply butt the edge of the fabric against the guide and sew. It is an absolutely foolproof way to make accurate $\frac{1}{4}''$ seams. Plus, the foot allows an unobstructed view of the fabric edges along the entire seam length, an advantage that prevents the fabric from shifting when crossing seams or doing delicate matching.

A more common method to stitching $\frac{1}{4}''$ seams is to guide the edge of the fabric along the edge of the regular presser foot. The problem is that not all presser feet are a true $\frac{1}{4}''$. On some machines you can compensate for the foot width by adjusting the needle position. As an alternative, you can use specially designed feet that accurately measure $\frac{1}{4}''$ or a customized $\frac{1}{4}''$ seam allowance (see quilting and seam guides in Chapter 1) when making templates. Using the foot edge as a $\frac{1}{4}''$ guide does not guarantee straight seams. Stitching tiny pieces, crossing seams or pins, can tug the fabric under the foot. You may start out on a true $\frac{1}{4}''$ inch, but unless you make an effort to watch the edges of the fabric, they may slip under the foot, distorting the seam.

SUPERACCURATE PIECING

Closely approximating hand piecing, this superaccurate method concentrates on the finished piece rather than slight variations in the seam allowances. This technique is slower than the previous method but is unequaled in intricate piecing or inset pieces.

The no-bridge foot is required to see clearly the matching dots. The dots marked on the fabric are the stitching guide. Pin the correct dots together, not trying to match up the seam allowances. Sew from dot to dot. The no-bridge foot enables you to see the dots and stitch up to the pin without interference from the foot.

BASIC PIECING DIRECTIONS

To sew, set your machine for a normal straight stitch. Choose the presser foot according to your method of piecing. When sewing pieces together, use chaining to save both time and thread. To chain, stitch one seam, stopping a stitch or two before the edge of the fabric. Without lifting the presser foot, slip the next pieces under the toes of the foot. As you finish stitching the first piece the feed dogs will catch the next piece, moving it under the foot to be sewed. A short length of thread chain will separate the pieces. Sew all the pieces you can at one time. Remove them from the machine and clip the blocks apart.

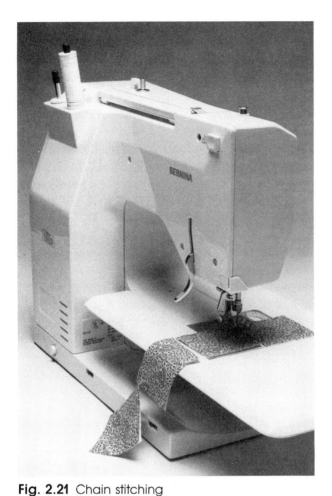

Fig. 2.21 Chain stitching

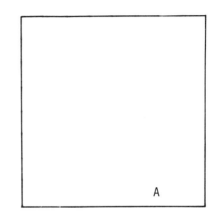

Fig. 2.22 Square and triangle before seam allowance is added

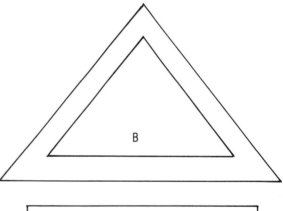

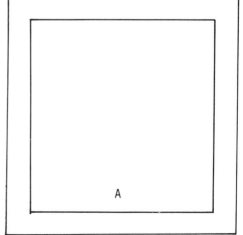

Fig. 2.23 Square and triangle in 2.22 after seam allowance is added

Stitching identical squares to squares, or triangles to triangles, is not difficult. Obviously you must match all the edges of the pieces and stitch the $\frac{1}{4}''$ seam. However, seaming triangles to squares or stitching any nonidentical pieces can be confusing. When you try to line up the seam allowances there is a discrepancy in the length of the pieces. It just doesn't look right. How can one piece be longer than the other and the block still fit together, and more important, how do you line up the seam allowances? Where does the extra fabric go? At the beginning of the seam? At the end?

For the answer, look back to when the seam allowances were added to the pieces. As an example use square A and triangle B. Before adding the seam allowances it is easy to see that the pieces will fit together (Fig. 2.22). When you add the $\frac{1}{4}''$ seam allowance the triangle suddenly becomes larger than the square (Fig. 2.23). There must be a perfectly clear explanation for this phenomenon, but, thankfully, we don't have to understand the geometry to accept the results. On simple shapes, use the excess seam allowance as a placement guide. Place square A on triangle B. In the illustration the square is transparent so you can see how the seams line up. Notice how the seam allowance on the triangle extends beyond the square. The excess seam allowance makes two tiny triangles on either ends of the seam.

On simple patterns, like this square and triangle, lining up the seam isn't difficult if you look in the right place. Notice where the tiny triangles formed by the excess seam allowance meet the edge of the square. To me the intersection of the overlapping of pieces looks like a V. The spot they touch is the bottom of the V. To correctly line up the seam, the V formed by the intersecting seam allowances should be on the $\frac{1}{4}''$ seam line. This simple method is used in most of the block directions.

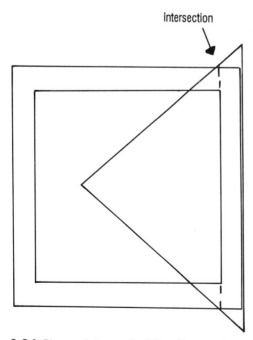

Intersection

Fig. 2.24 Pieces intersect at the $\frac{1}{4}''$ seamline

There are other ways to handle this problem. My favorite is using the corner dots to line up the seams. I pin the two pieces together using the dots as my guide.

This method is used for more complex patterns, like the Dutch Rose.

Most seams are sewn simply from edge to edge. The exception is inset piecing, like the corner block in eight-pointed stars. The seams start and stop $\frac{1}{4}''$ from the edges of the piece. The corner dot on the template and corresponding mark on the fabric indicate the exact place to start and stop. Securely knot the stops and starts by backtacking two or three stitches or by using the auto knot feature on the machine.

Eventually you are going to make a mistake that will have to be ripped. Ripping is a necessary evil. The trick is to rip the stitches without distorting the pieces. I use a sharp fine seam ripper. I slip the point of the ripper under a stitch and cut the thread. I do this every fifth or sixth stitch. Then I slip the point of the ripper under an uncut thread and pull. Voilà! The clipped thread slips out of the seam without any damage to the fabric.

Pressing Seams

Press with care and keep in mind that "less is best." Pressing can cause as many problems as it solves. Overzealous pressing can stretch the bias edges, distorting the entire block. Spray-starched fabrics don't require heavy pressing. Finger pressing is often adequate. To finger press, pinch the seam open or to one side between your fingers and thumb. Move your fingers along the seam line. The heat, moisture, and pressure from your fingertips and nails act like a mini-iron. A quick touch with a steam or dry iron can also be helpful. The trick is to move the iron in an up-and-down motion, not slide it across the fabric. Always press from the back. Whatever pressing method you choose, press as you go along. Crossing unpressed seams causes seam wells or inexact matches. Good pressing makes good stitching.

Seams can be pressed open or to one side. Both methods have advantages, and often blocks have seams pressed both ways.

Seams pressed to one side are traditional. The seams are strong and don't allow the batting to beard along the seam lines. It is also the fastest and simplest way to press. Press the seams toward the darker color. This method is the best choice for joining squares or rectangles but can be bulky and difficult for matching triangles and diamonds.

Pressing seams open is controversial. It flies in the face of hundreds of years of tradition. Although time-intensive, the results are well worth the effort. Open seams produce a smooth quilt top that lays flat and hangs straight. They make matching points highly visible and difficult matches, like inset piecing, a snap.

Open seams are slightly weaker, as there is more stress on the threads and fabric. Machine quilting adds strength to the quilt and reinforces the open seams. Machine stitching is a strong, lock stitch in comparison to the running stitches used in hand quilting. The locked quilting stitches compensate for the weaker piecing seams.

Stitch-in-the-ditch quilting is the single exception. Stitching along the open seam breaks the piecing threads. Use stitch-in-the-ditch quilting exclusively on seams pressed to one side.

Pinning and Matching

Proper pinning is the key to accurate matching. Surprisingly, there is a right and wrong way to use pins. In general, pin perpendicular to the seam and never sew over a pin. Slide pins out of the fabric as they move under the presser foot. Pin only when necessary on long seams or for involved matching.

Matching intersecting seams. Matching straight seams that cross at 90-degree angles, often called keying a seam, is used for squares and rectangles. The seams are pressed to one side and in opposite directions to facilitate the match. Line up matching seams and slide them together. The shallow rise from the opposing seam allowances helps to form a tight match. Pin through the seam allowance that will reach the needle first.

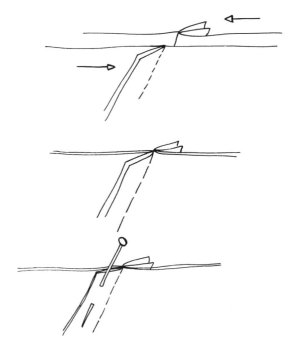

Fig. 2.25 Matching seams pressed to one side

The keyed match must be modified when working with pressed open seams. There is a trick that makes this a simple match. When matching a seam pressed to one side with an open seam, tip the open seam allowance to one side. Treat the match as a simple keyed match. Slide the

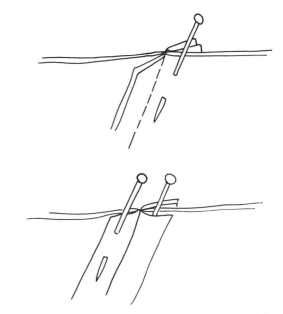

Fig. 2.26 Matching seam pressed to one side with open seam

seams together. Secure the match by pinning, using one pin in the seam allowance that will remain pressed to one side. Open the other seam allowance and pin the other side of the match. There are three seam allowances on one side of the match and a single seam allowance on the other side.

Keying also works for two seams that are pressed open. Tip the seams to one side and in opposite directions. Treat the match as a simple keyed match. Secure the match by pinning the block, *not* the seam allowances. That way the seam allowances can be stitched as open seams. Keying makes an easy perfect match, and the open seams result in a flat block.

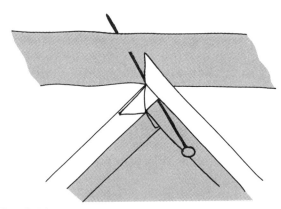

Fig. 2.28 Pin matching points

or to scratch the bed of the machine. Stitch right up to the pin, removing it as the needle secures the match. Always sew a thread or two to the right of the match. It may look like you missed the match from the wrong side, but the slight misstitching will insure sharp points.

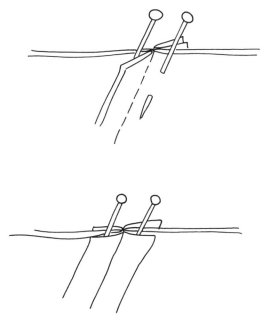

Fig. 2.27 Matching open seams

Matching diagonal seams. This method is used for triangles, diamonds, eight-pointed stars, and any multiple-piece matches. Use a stab pin to secure the match and sew with an open-toe or no-bridge foot. Open seams increase accuracy. Skewer the matching points with a stab pin. Leave the pin standing in that point. Don't tip the pin over or try to bring the point back into the fabric. Pin conventionally on either side of the stab pin. As you approach the stab pin, tip it up. Be careful not to pull the pin out

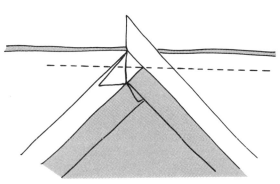

Fig. 2.29 Stitch up to pin

Inset piecing. Use where three seams come together, as in the corner blocks of the Le Moyne Star or Attic Windows. Traditionally done with two separate lines of stitching, inset piecing is easier to accomplish when machine stitching with a single line. Sew together the two pieces, bracketing the inset. Remember to start and stop $\frac{1}{4}''$ from the edges and knot. Press open the seams. Sew with the inset piece on the bottom and the two-seamed pieces on the top. Line up the first edges, sewing toward the open seam. Stitch the first half of the seam, stitching toward the corner. The last stitch before turning the corner should fall off the folded edge of the top

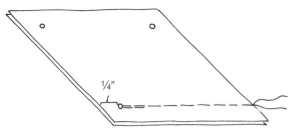

Fig. 2.30 Stitch two pieces together, stopping ¼″ from edge

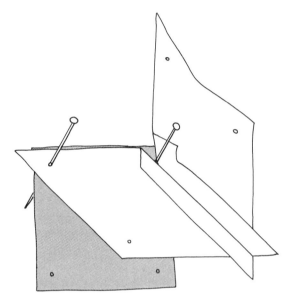

Fig. 2.31 Line up first edges with inset piece on bottom

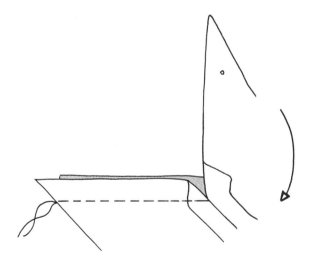

Fig. 2.32 Last stitch before corner falls off folded edge of top fabric

fabric. Stop with the needle lowered in a single layer of fabric, the inset piece. Lift the presser foot, turn the corner, and line up the seam allowances. Lower the presser foot and continue sewing.

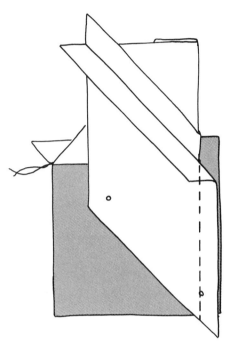

Fig. 2.33 With presser foot raised, line up seam allowances when turning corner

Curves. All curved templates and pieces should have a middle or center mark for matching curves. The straight stitch presser foot, with its unobstructed view of the seam allowances, is the best choice. This method uses only three pins. Any more pins would interfere with the stitching. Sew with the convex curve on top (curves outward). Place the first pin about ¼″ from the start of the seam. Pin at the middle mark and about ¼″ from the ends. The bias edge of the upper piece will stretch to fit the lower curve. Sew slowly. Use the point of a pin or your scissors tips to help align the seam allowances. Sew up to the pin, before sliding it out from under the presser foot. If necessary, lift the foot to release the pin.

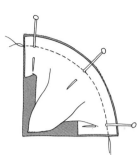

Fig. 2.34 With convex curve on top, pin at middle mark and ¼" from ends

In place of scissor tips, you can use a hemostat to help align the seam allowances. A hemostat looks like embroidery scissors but works like a delicate tweezer. Its locked grip holds securely in the tightest places. Originally designed as a surgical tool, they have been appropriated by everyone from anglers to sewers. The hemostat is a common accessory for an overlock machine and is readily available at fabric sewing stores.

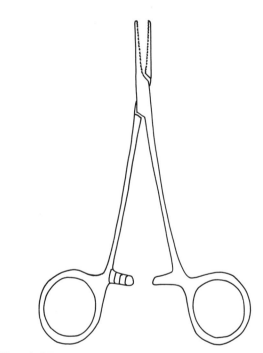

Fig. 2.35 Hemostat

Perfect Matches and Perfect Blocks

Whenever I read instructions, attend a class, or see a prize-winning quilt, it seems the work featured is always perfect. Yet no matter how hard I try, my work is *never* perfect. The blocks are slightly skewed, I have to ease pieces, some seams aren't straight, and sometimes the matches just don't match! Does this sound familiar?

Take heart. As any honest quilter will tell you, there is no such thing as perfect piecing. Quilting mistakes multiply like rabbits. We can't copy the pattern perfectly, we don't cut accurately, and it is impossible to sew absolutely straight. All together these mistakes spell trouble. If you wait until you're perfect to make your first quilt, you will never be a quilter. My best advice is, don't be too hard on yourself. Remember, quilt making is supposed to be fun. Just do the best you can. My favorite saying about perfection is: "You can't see the saddle on a trotting horse." Any mistake you can't see from across the room isn't really a mistake.

Quilting Methods

I piece the entire top before quilting. I don't like—and don't ever use—quilt-as-you-go methods. They require hand stitching and limit the number of options for setting blocks in the quilt. Quilting the whole quilt means you will be handling the entire quilt as you sew. For a king-size quilt you will have 120" × 120" on the machine at one time. Don't panic! It is not as difficult as you might think.

MARKING, LAYERING, BASTING

Take time before marking the quilt to do a final press. Trim away any errant threads or fabric tails. Mark all the quilting lines on the quilt top. Use bold, easy-to-see markers. Transferring the pattern as you stitch is impractical for machine quilting.

To transfer the pattern to the quilt use quilting templates or a paper pattern and light box. Quilting templates are lightweight plastic sheets with the design cut or burned out. Place the stencil over the right side of the quilt and draw through the slots in the stencil onto the fabric. Stencils can be purchased in many designs and sizes. Or, make your own using a double-bladed knife or stencil burning kit.

You can make paper patterns and a light box from things found around the house. Pattern designs are drawn on plain paper with a dark permanent marker. For large or complex designs draw the design on freezer paper, which is white, strong, and comes on a roll. It can be cut and taped to fit any pattern size. A light box can be made from a table with an extension leaf. Split the table in the center as you would to insert the leaf, but in place of the leaf use a large piece of glass, such as from a storm window or a storm door. Place a lamp on the floor under the glass. Tape the pattern to the top of the glass, turn on the light, and place the quilt over the pattern. The light allows you to clearly see and trace the pattern on even the darkest fabrics.

When you have completed marking the quilting pattern on the top, make quarter marks on the batting and backing to help you layer the quilt for basting. The quarter marks are a guide for layering the top, batting, and backing. To quarter the marked top, fold the quilt top in half the long way and in half the short way. Mark along the edges with safety pins. Spray starch the backing and mark the quarters. Also mark the quarters on the batting. Polyester batting can wrinkle or crease in its packaging. Open the batting and allow it to relax before using it, or, to speed things up, tumble it in a cool dryer with a damp terry towel.

Basting the Layers

The three layers of the quilt must be held together during quilting. Pleats and tucks in the backing are common problems with machine quilting. Stretching the backing before basting is a key step to obtaining a smooth, unpleated backing. The secret is in working with another person to stretch the backing. Quilt layering and basting can be done on a table or on the floor.

Layering and basting on the floor. When working on the floor, choose a clean vinyl floor slightly larger than the quilt. Place the quilt back right side down on the floor. You and your helper are at the center marks, on opposite ends of the quilt. Both pull gently on the quilt back and securely tape it the floor. Two-inch masking tape works well. Next, move to the other two sides of the backing, find the center marks, and repeat the procedure. Work around the entire edge of the backing, taping at 6″ intervals. Always pull on the straight of grain, never on the bias. When the backing is stretched, layer the batting and line up the quarter marks. Pat the batting in place but do not stretch it. Place the quilt top right side up over the backing and batting, using the quarter marks as a guide. Do not stretch the top but smooth it over the other layers.

To baste, use safety pins or a hand-sewing needle and thread. Start in the center of the quilt. Slowly kneel or lean on the quilt to reach the center. Move carefully. Don't shift the layers or pull the backing loose from the floor. Check the quilt frequently to ensure a smooth baste. Baste 4″ apart on your first quilt. As you become more skilled, you may use less basting.

Layering and basting on a table top. This method, my personal favorite, doesn't require large empty floor space or crawling on hands and knees. To baste on a table, you need a table at least one-third the size of the finished quilt. I use an 8′ × 30″ lunch table. The table you choose needs a 1″ lip on all the edges and a surface that will not be marred by pin scratches.

Begin by centering the quilt back right side down on the table top. You and your helper are at the center marks on opposite sides of the table. Gently stretch the backing. Use a 1″ paper clamp to hold the back to the lip of the table (if the table is longer than the quilt, tape the quilt to the table top). Move to the opposite side of the table and repeat the process. Work around the entire quilt, clamping about every 12″. Pull only on the straight of grain, never the bias.

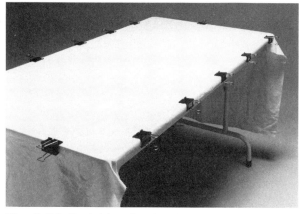

Fig. 2.36 Stretching the backing on a table top

Using the quarter marks, center the batting over the backing and pat in place. Then layer the quilt top, right side up, on top of the backing and batting. Baste at 4″ intervals, using safety pins or hand-basting stitches. Start in the center and work out to the edges. Baste the center third of the quilt. To remove the quilt from the table, gently turn back the top and batting to expose the clamps holding the backing to the table. Always open the clamps to remove them. Metal clamps can tear the backing if they slide on the taut fabric.

Fig. 2.37 Basting the second third

Slide the quilt across the table top, bringing one of the undone thirds to the table top. Clamp the backing to the table on the three loose sides. Do not clamp the side that is already basted, and never put a clamp over the quilt top or batting. Smooth the batting and top over the taut backing and baste. When the second third is finished, repeat the procedure for the last third.

In general, when hand basting or pinning do not baste across a stitching line or heavy seam. If possible, place the basting in a grid or in rows for the most uniform coverage. Remove pins or basting as the quilting approaches them. Always finish basting by turning the quilt back over the batting and quilt top, and safety pin it in place on the right side of the quilt. This step encases the batting and prevents the excess backing from catching in the quilting.

Fig. 2.38 Detail of the pin-basted quilt

Extra-thick Batting and Large Quilts

The small amount of space between the inside of the machine head and the needle can limit the types of batting we can use. As a rule of thumb, half the batting and quilt must fit easily into the space. On extra-thick batting or very large quilts, the bulk of the quilt must be reduced. The easiest method is to quilt one-third of the quilt at a time. Cut your batting into thirds the long way. Stretch the *entire* backing as you normally do. Place one-third of the batting over the center of the backing. Next, layer the *entire* quilt top, but only baste the center third of the quilt. After basting, roll the backing and top toward the center until you reach the section with the batting. Pin the excess backing and top together. Quilt the center third of the quilt, but stay at least 1″ from the edge of the batting.

Upon completing the center section, unroll the edges of the quilt and stretch the backing for the second third of the quilt. Butt the second piece of batting against the first and hand-whip the butted edges of the batting to prevent them from shifting as the quilt is used or washed. Finish layering and basting. Quilt that third and repeat the process with the last third.

SETTING UP YOUR WORK AREA

Aching wrists and sore fingers are the lot of hand quilters, while machine quilters suffer from backaches and headaches. Finding a comfortable working arrangement can go a long way toward alleviating fatigue and reducing stress.

If you find sewing at the machine uncomfortable, a brief anatomy lesson may show you why you're having trouble. Your head and upper body make up about one-fourth of your body weight. The shoulder muscles and spine support that weight all your waking hours. Everything is fine as long as your head and arms are centered over the spine. When you sew, however, the design of the cabinet or the habits of a lifetime have you bending your head and rolling slightly forward to see the work. Your head is no longer being supported by your spine, but by the neck muscles. To add more injury, your hands and arms are held in mid-air in front of your body. The shoulder muscles have the unenviable task of supporting the weight of your arms plus controlling the extremely delicate movement of your hands and fingers. To realign everything you need to sit up straight, lean forward from the waist, and rest your elbows on the table.

For quilting use your machine as a portable. Remove it from the cabinet and place it on a table large enough to hold most of the quilt. The table should not be against a wall.

The most comfortable chair is a secretarial chair with adjustable height and backrest. The chair should be adjusted so the height of the table is slightly above your waistline. The chair back should push against the small of your back, giving you a gentle reminder to sit up straight.

For basic quilting, sit directly in front of the needle, not in front of the center of your machine. Push the machine back from the front edge of the table about 6″. The machine may seem miles away from you, but the 6″ gives you place to rest your elbows and forces you to lean slightly forward. Rest your elbows on the table top, or at least, rest your arms on the table edge. Your elbows should be about 20″ to 24″ apart, with your finger tips near the presser foot. Make a conscious effort to keep your arms in contact with the table. Use books to prop up your elbows if your arms are too short to reach from the table to the presser foot (I've used the metropolitan telephone directory for years).

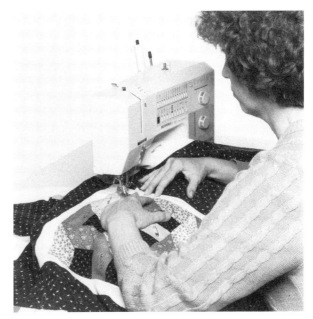

Fig. 2.39 Working position for machine-guided stitching

MACHINE-GUIDED QUILTING

Quilting methods are divided into two types: machine-guided and free-motion. Machine-guided quilting is like regular sewing. It is the place to begin. The machine does most of the work, including sewing straight with a perfect-length stitch. Machine-guided quilting is used for straight-line quilting like channel, grid, hanging diamonds, outline quilting, and stitch-in-the-ditch. Its major drawback is that it requires frequent pivoting of the quilt. Turning a small quilt 180 degrees is not a problem, but constant rotation of a full-size quilt can be aggravating, if not impossible. Practice on a 15″ square of backing, batting, and top to perfect your skill.

Set up the machine for machine-guided quilting by choosing the walking foot or the regular sewing foot. Set the machine for straight stitching with an average-length stitch. Position the quilt on the machine in the place you wish to start. Hold onto both the bobbin and top thread tails as you begin to sew. If you're in the middle of a section, press the top thread behind the foot to hold it. Every line of stitching must be knotted at the beginning and the end. Use auto knot for securing the threads. For machines without auto knot, shorten the stitch length to a very short stitch. On some machines this is almost zero; on others it may be in the fine setting or buttonhole setting. Stitch with the shortened length for the first ¼″ of the quilting line, then return the machine to the original length and continue sewing. About ¼″ before the end of the quilting line, shorten the stitch length and finish the line. This knot is inconspicuous and impossible to remove.

Handling Fabric

Sew with your elbows out and the three middle finger tips touching. Use your fingertips to guide the fabric, not the side of your hand or thumb. With a light touch, nudge the quilt top towards the presser foot. Move only the top, not the batting or backing. The top should form a small raise or "bubble" in front of the presser foot, and

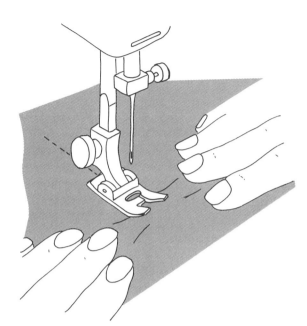

Fig. 2.40 A small bubble is created in front of the presser foot

Fig. 2.41 Close-up of bubble

there may be smaller bubbles between your finger. Press down and pull out with your fingertips to flatten the bubbles and hold them in place. Stitch in the space between the fingertips of your right and left hands. The fabric should look like it will be stitched in a pleat. Don't lift your fingers off the fabric until the needle is even with the index fingers. Stop sewing momentarily with the needle lowered in the fabric to repeat the process.

With practice this can be done in a smooth line of sewing. The key is to always have one hand on the quilt at all times. Think of it as walking: you would never have both feet off the ground, so don't lift both hands off the fabric.

When this is done correctly, the quilting line should have infinitesimal creases running perpendicular to the line but no pleats. This method of feeding the fabric to the foot compensates for the feed dogs pulling the backing fabric. The bubble method prevents the pleats that occur when crossing stitching lines, like grid quilting. It also alleviates sheering—the diagonal folds or pull lines that form between adjacent lines of stitching. Previously, the only method to prevent these lines was to follow a complex stitching sequence. Using the bubble method, it is not necessary to begin all the lines of stitching on one edge or to alternate them end for end.

Stitching Sequence

It is impossible to give the stitching sequence for every quilt pattern, but some general rules can help you decide on the sequence to use on your quilt.

When possible do the machine-guided portions of the design first. Think of the initial lines of stitching as a continuation of basting. Get as much of the quilt stitched in place as possible by these first lines. Use the quilting to divide the quilt into halves, quarters, and eighths, working smaller and smaller sections. The first line should be vertical or diagonal. Work the inside of the quilt before doing the borders, and keep all areas quilted evenly.

Managing Quilt Bulk

The size and weight of the quilt can be overwhelming. The question I'm most frequently asked is how I get the entire quilt on the machine. The key is making good use of the table and in the pliability of the quilt. The 36″ around the edges of the quilt are easy to stitch. That means a quilt up to 72″ wide won't give you much trouble. The

initial three or four lines of quilting are the worst to stitch. No matter how well you've basted, the quilt still acts like three separate pieces of fabric until those first lines are completed. Don't judge machine quilting until you've done a few lines; it will get easier.

There are many ways to handle a quilt. For machine-guided quilting I recommend you accordion-pleat the edge that must fit under the head of the machine. Keep it open and soft. A tight roll will make the quilt stiff and hard to handle. Fold it only where it is in the machine. Allow the pleats to fan out in front and back to keep the quilt manageable. Hold the quilt in your lap. Lift sections to the height of the presser foot as you sew. Stop with the needle in the fabric when you readjust the folds.

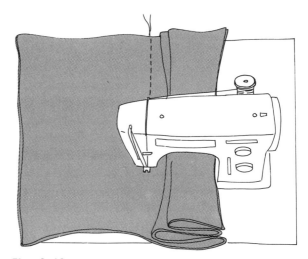

Fig. 2.42 Accordion-pleat quilt under the machine

FREE-MOTION QUILTING

Free-motion, or free-hand, quilting is the most like hand quilting. The stitch formation, size, and location depend solely on the quilter's skill. It is excellent for intricate curved designs. Free-motion quilting is used for motifs like feathered wreaths and floral designs, outline quilting, and backgrounds like stipple or echo. It can be used for short lengths of straight-line quilting but is unsuited to long accurate lines of straight stitch. The sewer's ability to move in any direction without turning the fabric makes this method the logical choice for large projects. Free-motion quilting is the creative part of machine quilting. It's like learning to color with crayons, read, and write all at once. It opens an entire new world by giving you complete control of the machine.

The best place to start is by stitching your name over and over again on a 15″ square of backing, batting, and solid-colored top. Set up the machine for straight stitch, with your stitch length at zero. Use the darning foot and lower or disengage the feed dogs. Place the quilt on the machine where you wish to begin. Start near the center of the 15″ square. Lower the presser foot. Don't bother to put the needle thread through the presser foot—it will be cut off later (see Fig. 2.43). Gently holding the

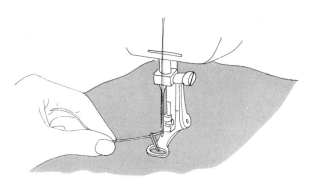

Fig. 2.43 Tug top thread to pop bobbin thread through the quilt layers

needle thread in your left hand, take one stitch and stop with the needle at the highest point. Tug on the top thread to pop the bobbin thread through the quilt. Grasp the two threads and hold them to the left of the foot. Every line of stitching must be knotted. To knot, run the machine at a high speed while moving the fabric slowly for about $\frac{1}{8}″$ to $\frac{1}{4}″$. This method results in the same tiny stitches used for knotting in other techniques. After the knot is made, clip the thread tails before they get caught in the stitching. Repeat the knot at the end of the stitching line.

Handling Fabric

Place your left hand behind the foot, circling it with the thumb and fingers. With the right hand about 2″ in front and to the right side of the presser foot, pinch an inch of fabric. The pinched fold should follow an imaginary line from your left shoulder to the spool pins on the machine. Both hands guide the fabric, but the left hand acts like a hoop, keeping the fabric taut and smooth, while the right hand does the majority of the guiding.

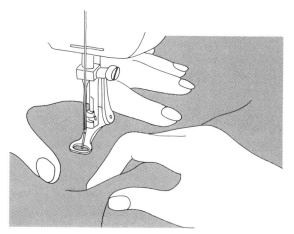

Fig. 2.44 "Pinch an inch" of fabric

A lot of things are happening at once. The stitch size and placement is determined by coordinating your hands and feet. At first it is like trying to pat your head while rubbing your stomach. Become aware of the machine speed and your hand movement. Don't only watch but use other senses, like touch and hearing. Listen to the sound the machine makes at different speeds and feel how tightly you're holding the fabric.

Start the machine running, taking a couple of stitches, before you move your hands. That way you're only concentrating on one thing at a time. Run the machine at a moderate speed. Move your hands and arms in a relaxed, flowing manner. Don't hold the fabric too tightly or press down too hard on the machine. The single most important step is to *relax*. If everything is coordinated, the stitches should be the size of a regular stitch.

Practice by writing your name in script. I do this warm-up every time I quilt. Don't write it out first in pencil on the fabric. Try to think of it as signing your name. You wouldn't pencil your signature on a check and then go back and copy it in ink, so don't copy it when you quilt. The letters should be about ¼″ high. To move to a new letter or word, knot the thread. Stop with the needle at the highest position. Lift the presser foot, and move the fabric just enough to get to the correct location. Lower the presser foot and lower the needle into the fabric. Knot the thread. Continue stitching as you did at the beginning. After all the words are stitched, go back and clip the connecting threads close to the quilt.

Running the machine too quickly or moving your hands too slowly will result in 500 stitches to the inch. The tiny stitches make a grainy or sandy-looking bobbin thread and can cause the top thread to break frequently. This is a good way to stitch if you feel like you're totally out of control of where you're going, but it is a hard habit to break. If you run the machine too slowly or move your hands too quickly, you'll get three stitches to the inch. Curves will have corners instead of smooth lines, and the whole name will look scribbled. When you sew like this you'll feel like you're out of control, but it is a great practice to improve your stitch quality.

Fig. 2.45 Name stitched with uniform-size stitches

Fig. 2.47 Sewing too slowly or moving fabric too quickly

Fig. 2.46 Another type of word stitching with duplicate lines

To improve the stitching don't turn the fabric at corners or curves. You may move forward, backward, or side to side, but do not turn the fabric. The advantage is you can stitch in any direction without turning the fabric.

Watch where you are going, not where the needle is going. Zeroing in on the needle or presser foot is like watching your feet when you walk—not the most efficient way to get around.

Most important, remember to blink, breathe, rest your elbows, and relax. It sounds odd but many beginners forget to breathe and blink regularly. The result is a shocking headache and burning eyes.

Machine quilting is not dangerous, but beginners should watch a few things: First, don't put your fingers under the needle. It sounds too obvious to point out, but many beginners become so involved in stitching, they don't watch where they are sewing. Second, keep your right index finger away from the needle clamp. Having a firm grasp of the fabric will save you from catching your finger on the needle clamp as the needle raises. There is simply not enough room for your finger between the clamp and the head of the machine. It's never serious to be caught, but it does hurt. Third, don't lean too close to your machine. This is a standing joke in my classes. A small percentage of people, like myself, get so close to the machine they hit the thread takeup. The shock of being hit on the forehead is nothing compared to having your hair pulled by catching it in the take-up lever.

Stitching Sequence

Do the machine-guided lines first, then the motif or outline quilting, and last, the background quilting. It is important that all areas of the quilt are evenly quilted, from the largest areas to the smallest. Machine quilting, especially background or filler quilting, puckers the quilt. Done out of sequence, the pucker would prevent flat quilting of the surrounding areas. Work from the center of the quilt to the outside edges, and don't bind the quilt until all the quilting is completed.

Handling Quilt Bulk

The technique used for handling a full-size quilt when doing free-motion quilting is completely different from that of machine-guided quilting. Combining the techniques used in commercial quilting with our home machine can result in an easy, painless method of quilting that frees us from the weight of the quilt. I devised this method when I developed back problems from sewing for long stretches of time. Although unorthodox, most quilters find this method best for free-motion quilting.

Angle the machine to slide the right front corner of the machine off the table edge. Continue turning the head of the machine until the needle is at ten o'clock and the body of the machine is at four o'clock. Wrap your arms around the body of the machine, and reach your hands toward the needle. Hug the machine to the hollow in your shoulder. If you have long hair you might find it advantageous to tie it back out of the way of the hand wheel. With the machine in this position, the entire weight of the quilt is on the table. Stitch as you did before, but the left hand is now at the front and left of the presser foot, while the right hand is to the back and right of the foot.

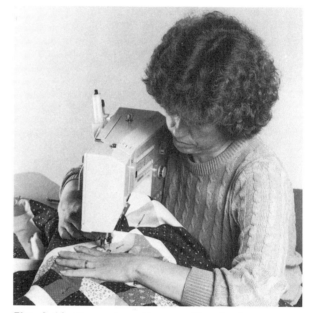

Fig. 2.48 Correct working position for free-motion quilting

CHAPTER 3

Dictionary of Quilting Patterns

To make an informed decision on the style of quilting and the method to use requires basic knowledge of quilting patterns and names.

Motif Patterns

Motif designs look like the drawing in Fig. 3.1. Styles include feathered wreaths and borders; floral and nature designs (pineapples, sea shells, flowers, hearts, and birds or animals); nautical designs (cabled border, twisted ropes, ships, and anchors); and patriotic designs (eagles, stars, and buildings). The list is endless and encompasses any line drawing you'd like on your quilt, from a simple continuous line design to an intricate pencil sketch.

Fig. 3.1 Typical quilting motif

Motifs usually are quilted in plain areas or over simple pieced shapes. Stitching is most apparent on light-colored fabrics. These patterns are used to highlight the skill of the quilter. Motif quilting is best done by free-motion quilting. Complex designs may require that small sections of the pattern be stitched over more than once to get to the next part of the design. The trick is stitching on the same line twice. Luckily, the batting helps conceal any small errors. Don't try to match lines stitch for stitch. Just get as close as possible to covering the original line. Any line drawing can be machine quilted, but not every design is a successful quilting pattern. The key is to choose the quilting pattern that enhances the piecing. Consider the scale of the quilt. Match the scale of the quilting pattern to the piecing. The edge of the quilting pattern should be $\frac{1}{4}''$ on small pieces to 1″ on large pieces away from the edges of the piecing. When the quilting design is too large, the design looks squeezed into the space. On the other hand, a tiny design in the middle of a large blank space is undesirable.

Outline Quilting

While motif quilting is for plain open spaces, outline quilting highlights the piecing. There are four basic types of outline quilting.

Stitch-in-the ditch. This is a simple form of outline quilting, in which stitches follow the seam line, usually just a fraction of an inch into the piece and away from the seam (Fig. 3.2). Staying a small distance from

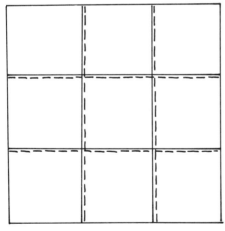

Fig. 3.2 Stitch-in-the-ditch

the seam makes the quilting stronger and is less apt to break the piecing seam. Stitch-in-the-ditch quilting shows the least of any form of quilting, and is excellent for

quilting tiny pieces where heavier forms of quilting are unacceptable. Exclusive use of this method can result in a quilt that looks unquilted and unfinished. Stitch-in-the-ditch can be done in machine-guided or free-motion quilting.

Traditional outline. Traditional $\frac{1}{4}''$ outline quilting is the most common form of pieced quilting. Each piece or shape in the block is quilted around with a line of stitching that is $\frac{1}{4}''$ from the seam. This line of stitching is very exact and requires careful turning of corners and curves to maintain the perfect $\frac{1}{4}''$ space. This method is *always* done machine guided, using the edge of the presser foot as a stitching guide.

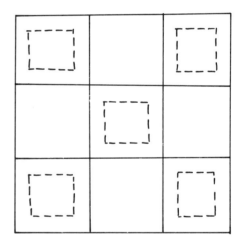

Fig. 3.3 Traditional $\frac{1}{4}''$ outline

Exact corners can be a challenge to the most experienced quilter. We all know the frustration of having the stitch length not coincide with the corner. Approaching the corner, one stitch falls before the exact corner, the next beyond. The best way to handle this problem is by adjusting the stitch length. As you approach the corner, shorten the length so the machine is making stitches half the length of the normal stitches. Stitch to the exact corner. Turn the corner, return the stitch length to the regular setting, and continue to stitch.

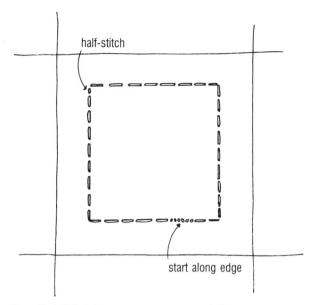

Fig. 3.4 Stitching corners successfully

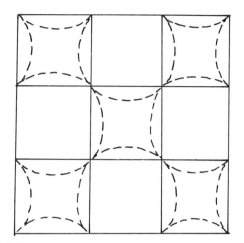

Fig. 3.5 Johannah's continuous curve

Another hint for perfect corners is never start at the corner, as knots are more conspicuous there. Start and stop stitching on the longest straight edge. The drawback to ¼″ outline is the constant turning required to stitch all the pieces in a single block. It is best suited to small projects or quilt-as-you-go methods.

Barbara Johannah's continuous curve. This unique and ingenious method of outline quilting was devised by Barbara Johannah. The basic premise is to connect the lines of ¼″ outline quilting by turning them into gentle curves that cross at the corners of blocks. This results in the look of ¼″ outline quilting without the fuss of machine-guided lines. The gentle curves are easy to stitch and are worked like puzzles. You must stitch as many lines as possible without doubling lines or breaking thread. Johannah's book (see Resource List) has a wealth of patterns and complete instructions on developing your own designs. It is one of the few books I simply can't do without. I've used this method frequently. It's often possible to stitch entire blocks of 30 or 40 pieces without breaking the thread. Although it isn't necessary to mark the quilting pattern on the blocks, I recommend

it for the beginner. Marking the pattern insures a modicum of uniformity. This method is best suited to free-motion quilting.

Modified continuous curve. I've combined stitch-in-the-ditch quilting and continuous-curve quilting. The result is a continuous quilting line approximately ⅛″ from the seamline. Unlike continuous-curve quilting, the quilting line never has to be marked, and mistakes are less apparent. The smaller scale works well on tiny pieces and unusual shapes. It is the perfect substitute for stitch-in-the-ditch quilting on patterns with open seams. The quilting is subtle without the disquieting, unquilted look of stitch-in-the-ditch quilting.

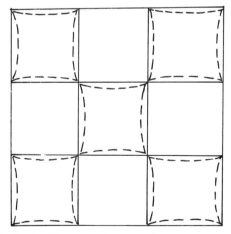

Fig. 3.6 Modified continuous curve

Filler Quilting

Filler quilting can be done in small sections of the quilt or in an overall pattern without paying attention to the piecing or appliqué pattern. Overall filler quilting had been considered passé. It is often seen in church group quilts from the 1930s. The recent revival of 1930s-style quilts has reintroduced this form of quilting. The most common types of filler quilting include:

Channel. Parallel lines of stitching, varying from $\frac{1}{4}''$ to many inches apart. The lines can be on the straight or bias of the quilt. Always done as machine-guided quilting, it uses the quilting guide to make evenly spaced rows.

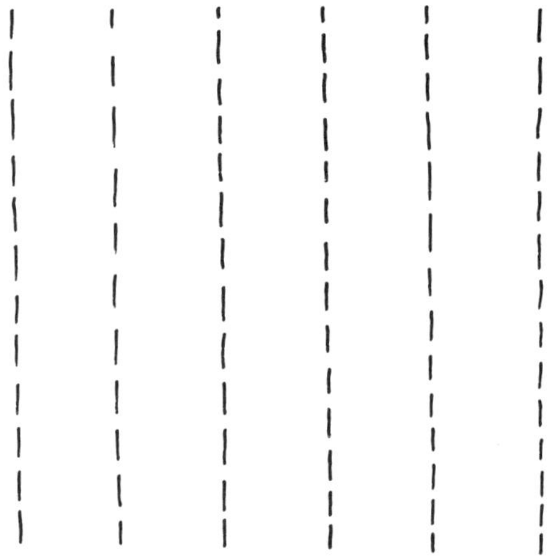

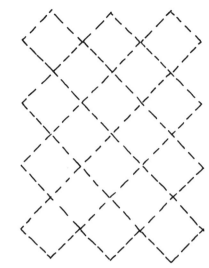

Fig. 3.8 Grid

Hanging diamonds. In a sophisticated version of the grid, the quilting lines cross at 45-degree or 60-degree angles. Both grid and hanging diamonds are machine-guided quilting. The quilting guide is not too successful in measuring these patterns, so I recommend you mark the quilting lines. At first glance these patterns appear deceptively simple. In reality complex mathematical calculations are needed to make the pattern fit the quilt top. Trying to line up

Fig. 3.7 Channel

Grid. Two sets of channel quilting stitched at 90-degree angles. This, too, can vary from $\frac{1}{4}''$ to large blocks of quilting.

For both channel and grid quilting, you may prefer a narrow zigzag to a straight stitch, as my editor uses.

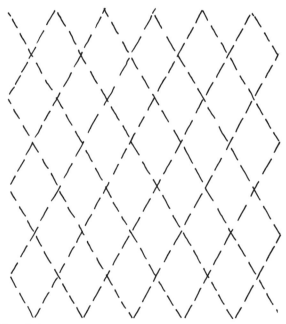

Fig. 3.9 Hanging diamonds

quilting lines with seams or corners can be overwhelming. The beginner should choose these patterns for small areas or, like the makers of antique quilts, pay no attention to where the quilting lines cross the piecing pattern.

Clamshell. The charm of this curved design, which is vaguely reminiscent of neat, overlapped rows of circles, is in its accuracy. From a distance clamshell quilting looks like a grid. In its diminutive size, it is also called thimble quilting; the thimble was used as a template for the design. Clamshell quilting can be done by free-motion machine-guided quilting.

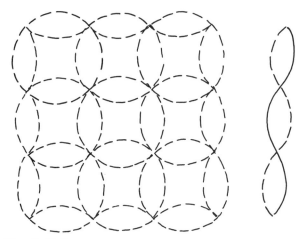

Fig. 3.11 Teacup

Fig. 3.10 Clamshell

Teacup. This curved design, a line drawing of the Double Wedding Ring piecing pattern, is composed of simple, overlapped circles. The name refers to the practice of using a teacup as the quilting template. Teacup quilting is done in gently curved lines that intersect to give the appearance of circles. It is easy to do by machine-guided or free-motion quilting. This basic idea is adaptable to stitch-in-the-ditch quilting of the pieced Double Wedding Ring.

Fan or Baptist fan. A simple pattern based on an arc, it is often marked using a dinner plate as the base line. The multiple lines of stitching in each fan shape follow the base line. The fans are overlapped and generally are in rows. Part of the charm of the pattern is that any imperfections are not readily apparent. Baptist fan is best suited to free-motion quilting. The design

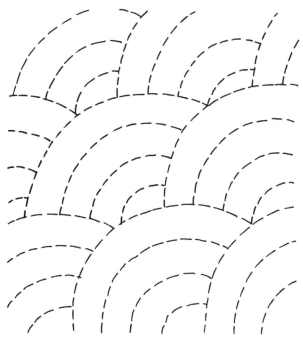

Fig. 3.12 Baptist fan

will require some areas to be double stitched. Working the design diagonally instead of in straight rows reduces duplicate lines and knotting.

Combination Designs

Most quilters use a combination of designs to complete their quilts. The best quilting has a variety of textures. The pieced sections can be done with stitch-in-the-ditch or outline quilting, while the plain areas are motif quilted. Often, motifs like feathered wreaths or borders are on a background of filler quilting (see the book cover). The fillers compact the fabric surrounding the motif, displaying the motif to its best advantage. The previous filler patterns, worked in small scale, are suitable backgrounds to motifs. Echo quilting and stipple quilting are also filler patterns but are traditionally designed as background for motifs rather than as overall patterns.

Echo. This quilting is a traditional choice for appliqué quilts. The most common form of echo quilting is Hawaiian quilting. Echo quilting surrounds an appliqué or a quilting motif with concentric lines of stitching.

Fig. 3.13 Echo

Each line forms a complete circle, not a single spiraling line. The lines can be any distance apart, but the usual range is from $\frac{1}{8}''$ to a few inches. The line carefully follows the edge of the original design on the first row of stitching, but on subsequent rows, the line becomes less and less like the original. The design is rarely marked on the quilt top but is worked by eye, using the edge of the darning foot or an arbitrary mark as a guide. Echo is best suited to free-motion quilting.

Stipple. Stipple quilting is often used as a background on trapunto or stuff-work quilts. The stitching gives a beautiful grainy or pebbled texture to the quilt while flattening the background. Although stippling is tedious by hand, it is fun and fast by machine. It is the one background that even a beginner can master.

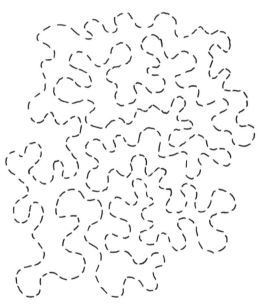

Fig. 3.14 Good even stipple

Stippling is a convoluted line of stitching. The secret is to have controlled chaos. The lines can be any distance apart, but remember, how you start is how you must finish. If the lines twist and turn at $\frac{1}{8}''$ intervals, all the stippling throughout the quilt must be that close together. Most quilters stipple at $\frac{3}{8}''$ intervals, which is close enough together to give a "hand" look without being overwhelming.

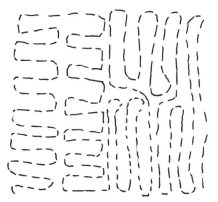

Fig. 3.15 Too-uniform stipple

In general, keep crosses to a minimum. Try to vary the stitch direction often enough to prevent a pattern from emerging. Think of the line of stitching as moving in two directions at once. The base line is a simple undulating line that does the actual filling in of the space. Superimpose scribbles on the baseline. You are now moving two ways at once, forward and side to side.

Of course stipple is not that cut and dried. Explaining how to stipple is like giving written instructions for riding a bicycle. The best way to learn is to experiment. Sew as fast as the machine will run. Tiny stitches give the desired effect. Too-large stitches will make the corners square instead of gently curved. Keep the stitches small and crossed lines to a minimum. Large stitches with frequent crosses look like sock darning!

Fig. 3.16 Poor stipple; too-large stitches make corners square instead of curved

In general, divide the area to be stippled into sections about the size of a silver dollar. Work around the edges of the section, then fill in the center, before moving to the next section. Remember, stippling puckers and can cause pleats where it joins a motif or piece. Starting on the edges of the section and working to the center will prevent problems. When combining stippling with outline quilting, use a large-scale, open stipple. Outline quilting doesn't pucker; stippling does. The results can be a fluted quilt. The pieced area will bow or dish, as if it is too large for the rest of the quilt. Large-scale or open stippling puckers less than compact stippling and is easier to blend with outline quilting. Work on developing your own style. Feathered motifs, outline quilting, or fillers require uniformity. Stippling encourages individuality and is as personal as your signature. No two quilters will stipple alike.

Patterns for Sashing and Borders

Sashing and borders require running patterns and pose special problems. There are corners to match, and the patterns must have an even number of repeats in a specified space. While outline quilting and fillers follow a strict pattern or are based on the piecing, the border and sashing designs are less structured and are open to personal interpretation.

Maintain balance between the areas of the quilt. Heavily quilted blocks require heavily quilted borders. Design elements need to be repeated in the different areas of the quilt. For example, if grid is used in the border, it should appear in the quilt body. The scale of the repeated elements can vary, but similar shapes give the quilting continuity.

Corners of borders or sashing can be handled three ways: One way is to ignore the problem and run the designs off the edges. Symmetry is not an issue with this method. The designs start and stop at seam lines or edges of the quilt without a thought about how the pattern fits the space. The quilter starts making the pattern at a seam line or edge and simply marks the running design along the length of the border or sashing. This is a common method of quilting on antique quilts. It is very easy and doesn't require math or drawing skills. Quilts stitched in this way have a charming folk art look.

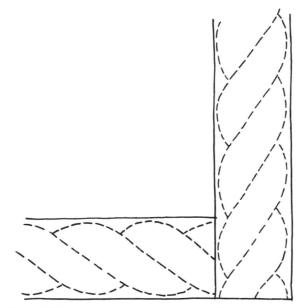

Fig. 3.17 Border designed to run off edges

A second way is to change the design at every corner. The simplest version of this idea is the corner square. Often the borders or sashing are quilted to make a square at the corners or joins. The long straight pieces of sashing or borders are quilted with a running pattern. The running pattern is stopped at the corner square and a motif, like flowers or feathered designs, is placed in the square. Slightly more sophisticated than the previous method, this pattern requires only the most basic drawing skills. The quilter starts marking the pattern at the midpoint of the border or

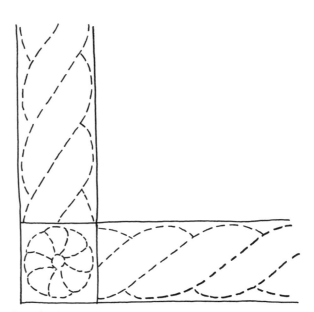

Fig. 3.18 Corner square with motif

sashing, then marks from the center to corner on each half of the border or sashing. This way, the design joins the corner squares at the exact same place in the repeat, giving the effect of careful planning without much work.

The third way is to continue the border pattern around the corner. This is the most sophisticated and complex method to corner quilting patterns. Many quilting pattern books have corner designs, but the repeats won't fit the length of every quilt. The secret is to start in the corners. The quilter marks the corners first and fills in the space along the straight edges. The straight edge can be handled two ways: (1) Stretch or squeeze the design to fit evenly into the available length by omitting or lengthening small sections of the pattern; or (2) intro-

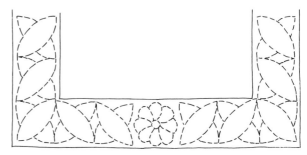

Fig. 3.19 Border designed to continue around corners

duce a different motif at the midpoint of the border or sashing. The extra motif acts like the corner square in the previous method. It joins two mismatched designs into one cohesive design. Fitting the quilting pattern to the borders or sashing requires math and drawing skills.

For the projects in Chapter 5, I've chosen the first method of marking sashing and borders, with one slight variation. I suggest you start marking the pattern at the midpoint and work toward the seams or quilt edges. That way the pattern will appear symmetrical. If you would like to try other designs, see the Bibliography for a list of quilting pattern books.

CHAPTER 4

12 Blocks: Patterns and Directions

This chapter gives patterns for one dozen 12″ blocks. Each pattern gives the piecing instructions, plus instructions for appropriate quilting designs. The patterns are presented in order of difficulty and represent diverse methods of piecing and quilting that can be transferred to many other quilt patterns.

All yardages are given for the blocks and projects. Yardages for the blocks are given in sets of blocks that correspond with the requirements for the projects in Chapter 5. The projects range from simple one-block pillows to an eighty-one block king-size quilt. The only math required is simple addition to add the block yardage to the project yardage. Knowing how to figure yardages is an important skill, but it can be a formidable task for even the accomplished quilter. I know very few quilters who can truly say they enjoy the process, so I have made it as easy as possible to determine the correct amount of fabric. If you would like to know more about determining yardages, see the Bibliography for a list of books that can help you.

- ♥ $\frac{1}{4}″$ seam allowances are included throughout
- ♥ All yardages based on 44″–45″ cotton fabric, but assume only 42″ usable
- ♥ Cutting and stitching directions are for a *single* block; when making a number of blocks, cut and sew all like pieces at the same time

1. Snowflake

Snowflake has three templates and nine pieces. It is made in three colors: a light, dark, and an accent. It is an excellent mix of shapes for your first block. Two of the templates, the square and the triangle, are so simple they are best cut using the rotary-cut method, while the arrow shape that forms the *X* is best cut with a scissors using a paper or plastic template. The matches are easy. There are no points, only simple-to-sew 90-degree corners, and all the seams are straight.

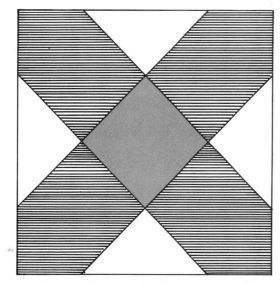

Fig. 4.1 Snowflake, in light, dark, and medium tones

Fabrics

For one 12″ block:

Template A: One strip $3\frac{5}{8}$″ wide in light color (4 triangles on the sides of the block)

Template B: One strip $4\frac{3}{4}$″ wide in accent color (for 1 center square)

Template C: One strip $4\frac{3}{4}$″ wide in dark color (4 arrows pointing to the block corners)

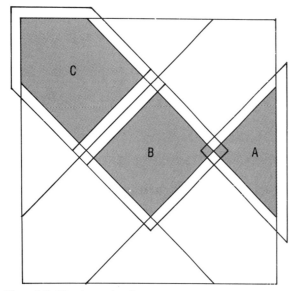

Fig. 4.2 Piecing chart

Cutting

1. Make a paper template of piece A. Tape the template to the 90-degree corner of your triangle. From light-colored strip A, cut four triangles the size of template A. Notice the straight of grain is parallel to the long edge of the triangle.

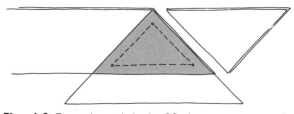

Fig. 4.3 Tape template to 90-degree corner of triangle

2. From strip B, cut one square $4\frac{3}{4}$″. This is the center square in an accent color.

3. Make a paper template of piece C. With careful pinning you can cut two pieces at once. Cut four piece Cs from the dark color.

4. When you have all the pieces cut, lay them together to form a block. This will give a clear idea of what the block will look like when it is finished and a point of reference when stitching the block together.

Piecing

5. Stitch piece A to piece C. A small corner of triangle A will extend beyond piece C. That is correct. The edges of the pieces do not line up unless the pieces are identical. The excess seam allowance on triangle A

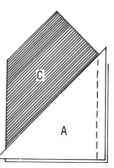

Fig. 4.4 Small corners of A will extend beyond C

Fig. 1 *Variable Star,* blocks set side-by-side

Fig. 2 *Variable Star,* blocks set with sashing and edged with prairie points

Fig. 3 *Hands All Around,* sashed with double borders

Fig. 4 *Lover's Knot,* side-by-side set without borders

Fig. 5 *Solomon's Puzzle*

Fig. 6 *Night and Noon,* alternating with *Plain Block*

Fig. 7 *Kansas Trouble,* alternating with *Wild Goose Chase* variation

Fig. 8 *Dutch Rose* pillow with double ruffle

Fig. 9 *Dutch Rose* wall hanging, sashed

Fig. 10 *Snowflake* quilt, matching pillow, made with striped fabric

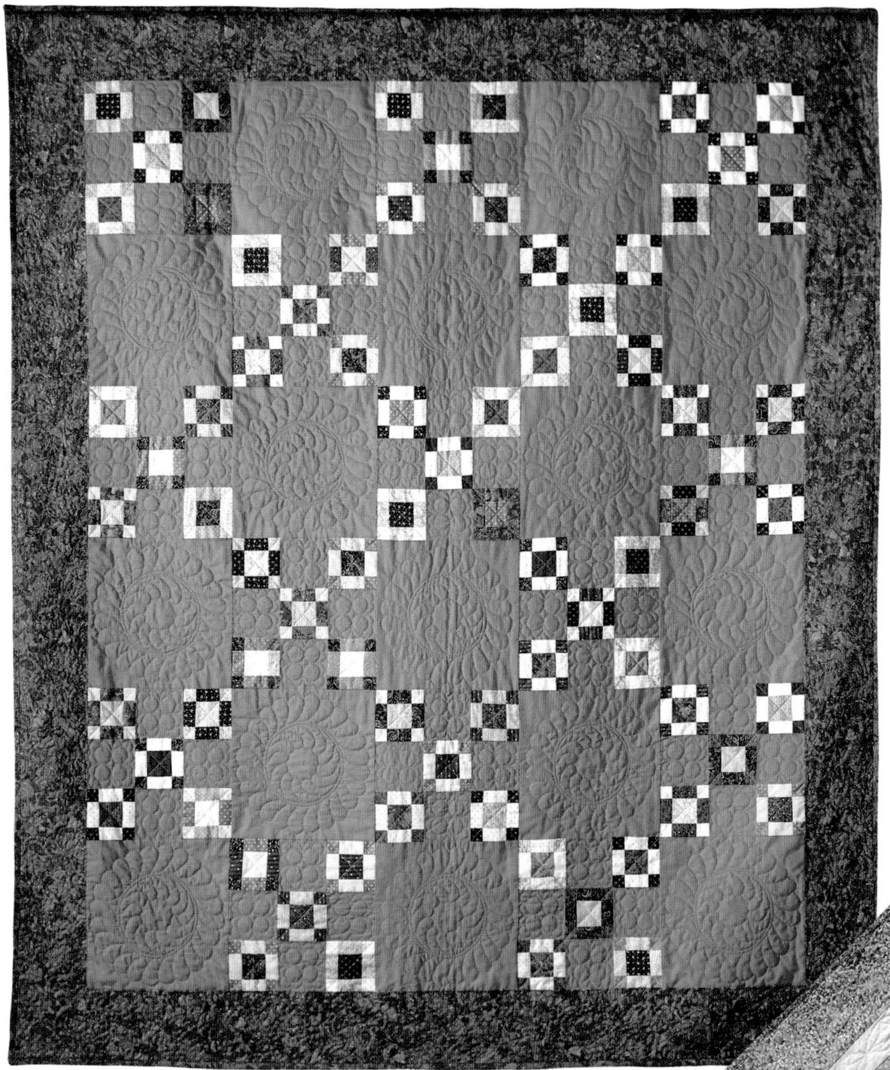

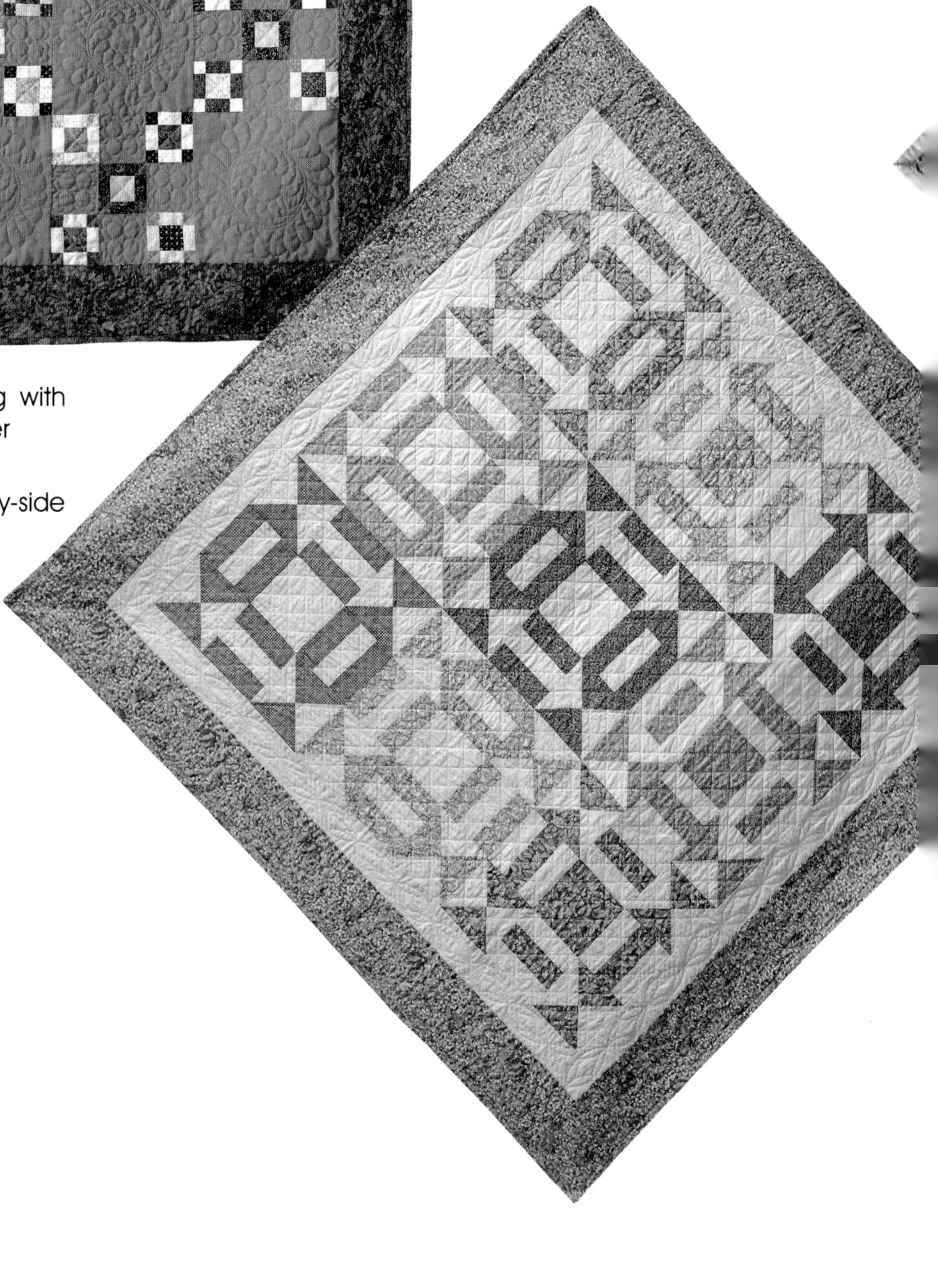

Fig. 11 *Puss in the Corner,* alternating with *Plain Block,* finished with a single border

Fig. 12 *At the Square,* blocks set side-by-side with double border

Fig. 13 *Plain Block* wall hanging, sashed with floral fabric

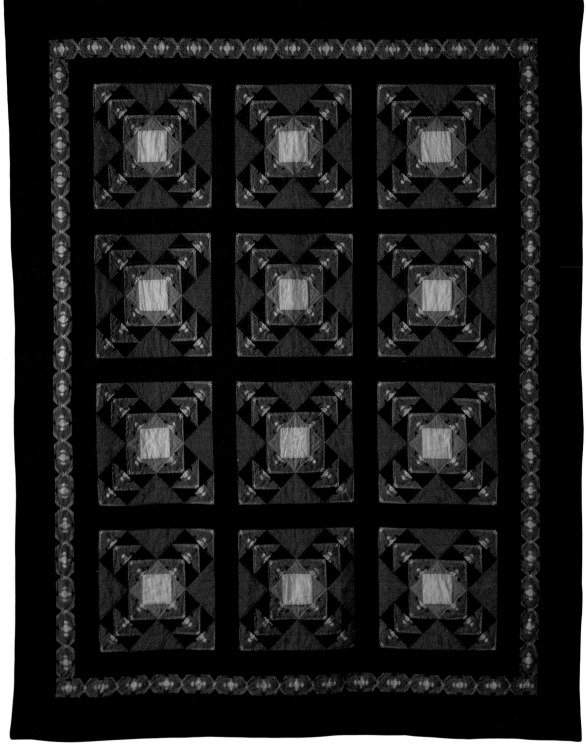

Fig. 14 *Wild Goose Chase,* blocks and border made with patterned fabric

should intersect piece C on the $\frac{1}{4}''$ seam line. For a more complete explanation see Basic Piecing Directions in Chapter 2. Join pieces A (light triangle) to piece C (dark arrow) to make two sections, A-C-A. Gently press the seams toward the dark fabric, pressing only the seam. One of the unsewn edges of triangle A is on the bias and may stretch if pressed.

6. Sew two Cs (dark arrows) to center block B to form a strip, C-B-C. Press the seam away from the center, toward the dark fabric.

7. Two seams remain to finish the block. Each of the seams have two simple keyed matches in the center block. Before stitching the seam, pin the matches. The seams have been pressed in opposite directions to make the match as easy as possible. Simply slide the right side of the seams together and pin. Don't worry if the center block is a slightly different size than piece C. After pinning the matches, pin the ends of the seam. A small corner of piece A will extend beyond piece C, as it did in the first step.

One of the pieces may be slightly longer than the other because of the bias edges on the light-colored triangles. Sew with the longer edge down. The feed dogs help to ease the excess fabric into the seam.

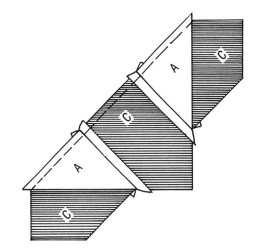

Fig. 4.6 Pin right sides together and stitch

8. Press seams toward the center.

Quilting

For the basic quilting design I have chosen the simplest form of quilting, machine-guided stitch-in-the-ditch. Its obvious

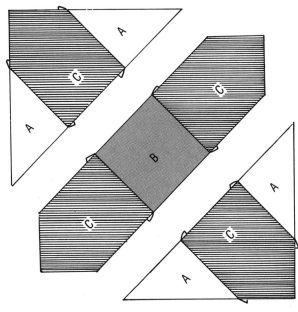

Fig. 4.5 Two seams will finish the pieced block

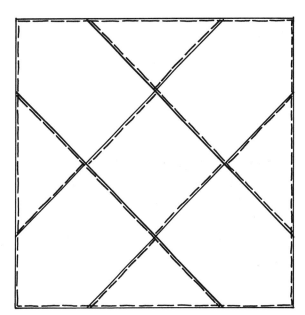

Fig. 4.7 Machine-guided stitch-in-the-ditch

advantage is that it doesn't require marking a quilting pattern on the block. You use the piecing seams and the block edges as the quilting guide. Because of the size of the pieces, the quilting lines will form a grid spaced about 4″ apart. Polyester batting is the best choice for the scale of quilting on this block.

Try to stitch as close as possible to the seam on the side of the seam that is a single layer of fabric—not on the side with the seam allowances. For blocks with high color contrast, use invisible thread.

The more accomplished quilter should see Fig. 4.8 for an additional free-motion quilting pattern to use in the center. Follow the numbered sequence for stitching order.

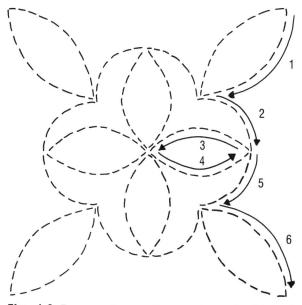

Fig. 4.8 Free-motion pattern; enlarge to fit block

Companion Blocks

Wild Goose Chase (see Fig. 4.64), Wild Goose Chase variation (Fig. 4.75), Variable Star (Fig. 4.33), and Plain Block can all be used as companion blocks. When joining Snowflake blocks, a secondary pattern

emerges. The side triangles form a square. The square is exactly the same size as the center block. The overall pattern gives the appearance of a lattice or woven design. Wild Goose Chase pattern is based on Snowflake. The diagonals of the blocks will intersect to form the same secondary pattern as that of simple Snowflake. When combined with Plain Block, the overall pattern loses its strong diagonal lines.

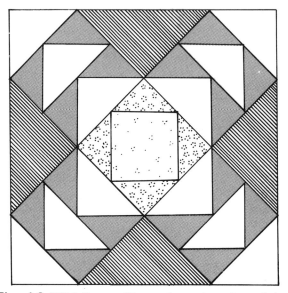

Fig. 4.9 Wild Goose Chase, based on Snowflake

Alternate Colors

This simple block is stunning in two colors. Reverse the colors: make the dark arrows light and the side triangles and center block a medium color. One of the loveliest quilts I've seen from this block was a baby quilt. Half the blocks were of a light print with solid blue triangles and center square. The other half were of light print and pink accents. The pieced blocks were set with sashing of the light print. The quilt was bordered in solid blue and the light print.

SNOWFLAKE

Number of strips needed to make the blocks:

						Number of Blocks						
		1	**4**	**6**	**9**	**12**	**30**	**35**	**48**	**56**	**64**	**81**
	Piece/Width					Number of Strips						
A	$3\frac{5}{8}''$	1	2	2	3	4	10	12	16	19	22	27
B	$4\frac{3}{4}''$	1	1	1	2	2	4	5	6	7	8	9
C	$4\frac{3}{4}''$	1	4	5	8	10	24	28	38	45	52	56

Yardages needed to make the blocks:

	Piece/Color					Yardages						
A	Light	$\frac{1}{8}$	$\frac{1}{4}$	$\frac{1}{4}$	$\frac{1}{2}$	$\frac{1}{2}$	1	$1\frac{1}{4}$	$1\frac{5}{8}$	$1\frac{7}{8}$	$2\frac{1}{4}$	$2\frac{3}{4}$
B	Accent	$\frac{1}{4}$	$\frac{1}{4}$	$\frac{1}{4}$	$\frac{1}{2}$	$\frac{1}{2}$	$\frac{5}{8}$	$\frac{3}{4}$	$\frac{7}{8}$	1	$1\frac{1}{8}$	$1\frac{1}{4}$
C	Dark	$\frac{1}{4}$	$\frac{5}{8}$	$\frac{3}{4}$	$1\frac{1}{4}$	$1\frac{1}{2}$	$3\frac{1}{4}$	$3\frac{3}{4}$	$5\frac{1}{8}$	6	7	$8\frac{5}{8}$

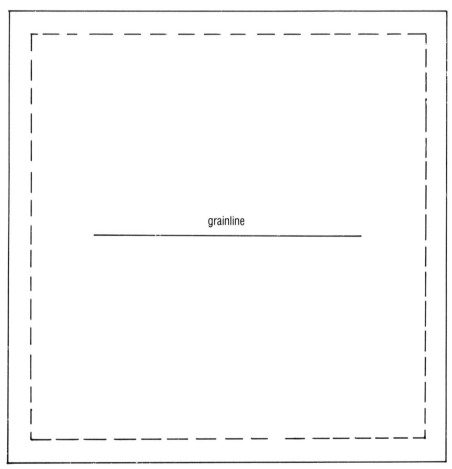

grainline

Fig. 4.10 Snowflake template B

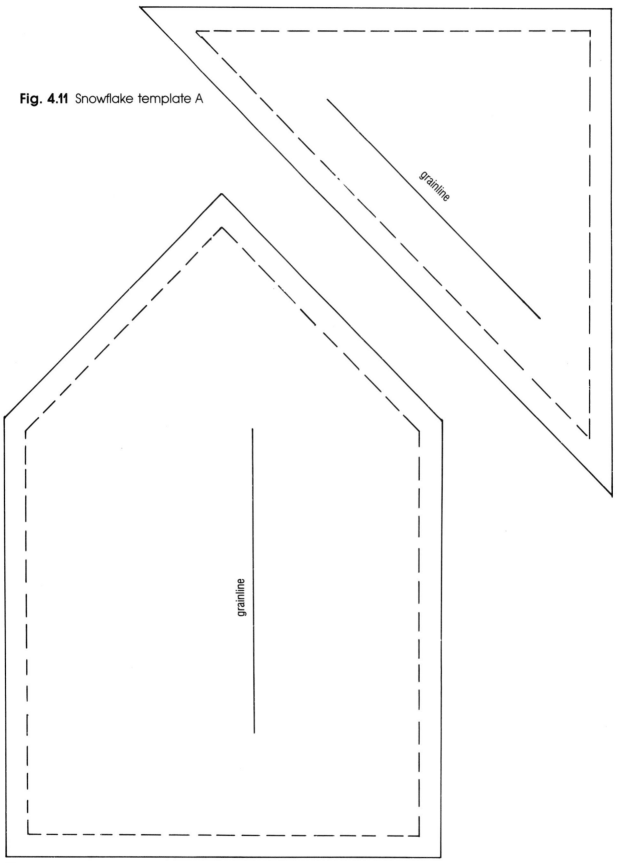

Fig. 4.11 Snowflake template A

grainline

grainline

Fig. 4.12 Snowflake template C

2. Puss in the Corner

Puss in the Corner is a variation of Double Nine Patch. The 12″ block is made of nine 4″ blocks. Five of the 4″ blocks also contain nine pieces. Like most Double Nine Patch patterns, this block is made with template-free strip piecing. The pattern is given in measurements, not pattern pieces. The entire block is rotary cut with simple straight seams and easy matches. The pattern uses four colors—a light, a medium, and a dark, plus an accent color.

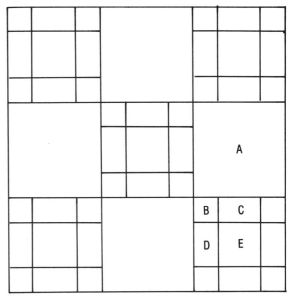

Fig. 4.14 Cut squares and rectangles in four colors

Cutting and Strip Piecing

To make the small pieced blocks:

1. Cut strip B (dark) and C (light) in half, resulting in strips approximately 21″ long.

2. Sew three strips together to form a strip B-C-B. The strip will be dark/light/dark. Press the seams toward the dark fabric.

3. Crosscut B-C-B into 1½″ strips. Cut ten strips. Set aside.

Fig. 4.15 Crosscut B-C-B into 10 strips

4. Cut piece D (light) and E (medium) in half, resulting in strips approximately 21″ long.

5. Sew three strips together to form strip D-E-D. The strip will be light/medium/light. Press the seams toward the medium fabric.

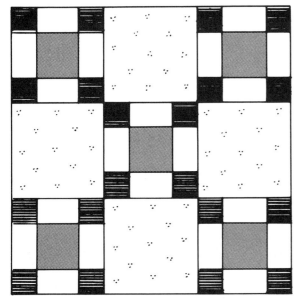

Fig. 4.13 Puss in the Corner

Fabrics

For one 12″ block:

Piece A: One strip 4½″ wide in accent color (4 plain blocks)
Piece B: One strip 1½″ wide in dark color (corners of pieced block)
Piece C: One strip 2½″ wide in light color (side rectangles of pieced block)
Piece D: One strip 1½″ wide in light color (side rectangles of pieced block)
Piece E: One strip 2½″ wide in medium color (center of pieced block)

6. Crosscut D-E-D into 2½″ strips. Cut five strips.

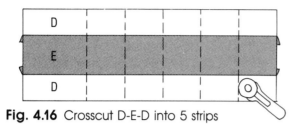

Fig. 4.16 Crosscut D-E-D into 5 strips

To complete the small pieced blocks:

7. You will make five 4½″ blocks. Each block contains two B-C-B strips and one D-E-D strip. The block has four simple keyed matches. The seams have been pressed in opposite directions to make the match as easy as possible. Before you sew, pin the matches. Slide the right sides of the seams together. Do not worry if pieces are not exactly the same size. If one of the edges is slightly longer than the other, sew with the longer edge down. The feed dogs help ease the excess fabric into the seam.

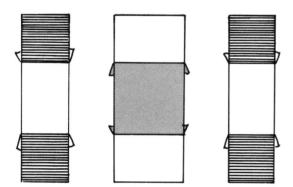

Fig. 4.17 Two B-C-B strips and one D-E-D strip ready to assemble

8. Sew five B-C-B strips to five D-E-D strips. Press the seams toward the center.

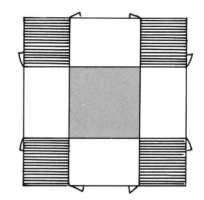

Fig. 4.18 With right sides together, stitch two lengthwise seams

9. Sew five B-C-B strips to the preceding sets. Press seams toward the center.

Cutting Four Plain Blocks

10. Cut four 4½″ blocks from strip A.

To complete the block:

11. Stitch three plain 4½″ blocks (piece A) to three 4½″ pieced blocks. Press the seams toward the plain block.

12. Stitch the remaining plain block to one of the preceding sets to form a unit that is plain-pieced-plain. Press the seams toward the plain block.

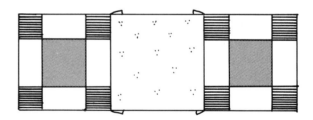

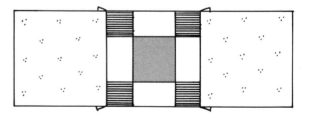

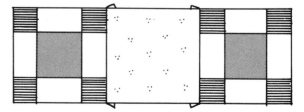

Fig. 4.19 Stitch two pieced-plain-pieced units and one plain-pieced-plain unit

13. Stitch the remaining pieced blocks to the sets made in Step 12, to form two units pieced-plain-pieced. Press seams toward the plain block.

14. Stitch the three units together to form a $12\frac{1}{2}''$ block. Use the opposing seams for easy matching. If some of the pieces are slightly longer than others, try to sew with the longer edge down. The feed dogs will help to ease the excess fabric into the seam. When the slightly longer piece is on top, gently stretch the fabric underneath. Grasp the fabric behind the foot and in front of the foot. Pull evenly with both hands. Don't affect the feed of the fabric; just stretch the shorter piece. Press the seams away from the center.

Quilting

The quilting pattern is a machine-guided bias grid, based on the piecing pattern. The grid is made by stitching corner-to-corner across the piecing. I recommend marking the quilting pattern on the block, as sewing perfectly straight lines without a guideline can be difficult. Either polyester or a cotton/polyester blend batting will work with this scale quilting pattern. Quilt following the numbered sequence shown. For the more accomplished quilter here is an additional free-motion quilting pattern for the plain areas (see Fig. 4.22).

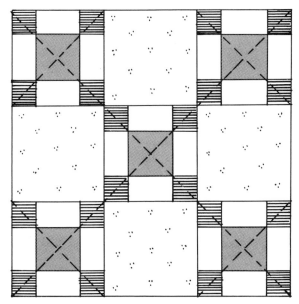

Fig. 4.20 Stitch corner-to-corner across pieced blocks

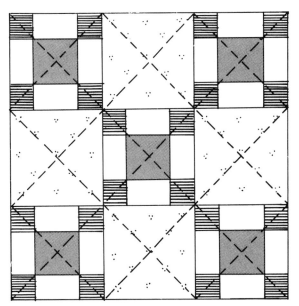

Fig. 4.21 Stitch across plain areas

Fig. 4.22 Free-motion pattern option for plain areas; enlarge to fit 4″ square

Companion Blocks and Sets

Puss in the Corner can be set with Night and Noon (Fig. 4.46) and At the Square (Fig. 4.23). Alternated with Plain Block, Puss in the Corner changes to a variation of Single Irish Chain. Alternated with a Plain Block or sashed is the easiest set for this block. Joining Puss in the Corner blocks forms a complex and interesting secondary pattern, but the matches along the block seams can be troublesome for the novice quilter.

Alternate Colors

Puss in the Corner makes a wonderful scrap quilt. The yardages and instructions are based on 42″ fabric, so you can substitute any combination of scraps as long as the fabric is the full width selvage to selvage. Like Single Irish Chain, this block is striking in two colors. The common arrangement is all light colors, except the center and four corners of the small pieced block. Reversing light and dark colors can give the pattern an Amish appearance.

PUSS IN THE CORNER

Number of strips needed to make the blocks:

		Number of Blocks										
		1	4	6	9	12	30	35	48	56	64	81
	Piece/Width	Number of Strips										
A	$4\frac{1}{2}''$	1	2	3	5	6	15	18	24	28	32	42
B	$1\frac{1}{2}''$	1	3	5	7	10	24	27	37	44	50	63
C	$2\frac{1}{2}''$	1	2	3	5	5	12	14	19	22	25	32
D	$1\frac{1}{2}''$	1	3	4	6	8	19	22	30	35	40	51
E	$2\frac{1}{2}''$	1	2	2	3	4	10	11	15	18	20	26

Yardages needed to make the blocks:

	Piece/Color	Yardages										
A	Accent	$\frac{1}{4}$	$\frac{1}{2}$	$\frac{1}{2}$	$\frac{3}{4}$	$\frac{7}{8}$	2	$2\frac{1}{2}$	$3\frac{1}{8}$	$3\frac{5}{8}$	$4\frac{1}{8}$	$5\frac{3}{8}$
B	Dark	$\frac{1}{8}$	$\frac{1}{4}$	$\frac{1}{4}$	$\frac{1}{2}$	$\frac{1}{2}$	$1\frac{1}{8}$	$1\frac{1}{8}$	$1\frac{5}{8}$	$1\frac{7}{8}$	$2\frac{1}{4}$	$2\frac{3}{4}$
C/D	Light	$\frac{1}{4}$	$\frac{1}{2}$	$\frac{1}{2}$	$\frac{3}{4}$	$\frac{3}{4}$	$1\frac{3}{4}$	2	$2\frac{5}{8}$	3	$3\frac{1}{2}$	$4\frac{3}{8}$
E	Medium	$\frac{1}{8}$	$\frac{1}{4}$	$\frac{1}{4}$	$\frac{1}{4}$	$\frac{1}{2}$	$\frac{3}{4}$	$\frac{7}{8}$	$1\frac{1}{8}$	$1\frac{1}{2}$	$1\frac{1}{2}$	$1\frac{7}{8}$

3. At the Square

At the Square is a combination of template-free and strip-piecing. It has simple matches with a limited number of points and straight seams. It serves as a good introduction to working with triangles. The pattern works well in two colors, a light and dark.

Fig. 4.23 At the Square, one light and one dark fabric

Fabrics

For one 12″ block:

Piece A: One square $4\frac{1}{2}″ \times 4\frac{1}{2}″$ in dark color (center square)

Piece B: One strip $1\frac{7}{8}″$ wide in dark color (2 of the three strips on the block sides)

Piece C: One strip $1\frac{7}{8}″$ wide in light color (1 of three strips on the block sides)

Piece D: One strip $2\frac{5}{8}″$ wide in light color (8 triangles in the corner unit)

Piece E: One strip $2\frac{5}{8}″$ wide in dark color (8 triangles in the corner unit)

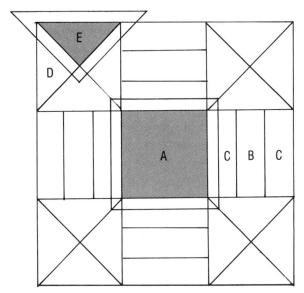

Fig. 4.24 Piecing chart

Cutting and Piecing

1. Cut strips B (dark) and C (light) in half, resulting in strips approximately 21″ long.

2. Sew three strips together to form a strip C-B-C. The strip will be light-dark-light as shown. Press the seams open.

3. Crosscut C-B-C into $4\frac{1}{2}″$ strips, as shown in Fig. 4.25. Cut four strips, set aside.

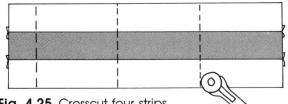

Fig. 4.25 Crosscut four strips

4. Make a paper template of piece D-E. Tape it to the 90-degree corner of the triangle. Cut eight triangles from both strip D (light) and strip E (dark). Notice that the straight of grain is parallel to the long edge of the triangle.

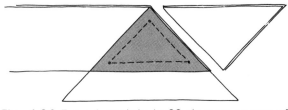

Fig. 4.26 Tape template to 90-degree corner of triangle

To make the corner blocks:

5. Stitch eight light triangles (D) to eight dark triangles (E) to make a larger two-colored triangle. Press seams toward the dark fabric. Gently press the triangles containing bias edges.

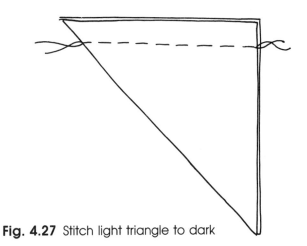

Fig. 4.27 Stitch light triangle to dark

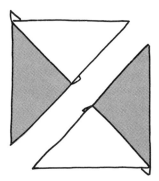

Fig. 4.28 Stitch together two two-color triangles

6. Join the two-colored triangles to make a $4\frac{1}{2}''$ square. Use opposing seams for easy matching. Before stitching, pin the matches. Press the seam open.

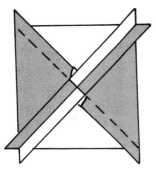

Fig. 4.29 Make a square from the triangle patches

To complete the block:

7. Lay the units together to form the block: this way you will have a clear idea of what the block will look like when it is finished and a point of reference when stitching it together.

8. Join two corner blocks to a striped piece. The dark stripe should join the light triangle. Do this twice. Ease any pieces that are slightly larger than the matching piece. Press seams open.

9. Join two striped pieces to the center square. The light stripe should join the dark square. Press seams open.

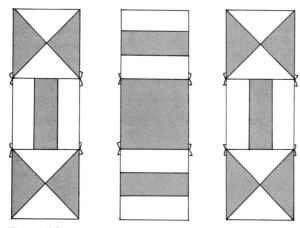

Fig. 4.30 Join striped pieces to plain and corner blocks

10. Stitch the final two seams to complete the block. The only difficult match will be where the triangles meet the center block. Use stab pins to secure the match. Pin through the corner of the triangle into the straight seam. Place a single pin on either side of the match. Sew with the triangle side up. Ease pieces as necessary. Press open seams.

Quilting

An overall quilting pattern, like a machine-guided grid, is a good complement to the diverse shapes in this block. Mark the grid on your block. The lines are $1''$ apart and are on the bias. On quilts with high color contrast, this is best worked with invisible thread. Low-loft polyester or cotton/polyester blend batting is best for the scale and density of the quilting.

Fig. 4.31 Overall quilting pattern complements diverse shapes

Companion Blocks and Sets

Companion blocks to At the Square include Puss in the Corner and Night and Noon (directions included in this chapter). Plain Block or sashing are suitable to this pattern and easy for beginners. Setting At the Square blocks side-by-side yields a complex secondary pattern that totally obscures the original block. The three strips on the side of the block join to make a six-strip square. The corner units form a Square in Square variation. The eight-point match at the corners can be difficult for a beginner.

Alternate Colors

The positive/negative look of At the Square depends on the two-color scheme. The colors can be reversed, substituting light colors for dark. Surprisingly, rather than making a drastic change, the reversal of colors merely darkens the block. At the Square can give a wonderful optical illusion by reversing the colors in every other block.

My favorite version of this pattern is a 1930s scrap quilt. All the blocks were two-color, but no two blocks were the same. The placement of colors apparently was determined by the amount of fabric available and alternated between the light and dark versions. The quilt was sashed with a putty-colored solid. The blocks were dusty blue, peach, and assorted shades of muddy brown prints, with assorted cream prints and muslins for the light colors.

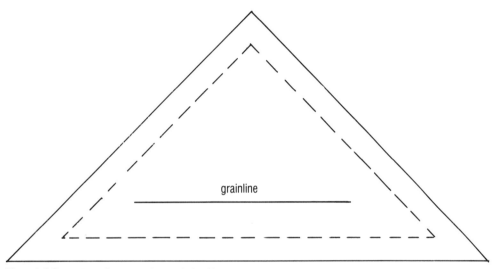

grainline

Fig. 4.32 At the Square template E

AT THE SQUARE

Number of strips needed to make the blocks:

		Number of Blocks										
		1	4	6	9	12	30	35	48	56	64	81
Piece/Width		Number of Strips										
A	$4\frac{1}{2}''$	1	4	1	2	2	4	5	6	7	8	11
B	$1\frac{7}{8}''$	1	2	3	5	6	15	18	24	28	32	42
C	$1\frac{7}{8}''$	1	4	6	9	12	30	35	48	56	64	81
D-E	$2\frac{5}{8}''$	1	4	4	6	8	20	24	32	38	43	54

Yardages needed to make the blocks:

Piece/Color		Yardages										
A-B-E	Dark	$\frac{3}{8}$	$\frac{5}{8}$	$\frac{3}{4}$	$1\frac{1}{8}$	$1\frac{3}{8}$	$3\frac{1}{8}$	$3\frac{3}{4}$	$4\frac{7}{8}$	$5\frac{3}{4}$	$6\frac{1}{2}$	$7\frac{1}{2}$
C-D	Light	$\frac{1}{4}$	$\frac{1}{2}$	$\frac{3}{8}$	$\frac{7}{8}$	$1\frac{1}{8}$	$2\frac{5}{8}$	$3\frac{1}{8}$	$4\frac{1}{8}$	$4\frac{7}{8}$	$5\frac{1}{2}$	7

4. Variable Star

Variable Star is one of those wonderful quilts that has only two templates, and all the pieces are rotary cut. The star is composed of sixteen 3″ blocks. Four of the blocks are plain; the other 12 are made of two triangles. Four colors are used for this version of the Variable Star: background color, a bright color for the star points, and two accent colors for the body of the star. Matching the points of the star is slightly more complex than the matches of previous blocks, but two-color squares are a basic component to many traditional patterns and mastering precise points is worth the effort.

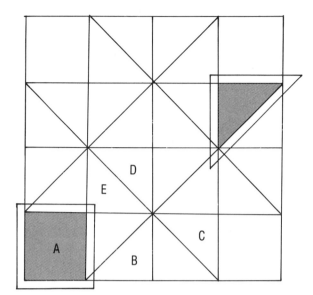

Fig. 4.34 Piecing chart

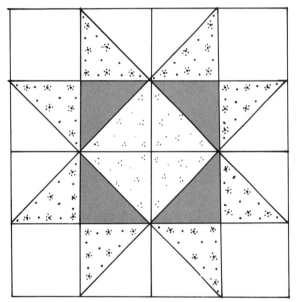

Fig. 4.33 Variable Star

Fabrics

For one 12″ block:

Piece A: One strip $3\frac{1}{2}''$ wide in background color (4 corner squares)

Piece B: One strip $3\frac{7}{8}''$ wide in background color (8 triangles for background of the star points)

Piece C: One strip $3\frac{7}{8}''$ wide in bright color (8 triangles for the star points)

Piece D: One strip $3\frac{7}{8}''$ wide in light accent (4 triangles for the interior square in the body of the star)

Piece E: One strip $3\frac{7}{8}''$ wide in dark accent (4 triangles for the body of the star)

Cutting

1. Cut four $3\frac{1}{2}''$ squares in the background color from strip A.

2. Make a paper template of triangle B-C-D-E. Tape it to a 45-degree angle triangle ruler. Cut eight triangles from both strip B (background color) and strip C (bright color). Notice the straight of grain is parallel to the short sides of the triangle.

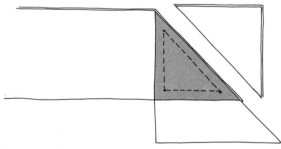

Fig. 4.35 Tape template to 45-degree-angle triangle ruler

3. Cut four triangles from both strip D (light accent color) and strip E (dark accent color). Cut as you did in step 2.

Piecing

To make the center of the block:

4. Stitch together the four D-E triangles to form four two-color squares. Press seams open.

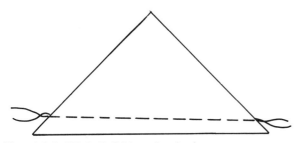

Fig. 4.36 Stitch D-E triangles to form square

5. Lay the stitched pieces together as indicated on the pattern. You will thus have a point of reference when stitching the block together. The interior block is light accent color in this version.

6. Stitch two sets of two. Before stitching pin the matches. Simply line up the seams across the entire piece. Use a stab pin at the seam line and a single pin in the body of the piece. Make sure the matched points meet at exactly the $\frac{1}{4}''$ seam allowance. Press seams open.

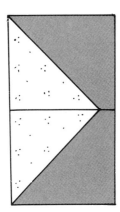

Fig. 4.37 Stitch two squares to form half the block

7. Stitch the two halves together to complete the block. Pin securely using the stab pin method. Press the seam open.

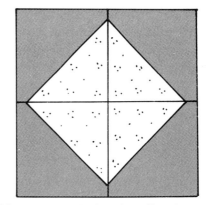

Fig. 4.38 Stitch two halves together to complete block

To make the star points:

8. Stitch together the eight B and C triangles to form eight two-color squares. Press seams open.

9. Arrange the star points and plain squares around the center square according to the pattern.

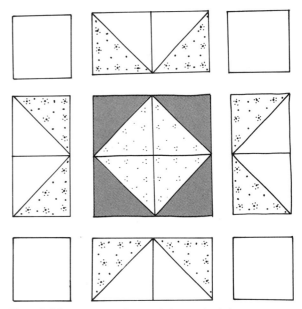

Fig. 4.39 Arrange star points and plain squares around center

10. Stitch the star points in four sets of two. Make sure the points meet at exactly the $\frac{1}{4}''$ seam allowance. Press seams open.

11. Stitch a plain square to either end of one set of star points. Repeat for another set.

12. Stitch two sets of star points to the center square. Eight points came together at this spot. Pin the match securely using the stab pin method (Fig. 4.40). As you sew you can only see one side of the match. For the best results, use a no-bridge presser foot. Do not remove the stab pin until the machine needle secures the match. Ease in the slightly longer pieces. Press seams open.

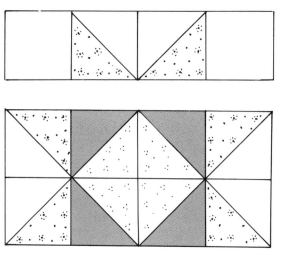

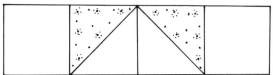

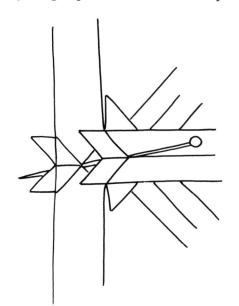

Fig. 4.40 Use stab pin method to secure eight points

13. Complete the final two seams. Pin the matches with stab pins. Press seams open.

Fig. 4.41 Ready-to-assemble block

Quilting

The open seams and triangle shapes make Variable Star the perfect choice for free-motion continuous curve quilting. Every triangle and square is outline quilted with continuous curve quilting. Follow the stitching sequence, starting in the lower left square. It is designed to permit stitching of the entire block without breaking thread, if invisible thread is used. It also is designed to allow each color section to be completed individually, so thread colors can be changed if cotton or polyester threads are used. For uniformity, mark the quilting pattern. A low-loft polyester or a cotton/polyester blend batting is suitable for the scale and density of quilting.

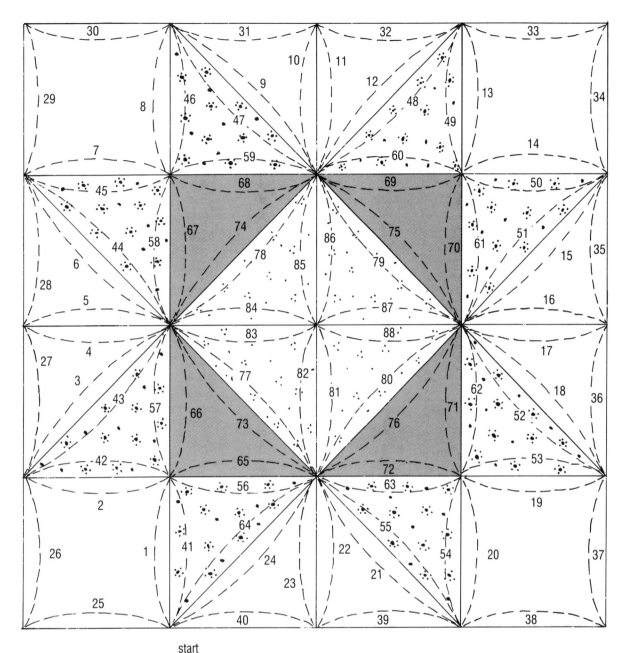

Fig. 4.42 Quilting pattern for Variable Star

Companion Blocks and Sets

Companion blocks include Wild Goose Chase and its variation and Snowflake. Plain Block or sashing are suitable companions for this block and can be effective. Setting blocks side-by-side is an easy option. The matches are no more difficult than the matches in the block. As a secondary pattern, the four corner squares make a larger square the same size as the star center. Variable Star is a wonderfully simple pat-tern. The pattern elements, the square and the two-color square, can be switched to allow creative interpretation of the design. As an example, the four corner squares can be replaced by two-color squares like the star center. Replacing the plain four corner squares with two-color squares radically changes the secondary pattern of the blocks. When setting the blocks side-by-side the altered corner squares form a unit identical to the center of the star. This gives

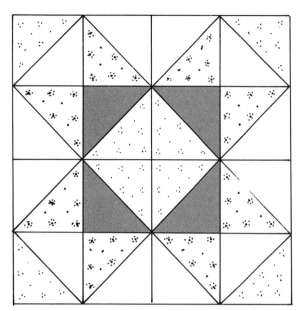

Fig. 4.43 Two-color squares in the four corners change the secondary pattern

the effect of overlaying stars. Where stars appear and disappear depends on the center upon which you focus. This altered block, done in two colors, results in an overall pattern unrecognizable from the original block.

Alternate Colors

The color choices for Variable Star can be as simple as two colors or as complex as multicolors. A two-color block in solid red and white is stunning when alternated with a plain white block. The primarily white quilt is the perfect showcase for intricate quilting. Another choice is alternating dark stars on a light background and light stars on a dark background. This is an excellent choice for a scrap quilt.

VARIABLE STAR

Number of strips needed to make the blocks:

						Number of Blocks					
		1	4	6	9	12	30	35	48	56	64	81
Piece/Width						Number of Strips					
A	$3\frac{1}{2}''$	1	2	3	4	5	11	13	18	21	24	30
B-C	$3\frac{7}{8}''$	1	2	3	4	5	12	14	20	23	26	33
D-E	$3\frac{7}{8}''$	1	1	2	2	3	6	7	10	12	13	17

Yardages needed to make the blocks:

Piece/Color						Yardages					
A-B	Background	$\frac{1}{4}$	$\frac{1}{2}$	$\frac{3}{4}$	$\frac{7}{8}$	$1\frac{1}{8}$	$2\frac{1}{2}$	$2\frac{7}{8}$	4	$4\frac{5}{8}$	$5\frac{1}{4}$	$6\frac{5}{8}$
C	Accent 1	$\frac{1}{8}$	$\frac{1}{4}$	$\frac{3}{8}$	$\frac{1}{2}$	$\frac{5}{8}$	$1\frac{3}{8}$	$1\frac{5}{8}$	$2\frac{1}{4}$	$2\frac{5}{8}$	3	$3\frac{5}{8}$
D	Accent 2	$\frac{1}{8}$	$\frac{1}{8}$	$\frac{1}{4}$	$\frac{1}{4}$	$\frac{3}{8}$	$\frac{3}{4}$	$\frac{7}{8}$	$1\frac{1}{8}$	$1\frac{3}{8}$	$1\frac{1}{2}$	$1\frac{7}{8}$
E	Accent 3	$\frac{1}{8}$	$\frac{1}{8}$	$\frac{1}{4}$	$\frac{1}{4}$	$\frac{3}{8}$	$\frac{3}{4}$	$\frac{7}{8}$	$1\frac{1}{8}$	$1\frac{3}{8}$	$1\frac{1}{2}$	$1\frac{7}{8}$

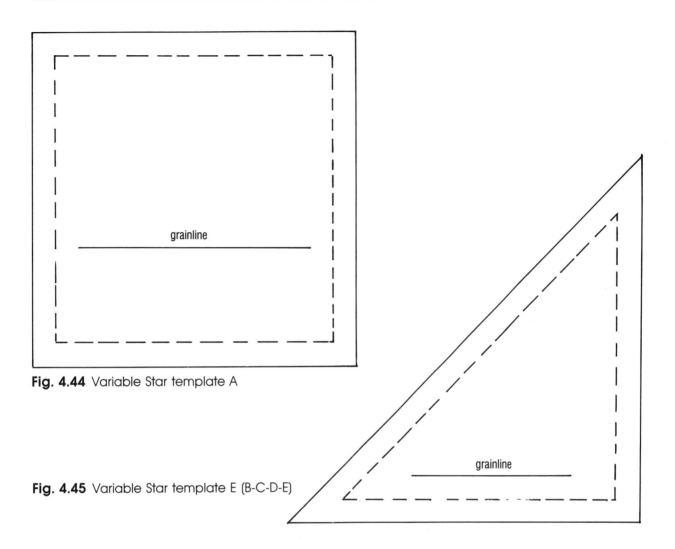

Fig. 4.44 Variable Star template A

Fig. 4.45 Variable Star template E (B-C-D-E)

5. Night and Noon

Night and Noon is an easy-to-piece block. Although most of the pieces are rotary cut, the corner squares combine strip piecing with hand-cut piecing. Combining techniques offers a simpler and faster way to piece many blocks. The block also has mirror-image piecing. This version of Night and Noon is done in five colors: a light, a dark, and three coordinating colors. There are a limited number of points to match, and all the seams are straight sewing. The real challenge of this block is the complex matches that result when setting the blocks side-by-side.

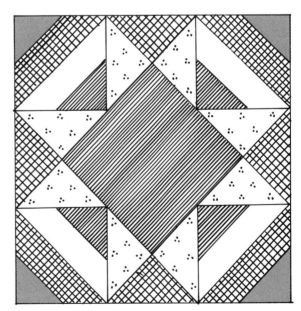

Fig. 4.46 Night and Noon

Fabrics

For one 12″ block:

Piece A: One $6\frac{1}{8}″$ square in dark color (for the center of the star)

Piece B: One strip $2\frac{5}{8}″$ wide in accent color 1 (for 4 triangles at the star points)

Piece C: One strip $2\frac{5}{8}″$ wide in accent color 2 (for 8 star points)

Piece D: One strip 2″ wide in dark color (1 strip in four corner squares)

Piece E: One strip $1\frac{7}{8}″$ wide in light color (1 strip in four corner squares)

Piece F: One strip $1\frac{7}{8}″$ wide in accent color 1 (1 strip in four of the corner squares)

Piece G: One strip 2″ wide in accent color 3. (1 strip in four corner squares)

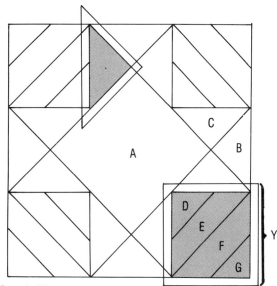

Fig. 4.47 Piecing chart

Cutting

1. Make a paper template of piece B. Tape it to the 90-degree angle on the triangle ruler. Cut four triangles the size of template B from strip B. Notice the straight of

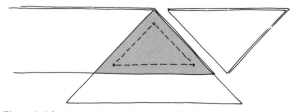

Fig. 4.48 Tape template to 90-degree corner of triangle

grain is parallel to the longest side of the triangle.

2. Cut eight triangles the size of template B from strip C. The straight of grain is parallel to the longest side of the triangle.

3. Sew the strips D-E-F-G together, in that order. Press seams open.

4. Make a plastic template of pattern piece Y. Place template Y on the reverse side of strip D-E-F-G as shown. Trace around the template to make four blocks. Hand cut blocks. By seaming, the waste fabrics can be used to form the corners for another block. The coloring of the waste block will be reversed from the original.

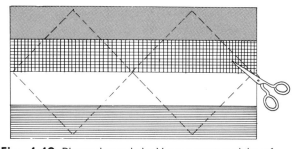

Fig. 4.49 Place template Y on reverse side of strip D-E-F-G

Piecing

Lay all the pieces together to form the block, which will be stitched into three sections and completed with two long seams.

5. Join C and B triangles on the short edges. Make four sets. Notice that two sets are mirror images of the other sets (Fig. 4.50). To make mirror-image pieces, sew with color C up on two of the triangles. Sew with color B up on the other two triangles. Press open seams.

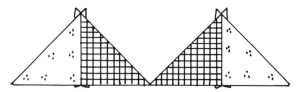

Fig. 4.50 Two C-B triangles are mirror images of the other two

6. Stitch the triangles from the preceding step to the corner block. The triangle pieces will be longer than the squares. To correctly place the triangles on the squares, the excess seam allowance at the point of the triangle should intersect the square at the $\frac{1}{4}''$ seam line. Press seams away from the corner block.

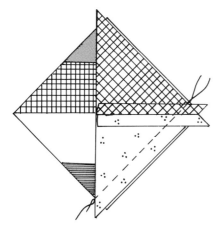

Fig. 4.51 Stitch first triangle to corner block

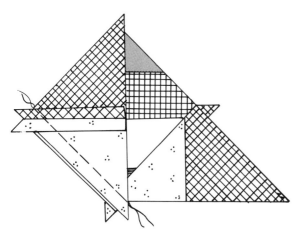

Fig. 4.52 Stitch second triangle to corner block

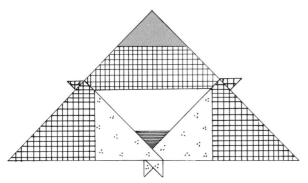

Fig. 4.53 Press seams away from corner block

7. Join two C triangles each to the adjacent sides of the remaining corner blocks. Press seams away from corners.

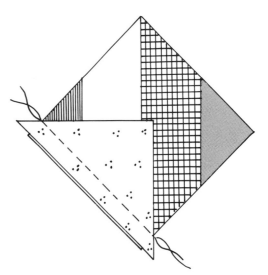

Fig. 4.54 Stitch first C triangle to remaining corner blocks

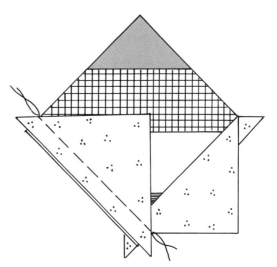

Fig. 4.55 Stitch second C triangle to remaining corner blocks

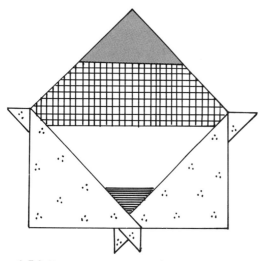

Fig. 4.56 Press seams away from corners

8. Stitch the corner pieces from the preceding step to opposite sides of the center block A. There is a match on this seam. Pin through the corner of block Y into the midpoint of block C. Stitch with the pieced block up. Press seams toward center.

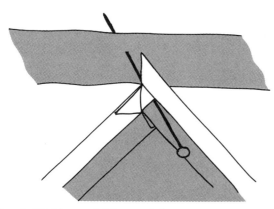

Fig. 4.57 Pin matching points

9. Stitch the final two seams to complete the block. Sew with the center section on the bottom. On this seam you will be matching a seam pressed to one side with an open seam. There is a trick that makes this a simple keyed match. Temporarily, tip the open seam allowance to the side opposite the other seam. Treat the match as a keyed match. Slip the seams together. Pin the match in the seam allowance that is pressed to one side. Open the other seam allowance, and pin the other side of the match. Sew the block together. Press seams toward center.

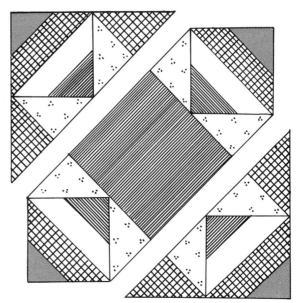

Fig. 4.58 Stitch two final seams to complete block

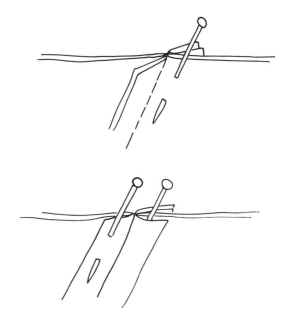

Fig. 4.59 Match seam pressed to one side with open seam

Quilting

Night and Noon's pieced corner block makes it important to choose a quilting pattern that accentuates the star and blocks rather than the individual piecing. The center block has a simple continuous line motif, done with free-motion quilting. The star points are outline-quilted with two lines of stitching using modified continuous curve quilting. One line is at the base of the points, outlining the center square. The

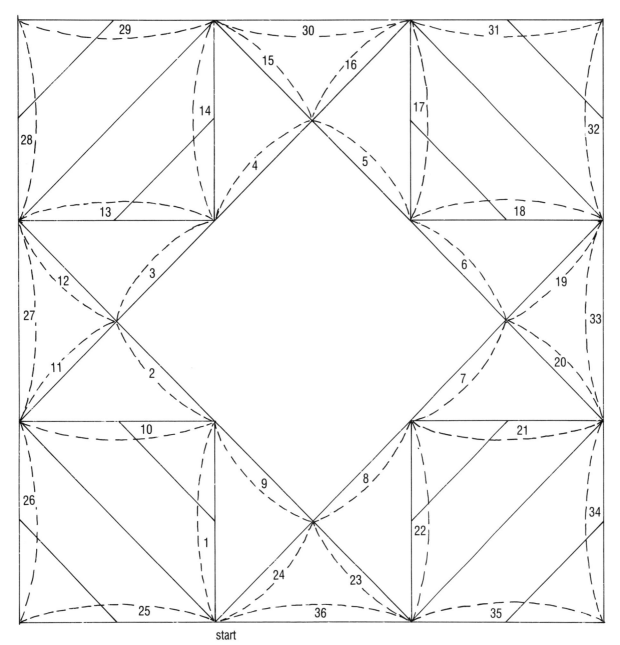

Fig. 4.60 Night and Noon quilting pattern

other line is outside the points, on the corner blocks, and triangle C. The edge of the block is also stitched with modified continuous curve quilting. Polyester batting is recommended for the scale of the quilting.

Companion Blocks and Sets

Plain Block (in this chapter) or sashing is recommended for the beginner. Night and Noon blocks make a marvelous secondary pattern when set side-by-side. The strips in the corner block form mitered squares. The real challenge comes with complex matches on the seams joining the blocks. Substituting Plain Block for the pieced corner Y on alternating blocks makes easier matches. At the Square (in this chapter) is another choice for an alternating block, or substitute the four-piece corner of At the Square for the pieced corner Y.

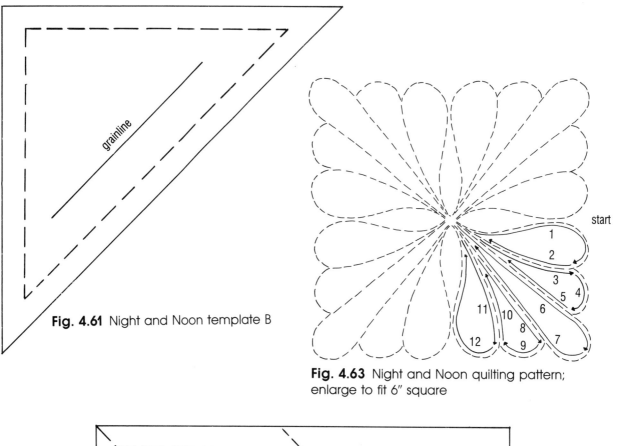

Fig. 4.61 Night and Noon template B

Fig. 4.63 Night and Noon quilting pattern; enlarge to fit 6″ square

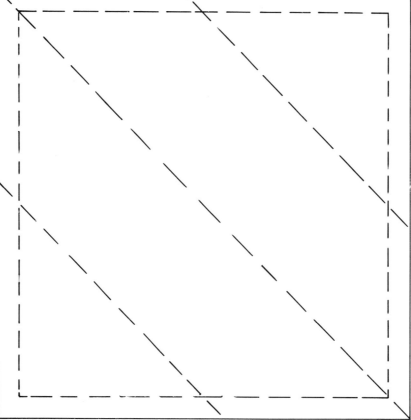

Fig. 4.62 Night and Noon template Y

NIGHT AND NOON

Number of strips needed to make the blocks:

		Number of Blocks										
		1	4	6	9	12	30	35	48	56	64	81
Piece/Width		Number of Strips										
A	$6\frac{1}{8}''$	1	1	1	2	2	5	6	8	10	11	14
B-C	$2\frac{5}{8}''$	1	2	2	3	4	10	11	15	18	20	25
D-G	$2''$	1	3	4	6	8	20	24	32	38	43	54
E-F	$1\frac{7}{8}''$	1	3	4	6	8	20	24	32	38	43	54

Yardages needed to make the blocks:

Piece/Color		Yardages										
A-G	Dark	$\frac{3}{8}$	$\frac{3}{8}$	$\frac{1}{2}$	$\frac{3}{4}$	$\frac{7}{8}$	2	$2\frac{1}{2}$	$3\frac{1}{4}$	$3\frac{7}{8}$	$4\frac{3}{8}$	$5\frac{1}{2}$
B	Accent 1	$\frac{1}{8}$	$\frac{1}{4}$	$\frac{1}{4}$	$\frac{1}{4}$	$\frac{3}{8}$	$\frac{7}{8}$	$\frac{7}{8}$	$1\frac{1}{8}$	$1\frac{3}{8}$	$1\frac{1}{2}$	$1\frac{7}{8}$
C-D	Accent 2	$\frac{1}{4}$	$\frac{3}{8}$	$\frac{1}{2}$	$\frac{5}{8}$	$\frac{7}{8}$	$1\frac{7}{8}$	$2\frac{1}{4}$	3	$3\frac{1}{2}$	4	$4\frac{7}{8}$
E	Accent 3	$\frac{1}{8}$	$\frac{1}{4}$	$\frac{3}{8}$	$\frac{3}{8}$	$\frac{1}{2}$	$1\frac{3}{8}$	$1\frac{1}{2}$	$1\frac{7}{8}$	$2\frac{1}{8}$	$2\frac{1}{2}$	3
F	Light	$\frac{1}{8}$	$\frac{1}{4}$	$\frac{3}{8}$	$\frac{3}{8}$	$\frac{1}{2}$	$1\frac{3}{8}$	$1\frac{1}{2}$	$1\frac{7}{8}$	$2\frac{1}{8}$	$2\frac{1}{2}$	3

6. Wild Goose Chase

This traditional pattern contains a common pattern element called Flying Geese, a rectangle made of three triangles.

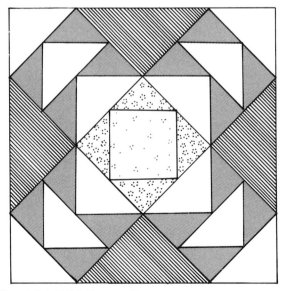

Fig. 4.64 Wild Goose Chase

Its counterpart, Square in a Square, a diagonally set square surrounded by four triangles, is used in the center of the block. The pieces are all rotary cut with simple straight seams. The matches around the center square are challenging. Properly matched, the center block and the four interior Flying Geese give the illusion of a third center square. In this version, a different color is used for every template in the block, totalling five colors.

Fabrics

For rotary cutting one 12″ block:

Piece A: One $3\frac{1}{2}''$ square (center square)
Piece B: One strip $2\frac{3}{4}''$ wide for flying geese (12 triangles)
Piece C: One strip 3″ wide (16 triangles for flying geese)
Piece D: One strip 3″ wide (4 triangles around the center square)
Piece E: One strip $3\frac{5}{8}''$ wide (4 side triangles)

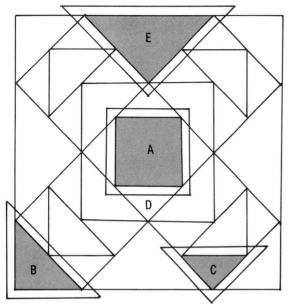

Fig. 4.65 Piecing chart

Cutting

1. Make a paper template of piece B. Tape it to the 90-degree angle on the triangle ruler. Cut 12 triangles from strip B. The straight of grain is parallel to the long edge.

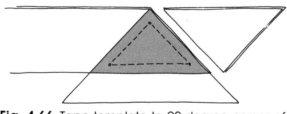

Fig. 4.66 Tape template to 90-degree corner of triangle

2. Make a paper template of piece C. Tape it to the 45-degree angle on the triangle ruler. Cut four triangles from strip C. The straight of grain is parallel to the short edges.

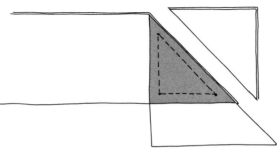

Fig. 4.67 Tape template to 45-degree angle on triangle ruler

3. Cut 16 triangles from strip D, using template C. The straight of grain is parallel to the short edges.

4. Make a paper template of piece E. Tape it to the 90-degree angle on the triangle ruler. Cut four triangles from strip E. The straight of grain is parallel to the long edges.

Piecing

5. Stitch two triangle Ds to opposite sides of the center square. The triangles will be too long for the square. To correctly match the pieces, the excess seam allowance at the points of the triangle should intersect the square at the $\frac{1}{4}''$ seam line. Press seams open.

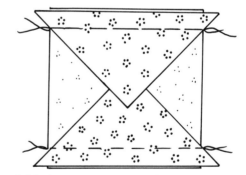

Fig. 4.68 Stitch two triangle Ds to center square

6. Stitch the remaining two triangle Ds to the center square. The triangle will be too large for the square. Line up the match as you did in the previous step. Press open seams. The center square in a square block is completed. Notice that the corners of the inner square are ¼″ from the edge of the block.

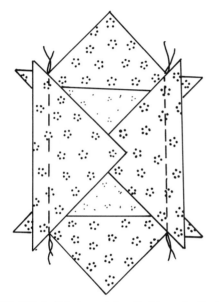

Fig. 4.69 Stitch third and fourth triangle Ds to center square

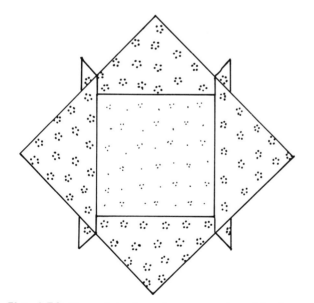

Fig. 4.70 Completed center square in a block

7. Join eight triangle Cs to eight Flying Geese Bs. Triangle B will seem to be too large for the Flying Geese. To correctly match the pieces, excess seam allowance at the point of triangle C should intersect piece B at the ¼″ line. Press seams open.

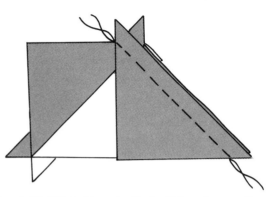

Fig. 4.71 Stitch triangle Cs to Flying Geese Bs

8. Join the remaining eight triangle Cs to the set made in the preceding step. Press open seams. Notice the point of the Flying Geese is ¼″ in from the edge of the piece.

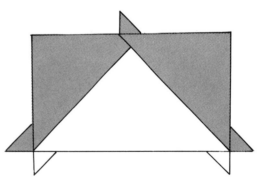

Fig. 4.72 Press open seams

9. Stitch together four sets of two Flying Geese. There is a match on this seam. Use a stab pin. Pin through the point of the Flying Geese into the base of the adjoining block. Sew with the match side up. Press seams toward the base of the large triangle. Join a single Flying Geese (piece B) to complete the unit. Press as with the previous seam.

10. Join two triangle Es to the Flying Geese unit. The triangle will be too large for the Flying Geese. Line up as in previous steps. Repeat once. Press seams toward the large triangle.

11. Stitch two Flying Geese units to the center square in square. Press seams toward the Flying Geese.

12. Complete the block by stitching the final two seams (Fig. 4.73). The matches will require careful pinning with stab pins. Pin all matches before starting to sew. Ease where necessary. Press seams away from the center.

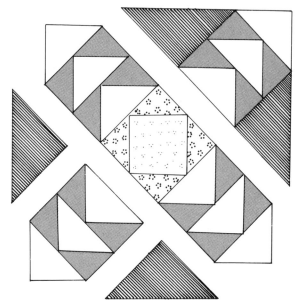

Fig. 4.73 Stitch triangle Es to Flying Geese unit, then stitch two final seams to complete block

Quilting

Wild Goose Chase is my favorite block to quilt. Free-motion continuous curve works well on the Flying Geese. The charm of this pattern is how easy it is to quilt all the pieces without having to break thread. You should be able to quilt this block without marking the pattern. Use invisible thread for blocks with high color contrast. Low-loft polyester batting is a good choice for this quilting pattern.

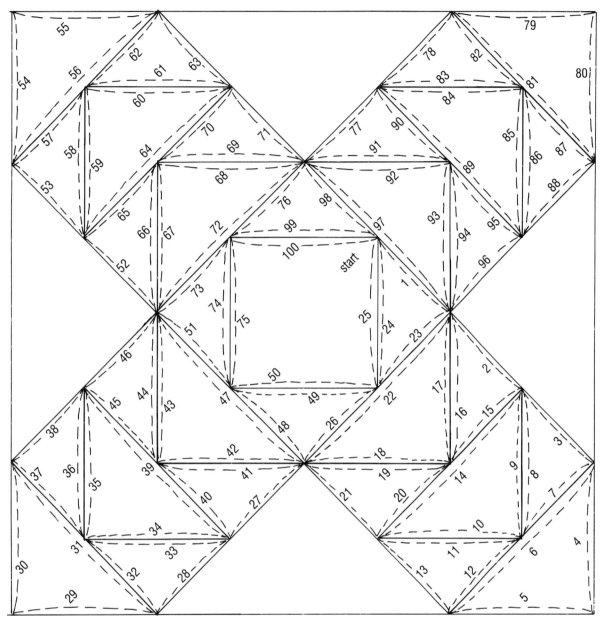

Fig. 4.74 Wild Goose Chase quilting pattern

Companion Blocks and Sets

Companion blocks include Wild Goose Chase Variation, Variable Star, and Snowflake. The Modified Wild Goose Chase is made by substituting a plain triangle for a unit of feathered geese and two side triangles. To cut the triangles for each block cut one square $9\frac{7}{8}''$. Cut diagonally to make two triangles. Quilt the plain triangles with a portion of the design from the Plain Block. Quilt the strip of Wild Goose Chase with continuous curve. Plain Block or sashing is a good choice for this pattern. Sashing stops the strong diagonal lines of this block. The Plain Block, a complement to the intricate piecing, gives an opportunity to display quilting skills.

Like Snowflake, Wild Goose Chase has a lattice effect when joined side-by-side. Alternating Wild Goose Chase with Snowflake accentuates the lattice effect.

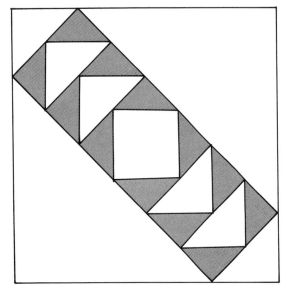

Fig. 4.75 Modified Wild Goose Chase

Alternate Colors

For a subtle effect, try the block in low-contrast colors or a monochromatic color scheme. A high-contrast, two-color block is striking.

A lovely antique quilt from the mid-1800s is done in navy and white. Everything is white except the Flying Geese and the center block. The Wild Goose Chase block alternates with a plain white block. The effect is a strong diagonal line reminiscent of an Irish Chain quilt.

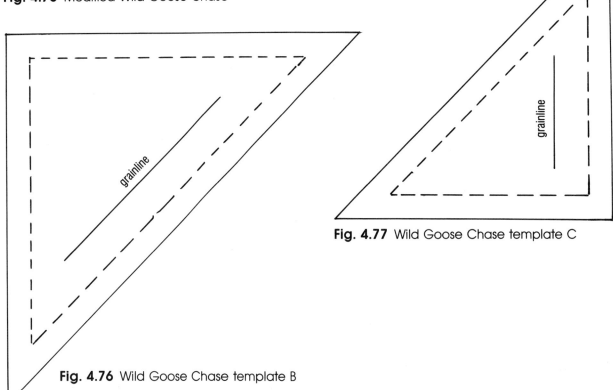

Fig. 4.77 Wild Goose Chase template C

Fig. 4.76 Wild Goose Chase template B

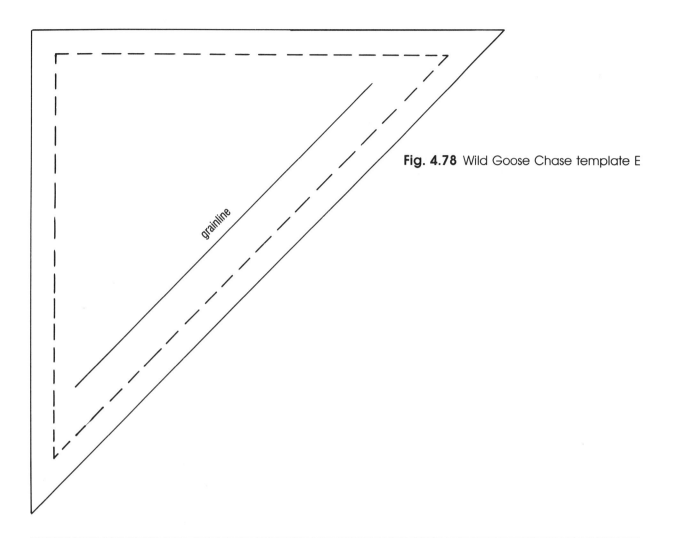

Fig. 4.78 Wild Goose Chase template E

grainline

WILD GOOSE CHASE

Number of strips needed to make the blocks:

		Number of Blocks										
		1	**4**	**6**	**9**	**12**	**30**	**35**	**48**	**56**	**64**	**81**
	Piece/Width					Number of Strips						
A	$3\frac{1}{2}''$	1	1	1	1	2	3	4	5	6	6	8
B	$2\frac{3}{4}''$	1	4	6	9	12	28	33	45	52	60	75
C	$3''$	1	3	4	6	12	20	24	32	38	43	54
D	$3''$	1	1	1	2	2	5	6	8	9	10	13
E	$3\frac{5}{8}''$	1	2	3	4	6	14	16	22	25	29	36

Yardages needed to make the blocks:

	Piece/Color					Yardages						
A	#1	$\frac{1}{8}$	$\frac{1}{8}$	$\frac{1}{8}$	$\frac{1}{8}$	$\frac{1}{4}$	$\frac{3}{8}$	$\frac{1}{2}$	$\frac{5}{8}$	$\frac{5}{8}$	$\frac{5}{8}$	$\frac{7}{8}$
B	#2	$\frac{1}{8}$	$\frac{3}{8}$	$\frac{1}{2}$	$\frac{3}{4}$	1	$1\frac{1}{4}$	$2\frac{5}{8}$	$3\frac{1}{2}$	4	$4\frac{5}{8}$	$5\frac{3}{4}$
C	#3	$\frac{1}{8}$	$\frac{3}{8}$	$\frac{3}{8}$	$\frac{5}{8}$	$1\frac{1}{8}$	$1\frac{3}{4}$	$2\frac{1}{8}$	$2\frac{3}{4}$	$3\frac{1}{4}$	$3\frac{5}{8}$	$4\frac{5}{8}$
D	#4	$\frac{1}{8}$	$\frac{1}{8}$	$\frac{1}{8}$	$\frac{1}{4}$	$\frac{1}{4}$	$\frac{1}{2}$	$\frac{5}{8}$	$\frac{3}{4}$	$\frac{7}{8}$	1	$1\frac{1}{8}$
E	#5	$\frac{1}{8}$	$\frac{1}{4}$	$\frac{3}{8}$	$\frac{1}{2}$	$\frac{5}{8}$	$1\frac{1}{2}$	$1\frac{3}{4}$	$2\frac{1}{4}$	$1\frac{5}{8}$	3	$3\frac{3}{4}$

WILD GOOSE CHASE VARIATION

Number of strips needed to make the blocks:

							Number of Blocks					
		1	4	6	9	12	30	35	48	56	64	81
	Piece/Width						Number of Strips					
A	$3\frac{1}{2}''$	1	1	1	1	2	3	4	5	6	6	8
B	$2\frac{3}{4}''$	1	2	3	5	6	14	17	23	26	30	38
C	$3''$	1	2	2	3	4	10	11	15	18	20	25
D	$3''$	1	1	1	2	2	5	6	8	9	12	13
E	$9\frac{7}{8}''$	1	1	1	2	2	4	5	6	7	8	11

Yardages needed to make the blocks:

Piece						Yardages					
A	$\frac{1}{8}$	$\frac{1}{8}$	$\frac{1}{8}$	$\frac{1}{8}$	$\frac{1}{4}$	$\frac{3}{8}$	$\frac{1}{2}$	$\frac{5}{8}$	$\frac{5}{8}$	$\frac{5}{8}$	$\frac{7}{8}$
B	$\frac{1}{8}$	$\frac{1}{4}$	$\frac{1}{4}$	$\frac{1}{2}$	$\frac{1}{2}$	$1\frac{1}{8}$	$1\frac{3}{8}$	$1\frac{7}{8}$	2	$2\frac{3}{8}$	3
C	$\frac{1}{8}$	$\frac{1}{4}$	$\frac{1}{4}$	$\frac{3}{8}$	$\frac{1}{2}$	$\frac{7}{8}$	1	$1\frac{3}{8}$	$1\frac{5}{8}$	$1\frac{3}{4}$	$2\frac{1}{8}$
D	$\frac{1}{8}$	$\frac{1}{8}$	$\frac{1}{8}$	$\frac{1}{4}$	$\frac{1}{4}$	$\frac{1}{2}$	$\frac{5}{8}$	$\frac{3}{4}$	$\frac{7}{8}$	1	$1\frac{1}{8}$
E	$\frac{3}{8}$	$\frac{3}{8}$	$\frac{3}{8}$	$\frac{5}{8}$	$\frac{5}{8}$	$1\frac{1}{4}$	$1\frac{1}{2}$	$1\frac{3}{4}$	2	$2\frac{1}{4}$	$3\frac{1}{8}$

7. Kansas Trouble

This two-color pattern serves as an introduction to bias strip piecing. The small two-color squares, commonly called sawteeth, are easy and accurately made with this advanced method of piecing. Sawteeth are a basic element in many designs, including Feathered Stars, Delectable Mountains, Ocean Waves, and Lady of the Lake. This block is cut using a combination of hand-cut template pieces and rotary-cut pieces. Except for the mirror-image piecing, this block is easy to piece, with basic matches and simple straight seams.

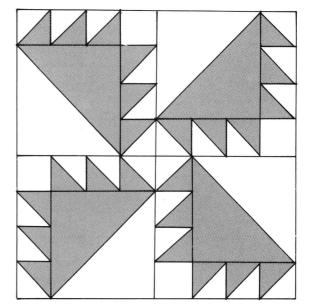

Fig. 4.79 Kansas Trouble

Fabrics

For one 12″ block:

10″ strip of both light and dark colors

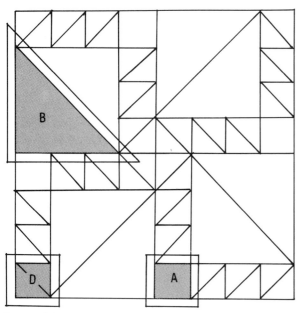

Fig. 4.80 Piecing chart

Cutting

1. Cut one 10″ × 10″ square of both fabrics. This will be used to cut the bias strips for the sawteeth. After cutting the squares, you should have two pieces approximately 10″ × 30″. Use them to cut the remaining pieces for the block.

2. Place the two 10″ squares right sides together. Cut on the diagonal to form two triangles. Stack the two light and dark triangles, lining up the bias edges. Cut the triangles into three bias strips, $2\frac{1}{4}$″ wide.

3. Using the remaining light-colored fabric, cut one strip 2″ wide by approximately 30″ long. Cut four 2″ squares, piece C.

4. Make a paper template of piece B. Tape it to the 45-degree angle of the triangle ruler. From both the dark and light re-

maining fabrics cut a strip $5\frac{3}{8}$″ wide by approximately 30″ long. Cut four triangles from each strip, piece B. Notice the grain-line is parallel to the short sides of the triangle.

Piecing

5. Stitch together the bias strips of matching length, one light to one dark, making six sets of two strips. Press open seams.

6. Make a plastic template of piece D. Mark the diagonal on the template.

7. Center the diagonal line on the template over the seam in the bias strips. Trace around the template with a fine-line fabric

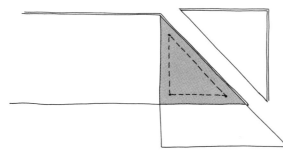

Fig. 4.81 Tape template to 45-degree triangle ruler

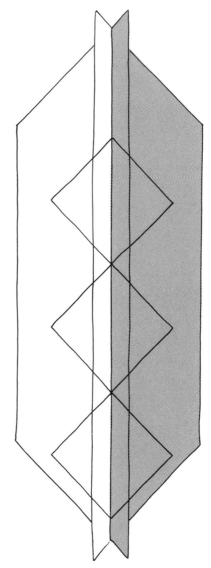

Fig. 4.82 Place template on wrong side to trace

marker. Mark the squares the entire length of all the bias strips.

8. Using scissors, cut out the squares. Don't cut into the waste fabric, because it will make a second row of pieces. Join the straight edges of the two waste pieces. Carefully press seam open. Trace and cut the second row of squares. This will yield 26 sawteeth (the pattern requires 24 per block).

Fig. 4.83 Trace along seam line and cut out pieces

9. Lay out the pieces to form the block. Notice that the sawteeth are stitched in sets of three and are mirror-image pieced. The diagonal runs from upper right to lower left

on half the blocks, while on the other half it runs from upper left to lower right. To sew the sawteeth in the correct order, it helps to stitch all the like sawteeth, then stitch the mirror-image sets. Press open seams.

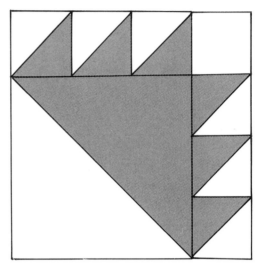

Fig. 4.84 Diagonal runs in opposite direction on half the sawteeth blocks

10. Join the plain square A to one end of half the sets of sawteeth. Press seam open.

11. Stitch the sets of three sawteeth to triangles B. Sew with the sawtooth side up for easier matching. Remember to stitch just to the right of the match to maintain sharp points. Press seam open.

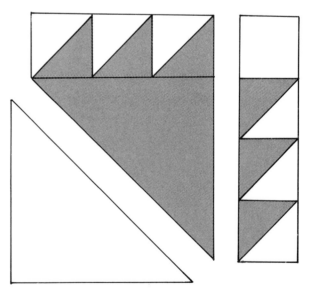

Fig. 4.85 Stitch sets of sawteeth to triangles B

12. Join the sets of square and sawteeth to triangles B. Sew with the sawtooth side up. Key the match at the plain square by tipping the open seams in opposing directions. Secure the match by pinning the *block,* not the seam allowances, so that the seams can be tipped open and stitched as an open seam. The keying makes a perfect match, and the open seam results in a flat block. Use stab pins for the other matches. Press seam open.

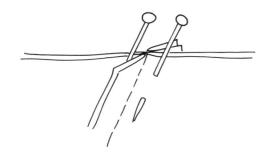

Fig. 4.86 Matching open seams

13. Complete the units from step 12 with a light-colored triangle B. The sawteeth require an unexpected match along the seam on triangles B. Stitch with the sawteeth up to see the match. Press seam toward the light triangle B. Pressing the seam toward the light color is irregular, but is preferable to pressing the seam against the pieced portion of the block. No matter how carefully the seam is sewn, small wedges of dark fabric always extend beyond the lighter seam allowance. Occasionally this whisper of darker fabric causes a shadow on the finished quilt. To determine if this is going to occur on your quilt, place the block over the batting. If there is a shadow, the seam will need to be carefully trimmed. Trim away a fraction of an inch on only the dark seam.

Brush away the snippets of fabric and recheck for shadows. If this doesn't correct the shadowing, press the seam open.

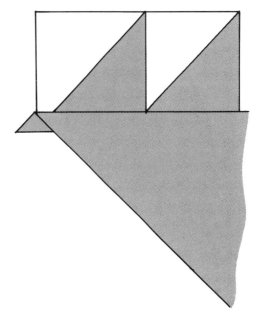

Fig. 4.87 An unexpected match along the seam on triangles B

14. Complete the block by stitching together the four sections. Sew with the sawtooth side up when possible. Press the seams away from the sawteeth. Check for shadowing on high-contrast colors.

Quilting

Modified continuous curve quilting is an excellent choice for the sawteeth. Stitch inside the dark triangles and squares. The scale fits the small pieces and accentuates the piecing. The two larger triangles are perfect for a free-motion motif. A low-loft polyester or cotton/polyester blend batting is a good choice for this pattern.

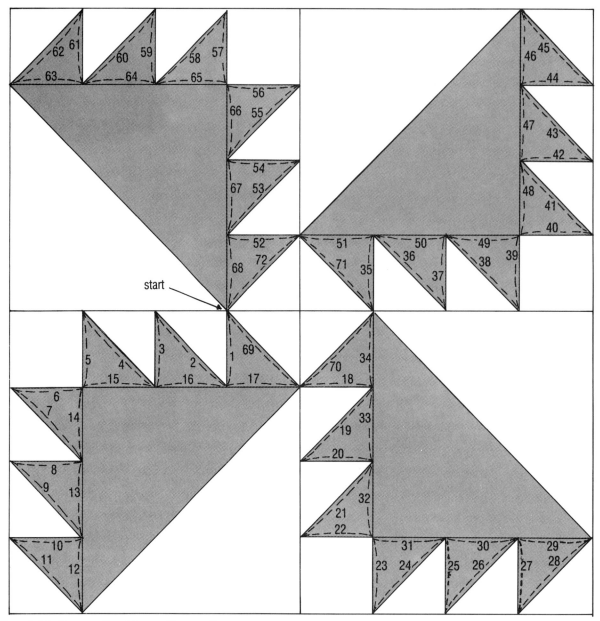

Fig. 4.88 Kansas Trouble quilting pattern

Companion Blocks and Sets

Plain Block (in this chapter) or sashing are an option for this block, but Kansas Trouble is not difficult to join side-by-side. A surprise companion to this block is a variation of Wild Goose Chase. The simplified Wild Goose Chase adds interest to the pinwheels of Kansas Trouble.

Alternate Colors

Unlike other blocks, there is no traditional color arrangement for Kansas Trou-

ble. It appears in two-color, three-color, and multicolor versions. The two-color version is very formal in high- or low-contrast fabrics. There are a number of three-color versions. The sawteeth can differ in color from that of the base triangle, or entire sections can alternate in color. Scrap versions of this design are charming, but the bias strip method excludes the use of "true" scraps and requires a selection of yardages or squares of fabric.

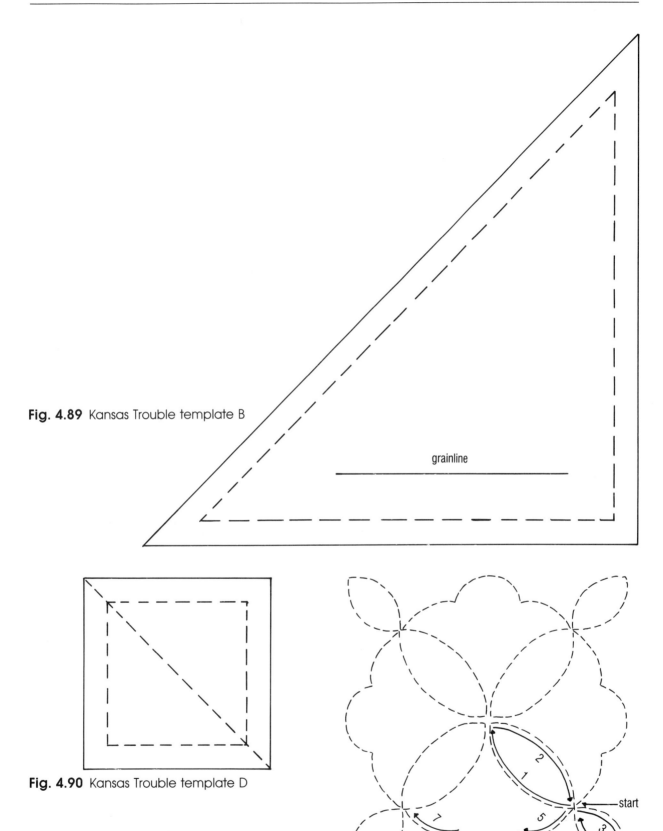

Fig. 4.89 Kansas Trouble template B

grainline

Fig. 4.90 Kansas Trouble template D

start

Fig. 4.91 Alternate block quilting pattern; enlarge to fit 4″ square

KANSAS TROUBLE

Number of strips needed to make the blocks:

		Number of Blocks										
		1	**4**	**6**	**9**	**12**	**30**	**35**	**48**	**56**	**64**	**81**
Piece/Width		**Number of Strips**										
A-B	$5\frac{3}{8}''$	1	2	2	3	4	9	10	14	16	19	24
C	2″	1	1	2	2	3	6	7	10	12	13	17
D-E*			10″	13″	20″	26″	$1\frac{3}{4}$	2	$2\frac{5}{8}$	$3\frac{1}{8}$	$3\frac{1}{2}$	$4\frac{3}{8}$

Yardages needed to make the blocks:

Piece/Color		**Yardages**										
A-D	Dark			$\frac{5}{8}$	$\frac{3}{4}$	$1\frac{1}{8}$	$1\frac{3}{8}$	$3\frac{1}{8}$	$3\frac{1}{2}$	$4\frac{3}{4}$	$5\frac{1}{2}$	$6\frac{1}{2}$
B-C-E			$\frac{3}{4}$	$\frac{7}{8}$	$1\frac{1}{4}$	$1\frac{5}{8}$	$3\frac{1}{2}$	$3\frac{7}{8}$	$5\frac{3}{8}$	$6\frac{1}{4}$	7	9

*To obtain the correct number of bias strips, the chart lists the width of the strip. For example, nine blocks require 20″; cut a strip of both colors, 20″ × 44/45″. 48 blocks require $2\frac{5}{8}$ yard; cut a strip of both colors, $2\frac{5}{8}$ yard × 44/45″. These strips will be bias-cut, following the block directions. The single exception to this is the yardage for one block (refer to block directions).

8. Solomon's Puzzle

Solomon's Puzzle belongs to a group of blocks often referred as Drunkard's Path variations. The blocks all share a common unit, a two-color block with a distinctive curved seam. Of the numerous ways to both cut and piece this block, I've chosen the traditional method that uses plastic templates and hand cutting. The curved seams can be challenging to stitch. With 16 curved seams in this block, the adage "practice makes perfect" is appropriate advice.

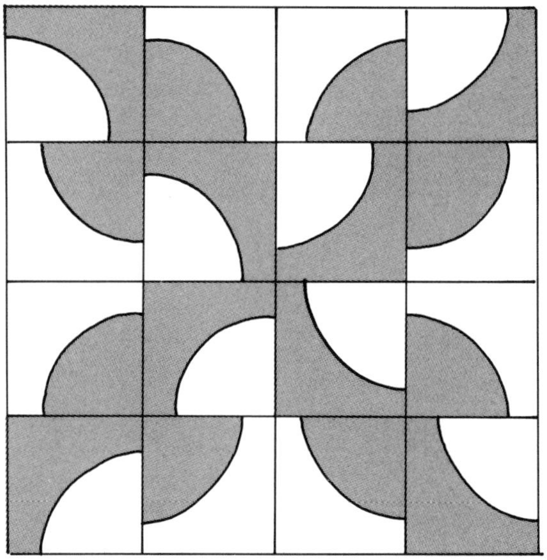

Fig. 4.92 Solomon's Puzzle

Fabrics

For one 12″ block:

Piece A and B: One strip $3\frac{1}{2}''$ wide (in both the light and dark color)

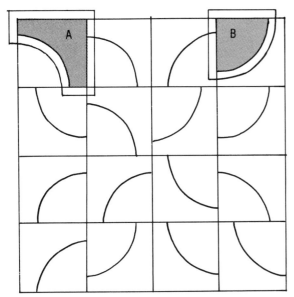

Fig. 4.93 Piecing chart

Cutting

1. Cut both strips in half to obtain two strips $3\frac{1}{2}''$ × (approximately) 20".

2. Make a plastic template of pieces A and B. Use a $\frac{1}{16}''$ punch to mark the three dots on the curves of both pieces.

3. Trace template A eight times on both the light and dark fabrics. Place as shown, using the straight edges of the strip as one edge of the pieces. This makes the tracing more accurate, reduces the amount of tracing and cutting necessary, and insures a uniform number of pieces across the width of fabric. Mark the three dots on all pieces. Cut on the lines.

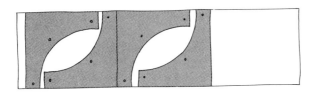

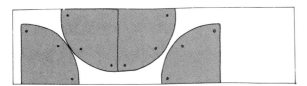

Fig. 4.94 Place templates on fabric and trace

4. Repeat the preceding step with template B.

Piecing

5. Piece together 16 two-color blocks using pieces A and B. See the section Pinning and Matching Techniques in Chapter 2 for complete directions on piecing curved seams. Press seams toward the dark fabric.

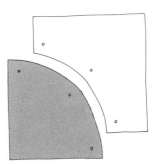

Fig. 4.95 With convex curve on top, pin at middle mark and $\frac{1}{4}''$ from ends

6. Lay the pieces together to ensure they are in the correct location, because in this complex block it is very easy to mis-stitch the pieces. Pin together the edges to be seamed. Stitch the units together in sets of two, working from top to bottom on one half of the block and chain piecing (see Basic Piecing Directions in Chapter 2). Do not cut the chain. Stitching the pairs in sequence and maintaining the chain preserves the proper order. Repeat for the other half of the block.

With high-contrast colors, especially with light colors like white and cream, press open seams to prevent shadowing of the darker color through the lighter. In other colorings press the seams to one side, alternating directions to facilitate the final matches.

7. Join the sets of two units to make a four-unit row. Do not clip the thread chain. Press as in the preceding step.

Fig. 4.96 Join sets of two units to make a four-unit row

8. Stitch the final three seams to complete the block. Use stab pins to match open seams. Key the matches on seams pressed to one side.

Fig. 4.97 Stitch final three seams to complete block

Quilting

One-fourth-inch outline quilting is the traditional choice for Solomon's Puzzle. Machine-guided stitching makes perfect $\frac{1}{4}''$ lines of quilting. The frequent turns and curves build cornering skills. The intricate machine-guided design is manageable on small quilts but cumbersome on large ones. As an alternative to machine-guided stitching, use modified continuous curve quilting about $\frac{1}{8}''$ from the seam line.

Fig. 4.98 Solomon's Puzzle quilting pattern

Companion Blocks and Sets

The name Solomon's Puzzle refers to the intriguing pattern of the individual pieces and of the blocks set side-by-side. The overall effect can be dizzying, and the number of curved seams may prove daunting for the beginner. Solomon's Puzzle alternated with Plain Block or sashing reduces the number of pieced blocks and provides plain fabric to show off the quilting. It has a strong diagonal line like Snowflake and Wild Goose Chase.

Alternate Colors

Solomon's Puzzle is a positive/negative pattern like At the Square. A two-color scheme accentuates that aspect of the pattern. Reversing the colors, light for dark, makes a startling change. On the original, dark designs float on a light background; the reverse appears to have light designs on a dark background. High-contrast colors give this block visual impact and will accentuate your piecing skills.

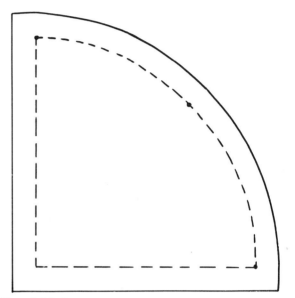

Fig. 4.99 Solomon's Puzzle template B

SOLOMON'S PUZZLE

Number of strips needed to make the blocks:

						Number of Blocks						
		1	4	6	9	12	30	35	48	56	64	81
Piece/Width						Number of Strips						
A-B	3½″	1	2	2	4	5	12	14	20	23	26	33

Yardages needed to make the blocks:

Piece/Color						Yardages						
A-B	Light	$\frac{1}{8}$	$\frac{1}{4}$	$\frac{1}{4}$	$\frac{1}{2}$	$\frac{5}{8}$	$1\frac{1}{4}$	$1\frac{1}{2}$	2	$2\frac{3}{8}$	$2\frac{5}{8}$	$3\frac{1}{4}$
A-B	Dark	$\frac{1}{8}$	$\frac{1}{4}$	$\frac{1}{4}$	$\frac{1}{2}$	$\frac{5}{8}$	$1\frac{1}{4}$	$1\frac{1}{2}$	2	$2\frac{3}{8}$	$2\frac{5}{8}$	$3\frac{1}{4}$

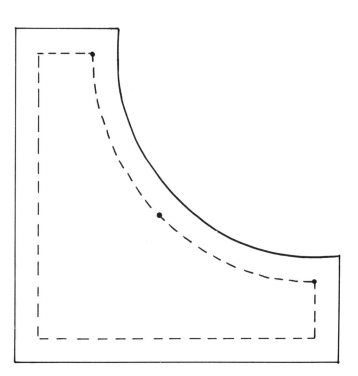

Fig. 4.100 Solomon's Puzzle template A

9. Hands All Around

An eclectic block, Hands All Around appears to contain a little of everything, as if it were two or three blocks merged into one. There are curved seams and pieces reminiscent of the Double Wedding Ring

pattern, with four diamonds on each corner set in squares and triangles like LeMoyne Star. Some of the pieces are rotary cut; others are hand cut. The matches and set-in pieces are not for the rank amateur but are well within the reach of the intermediate quilter. It is complex enough to be a challenge, yet easy enough to be fun to make. The mix of shapes and techniques make Hands All Around a great block. This version uses three colors: a background color, the star color, and a coordinate for the four curved pieces that circle the center.

Fabrics

For one 12″ block:

Piece A: For A, B, E (8 triangles on block edge)

Piece B: One strip $5\frac{5}{8}$″ wide (8 squares on block edges)

Piece E: In background color (1 center of block)

Piece C: One strip 4″ wide in star color (16 diamonds for star)

Piece D: One strip $2\frac{5}{8}$″ wide in coordinating color (4 curved pieces around center)

Fig. 4.101 Hands All Around

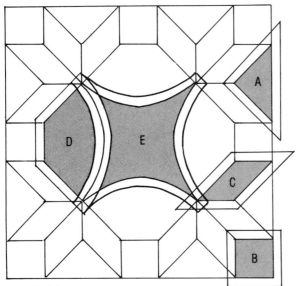

Fig. 4.102 Piecing chart

Cutting

1. Make paper or plastic template of piece E. Use a $\frac{1}{16}''$ punch to make the matching dots. Cut one piece from the background fabric, accurately marking the matching dots. This should leave a piece of fabric approximately $5\frac{5}{8}'' \times 34''$.

2. Cut a strip $2\frac{1}{8}'' \times 34''$ from the background fabric. Cut eight triangles A. The straight of grain is parallel to the long edge.

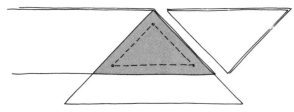

Fig. 4.103 Tape template to 90-degree corner of triangle

3. The actual measurement of square B is $2\frac{9}{16}''$. Most rulers are marked in eighths, not sixteenths. It is possible to estimate $2\frac{9}{16}''$ by locating the fabric edge between $2\frac{1}{2}''$ and $2\frac{5}{8}''$ on the ruler. Cut a strip $2\frac{9}{16}'' \times 34''$ from the background fabric. Cut eight $2\frac{9}{16}''$ squares.

4. Make a plastic template of piece C. Use a $\frac{1}{16}''$ punch to make the corner dots. Mark 16 diamonds on the star fabric. Mark the four corner dots on all pieces (Fig. 4.104). Hand cut on the line.

Fig. 4.104 Mark four corner dots on all diamond-shaped pieces

5. Make a plastic template of piece D. Make the matching dots with a punch. Mark four pieces on the third color, marking the matching dots on all pieces. Hand cut.

Piecing

6. Join the four curved pieces (D) to the center. Press seams away from center.

7. Stitch the diamonds in sets of two. To inset the squares and triangles, the seams joining the diamonds start at the dot, rather than at the fabric edge. Stitching toward the point, start at the dot and knot. At the point, sew through the matching dot and off the edge of the fabric. Press seams open. Press carefully to avoid stretching bias edges.

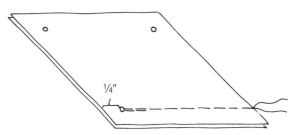

Fig. 4.105 Stitch, starting at the dot, then knot

8. Join diamonds into sets of four. Match seams to make the center. Sew and press as in step 7.

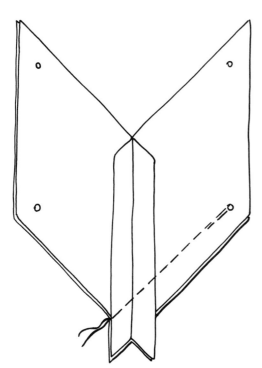

Fig. 4.106 Sew diamonds together, starting at dot and stitching through point

9. Inset triangle A. See the section Inset Piecing in Chapter 2 for complete instructions if you are unsure how to proceed. Press seams open.

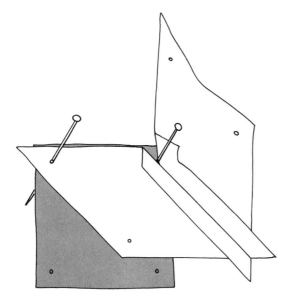

Fig. 4.107 Line up first edges, with inset piece on bottom

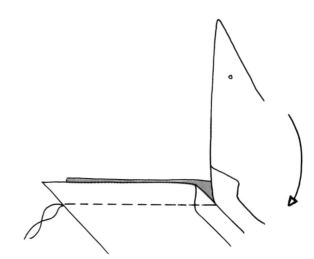

Fig. 4.108 Last stitch before corner falls off folded edge of top fabric

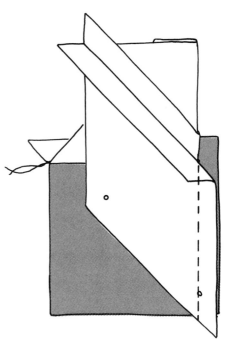

Fig. 4.109 With presser foot up, line up seam allowances before turning corner

10. Inset square B to form the block corners. Press open seams.

11. Stitch the half-star unit to the center unit. Match the star center and the seams on the center unit. Sew with the star unit up. The seam is from dot to dot; do not stitch to the fabric edges. Knot securely. Press open seams.

Fig. 4.110 Stitch pieces to center unit to complete block

12. Inset the square between two stars. This unique square is inset on three sides rather than the usual two. The three edges can be stitched without breaking thread. From the reverse side of the block, pin the square to the upper left-hand star. Stitch as usual, turning the corner between the star and block center. Line up second corner. Pin if necessary to secure. Stitch second side, joining the square to the block center. Turn corner. Stitch final seam, joining the square to the right-hand star. Press open seams.

Quilting

Continuous curve quilting is a good choice for diamond piecing. The open seams are strengthened by the quilting stitches. Quilt the half-stars and the background pieces around the stars. In the center the mix of curved and straight seams can be difficult to outline quilt successfully. The better choice is to treat the five pieces in the center block as a single unit. Use a free-motion motif for the center of the block. Choose a batting carefully. Continuous curve stitching on both sides of a seam and the frequent stitching across seam intersections can make the quilt stiff. Low-loft polyester or cotton/polyester blend batting is the best choice.

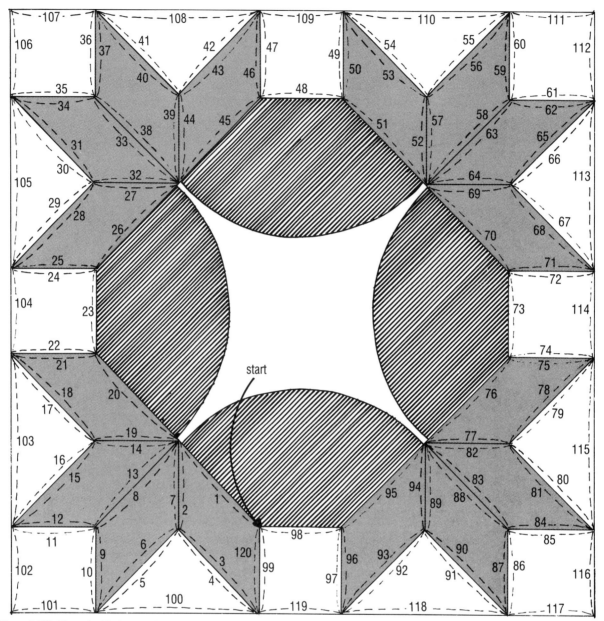

Fig. 4.111 Hands All Around quilting pattern

Companion Blocks and Sets

Plain Blocks or sashing are suitable. Setting the blocks side-by-side requires intermediate matches, like those used in piecing the block. The side-by-side setting forms exciting secondary patterns.

Alternate Colors

Three colors accentuate the piecing pattern. I've also seen the block in four colors, with the center piece different from the background. Hands All Around is a good choice for a scrap quilt. Most pieces are hand cut and marked and do not require a full width of fabric.

HANDS ALL AROUND

Number of strips needed to make the blocks:

		1	4	6	9	12	30	35	48	56	64	81
	Piece/Width											
A	$2\frac{1}{8}''$	1	2		5	6	15	17	23	27	31	39
B	$2\frac{9}{16}''$	1	3		5	7	16	19	26	30	35	44
C	$2''$	2	5		12	15	37	44	60	70	79	100
D	$2\frac{5}{8}''$	1	3		6	7	18	20	28	32	37	47
E	$5\frac{5}{8}''$	1	1	1	2	2	5	5	7	8	10	12

The columns **Number of Blocks** and **Number of Strips** span the data.

Yardages needed to make the blocks:

	Piece/Color					Yardages						
A-B-E	Background	$\frac{1}{4}$	$\frac{5}{8}$	$\frac{3}{4}$	1	$1\frac{1}{4}$	$2\frac{7}{8}$	$3\frac{1}{4}$	$4\frac{3}{8}$	$5\frac{1}{8}$	6	$7\frac{3}{8}$
C	#1	$\frac{1}{4}$	$\frac{3}{8}$	$\frac{1}{2}$	$\frac{3}{4}$	$\frac{7}{8}$	$2\frac{1}{8}$	$2\frac{5}{8}$	$3\frac{3}{8}$	4	$4\frac{1}{2}$	$5\frac{5}{8}$
D	#2	$\frac{1}{8}$	$\frac{3}{8}$	$\frac{3}{8}$	$\frac{1}{2}$	$\frac{5}{8}$	$1\frac{1}{2}$	$1\frac{5}{8}$	$2\frac{1}{4}$	$2\frac{1}{2}$	$2\frac{7}{8}$	$3\frac{3}{4}$

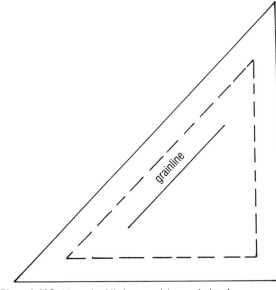

Fig. 4.112 Hands All Around template A

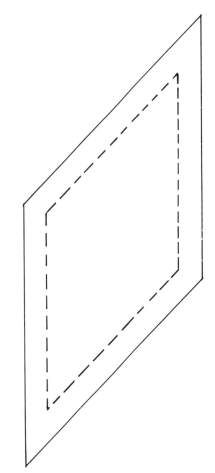

Fig. 4.113 Hands All Around template C

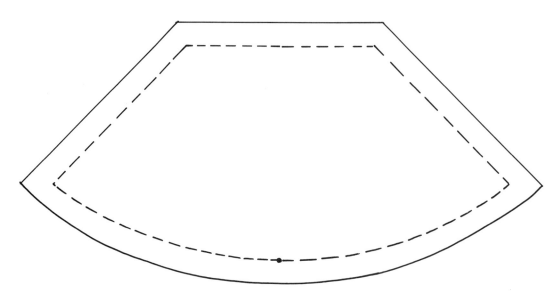

Fig. 4.114 Hands All Around template D

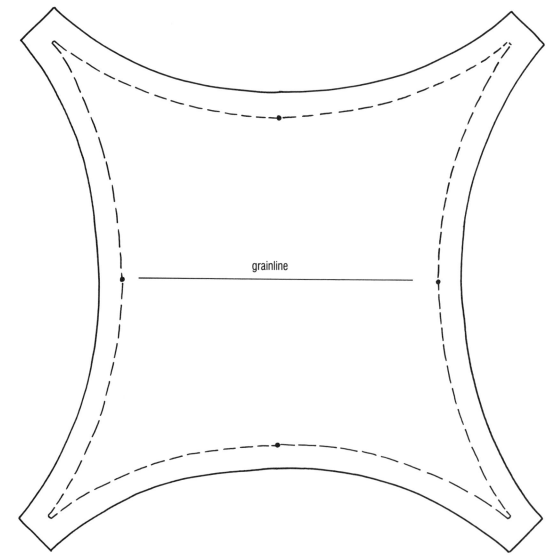

Fig. 4.115 Hands All Around template E

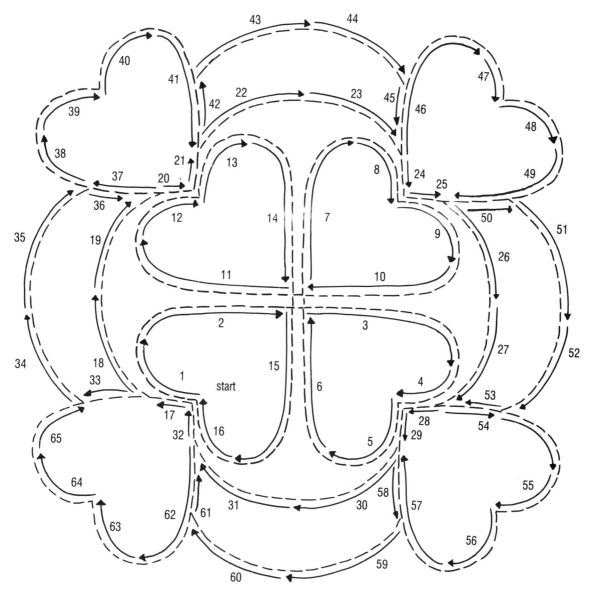

Fig. 4.116 Alternate block quilting pattern; enlarge to fit 7" square

10. Dutch Rose

The beauty of Dutch Rose is its elegant design. The block has three basic pieces: diamond, square, and triangle, with a total of 60 pieces per block. Don't be intimidated by the number of pieces. The piecing is only a repeat of techniques learned in preceding blocks, like insets and matching points. It requires patience, not new skills, and the resulting block is well worth the time. The square and triangle can be rotary-cut; the diamond is hand-cut. The pattern is given in two colors, a background color for the squares and triangles, and star color for the diamonds and four corner squares.

Fig. 4.117 Dutch Rose

Fabrics

For one 12″ block

Piece A: Two strips $1\frac{3}{4}$″ wide in star color (32 diamonds)

Piece B: One strip $1\frac{7}{8}$″ wide in background color (8 triangles)

Piece C: One strip $2\frac{1}{4}$″ wide in background color (16 squares)

Piece C²: One strip $2\frac{1}{4}$″ wide in star color (4 corner squares)

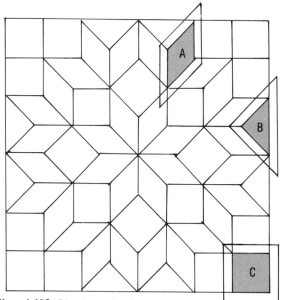

Fig. 4.118 Piecing chart

Cutting

1. Cut a plastic template of piece A. Use the punch to make the corner dots. Mark and cut 32 diamonds from the star color.

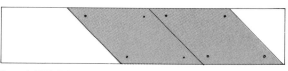

Fig. 4.119 Mark four corner dots on all diamond-shaped pieces

2. Cut eight triangles from strip B. The straight of grain is parallel to the long edge.

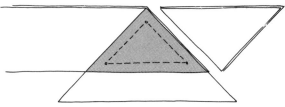

Fig. 4.120 Tape template to 90-degree corner of triangle

3. Cut sixteen $2\frac{1}{4}$″ squares from the background color.

4. Cut four $2\frac{1}{4}$″ squares from the star color.

Piecing

5. Lay the cut pieces out to form the block. Join the diamonds in sets of two. To inset the squares and triangles, start the seams joining diamonds at the dot rather than at the fabric edge. Start at the dot and knot, then stitch toward the point. At the point, sew through the matching dot and off the edge of the fabric. Press seams open.

Fig. 4.121 Lay out pieces to form the block

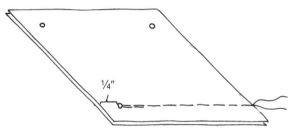

Fig. 4.122 Stitch, starting at dot, then knot

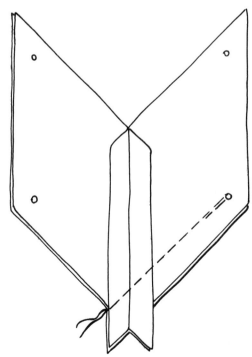

Fig. 4.123 Sew diamonds together, starting at dot and stitching through point

6. With four sets of two diamonds, stitch the center star. First stitch two sets of four, then the final seam. Match the seams using stab pins. Stitch slightly to the right of the match to insure a perfect center. For complete instructions see the section Inset Piecing in Chapter 2. Note that while both fabrics are dark, diagrams show contrast for clarity.

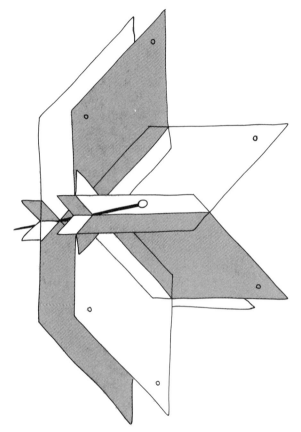

Fig. 4.124 Pin match two sets of four

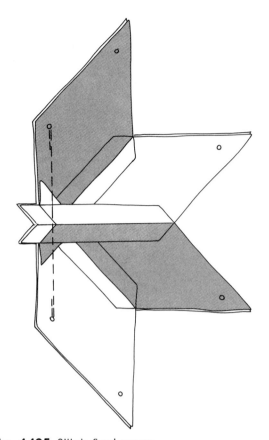

Fig. 4.125 Stitch final seam

7. Inset four background squares in the star, at alternating points. This portion of the block is the central star. (At this point, adding four triangles could make a simple 6″ LeMoyne Star block.)

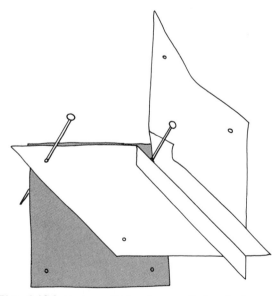

Fig. 4.126 Line up first edges, with inset piece on bottom

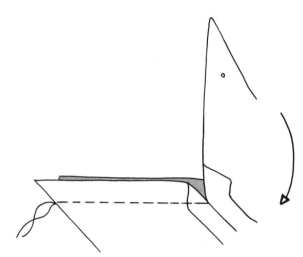

Fig. 4.127 Last stitch before corner falls off folded edge of top fabric

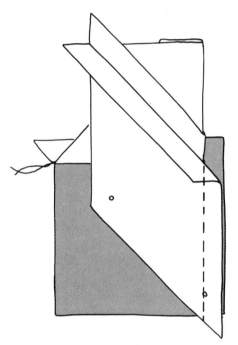

Fig. 4.128 With presser foot up, line up seam allowances when turning corner

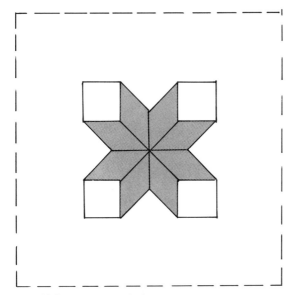

Fig. 4.129 The central star

8. The next section of block to be stitched is the corner. It is made of one set of diamonds and three squares, two of background color, one of star color. Join a background-colored square to a star-colored square. Sew edge to edge, since this is not an inset seam. Press seam open.

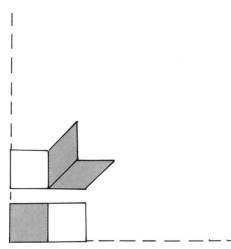

Fig. 4.130 Join background-colored squares to star-colored square and diamond set

9. Join a background square to the diamond set. Refer to the illustration and the piece layout. This will be an inset seam where the diamond joins the square. Start and stop sewing at the corner dots. Sew with the diamond side up. Press seam open.

10. Stitch the two squares from step 8 to the diamond and square unit from step 9. Match seams, using stab pins. This will be an inset seam. Start and stop sewing at the corner dots. Sew with the diamond side up. Press seams open.

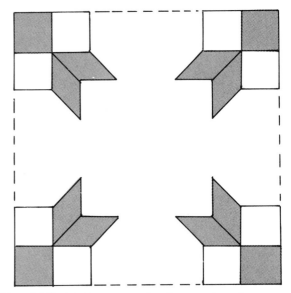

Fig. 4.131 Stitch squares to diamond and square unit

11. Join the corners to the background blocks of the central star. The square is inset between the diamonds. Press open seams. Set this portion of the block aside.

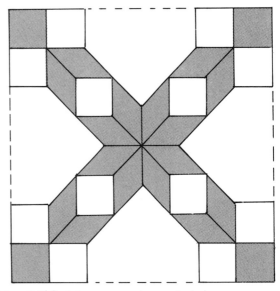

Fig. 4.132 Join corners to central star

12. The last sections to be stitched are the block sides. They are composed of two sets of diamonds, one square in the background color and two triangles. Join the sets of diamonds as illustrated. This will be an inset seam, so start sewing at the corner dot.

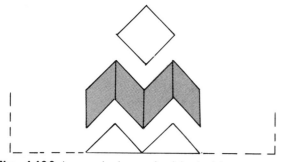

Fig. 4.133 Lay out pieces for block side

13. Inset the background square and the triangles as illustrated. Press open all seams.

14. The basically triangle-shaped block sides are inset on the central star. A single line of stitching runs from *X* to *Y*. Sew with the central star up and the block side down. There are three corners and two matches. Stab pin the matches as you sew. Press open all seams.

Fig. 4.134 Inset block sides with corners and central star

Quilting

Like Hands All Around, the diamonds in Dutch Rose are best quilted with continuous curve quilting. Modified continuous curve, $\frac{1}{8}''$ from the seam line, is appropriate for the number and size of pieces in this block. Choose to stitch either the background pieces or the star pieces. Quilting on the background accentuates the stars and requires the least amount of stitching. Polyester low-loft batting is recommended. Securely quilting the star quilts the piecing, but a cotton/polyester batting is needed to keep the quilt soft and pliable. Cotton thread is preferred for this density of quilting line.

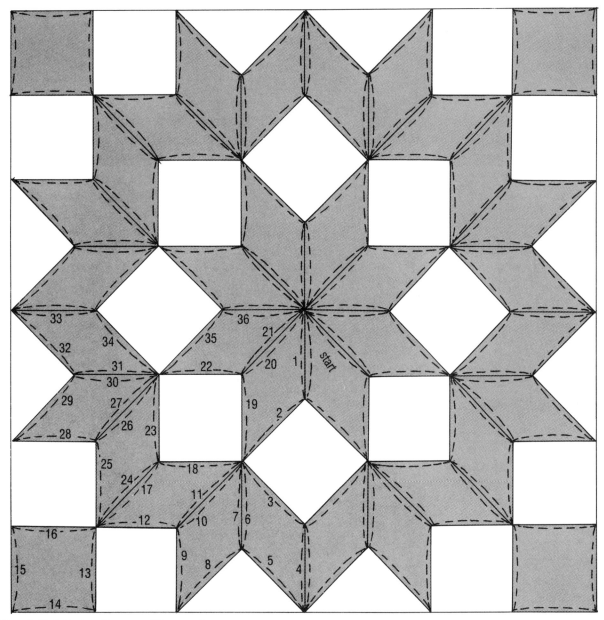

Fig. 4.135 Dutch Rose quilting pattern

Companion Blocks and Sets

Plain Block or sashing are excellent choices for Dutch Rose. Plain spaces are a perfect foil for the intricately pieced blocks. Plain block or sashing reduces the number of pieced blocks required for the quilt, an obvious consideration with a complex block. Joining the blocks side-by-side is suitable for this pattern, but the matches are complex. The major problem is maintaining the fine points on the diamonds. The overall effect of side-by-side joining can be overwhelming or confusing rather than awe-inspiring.

Alternate Colors

High-contrast colors give the piecing sparkle and excitement, but they also accentuate piecing flaws. On the other side, subtle colors or large prints can obscure the piecing. A two-colored block is a conspicuous choice. Another alternative is a three-colored block: the center star in one color, the outer rings of diamonds in a second color. Some antique quilts are scrap quilts, with the center star in one print. The outer ring of diamonds has alternate pieces in two coordinating prints. Stripes and linear-patterned fabric can give spectacular results by using mirror-image piecing.

For a kaleidoscope effect, use floral prints with a distinct pattern. Center the template over a portion of the pattern, for example a flower. Cut every diamond from the exact same place in the print. The pattern formed by the matched prints is always a pleasant surprise. Even unbelievably ugly fabric can yield beautiful stars.

The best approach is "cut and play." Buy extra fabric to allow for some waste when experimenting. The hand-marked and -cut method give more freedom than the rotary-cut method. Cutting single pieces from the center of yardage unmistakably wastes fabric, but a single print has dozens of possibilities. Rather than cutting all the pieces from the same portion of print, vary the location with every star or set of pieces.

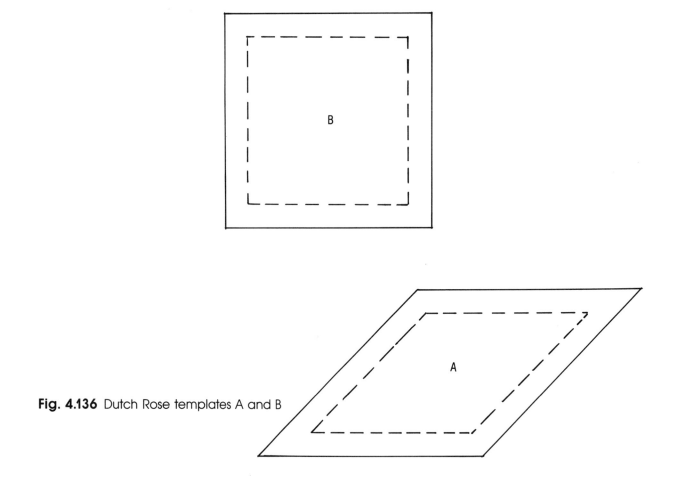

Fig. 4.136 Dutch Rose templates A and B

DUTCH ROSE

Number of strips needed to make the blocks:

						Number of Blocks						
		1	**4**	**6**	**9**	**12**	**30**	**35**	**48**	**56**	**64**	**81**
	Piece/Width					Number of Strips						
A	$1\frac{3}{4}''$	2	8	12	18	20	60	70	96	112	128	162
B	$1\frac{7}{8}''$	1	2	3	4	5	12	14	19	22	24	31
C	$2\frac{1}{4}''$ light	1	2	3	4	5	12	14	19	22	24	31
C^2	$2\frac{1}{4}''$ dark	1	1	1	1	2	3	4	5	6	7	9

Yardages needed to make the blocks:

	Piece/Color					Yardages						
A-C	Dark	$\frac{1}{4}$	$\frac{1}{2}$	$\frac{3}{4}$	1	$1\frac{1}{8}$	$1\frac{3}{4}$	$3\frac{3}{4}$	5	$5\frac{7}{8}$	$6\frac{3}{4}$	$8\frac{1}{2}$
B-C	Light	$\frac{1}{4}$	$\frac{3}{8}$	$\frac{3}{8}$	$\frac{1}{2}$	$\frac{5}{8}$	$1\frac{1}{2}$	$1\frac{5}{8}$	$2\frac{3}{8}$	$2\frac{5}{8}$	3	$3\frac{3}{4}$

11. Lover's Knot

Lover's Knot is a wonderful pattern, reminiscent of the 1930s. The block is a combination of strip piecing and template piecing. The block is cut much like Night and Noon, where the strips are pieced and then cut using a template. I've chosen a method of cutting that is fast and easy, but does waste fabric. If time is money, what is wasted in fabric is saved in time. There is mirror-image piecing on the bow. The original block had an appliqué center but I made it an easy inset piece. The block uses three colors: a background color and two coordinating pieces using a solid color and a print.

Fabrics

For one 12″ block:

Piece A and A^2: One strip 2″ wide in the solid coordinating color (for the ribbons and inside of the bow)

Piece B and B^2: Two strips $2\frac{3}{4}''$ wide in background color (for background around ribbons and bow)

Piece C: One strip $3\frac{3}{4}''$ wide in solid coordinating color (4 pieces of ribbon running into the knot)

Piece D: One strip 2″ wide of print coordinating color (8 pieces for the bow; four are mirror image)

Piece E: One square $2\frac{1}{2}''$ in solid coordinating color (center square of knot)

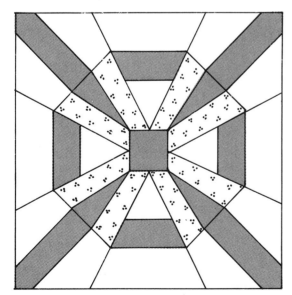

Fig. 4.137 Lover's Knot

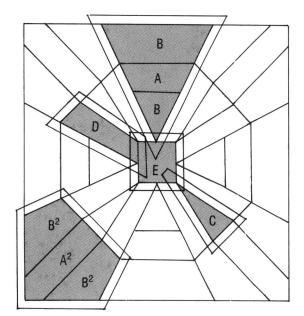

Fig. 4.138 Piecing chart

Cutting

1. Make a plastic template of piece D, marking the matching dot with a $\frac{1}{16}''$ punch and the top side of the template. Using strip D, cut four pieces right side up, and for the mirror image four pieces wrong side up.

2. Make a plastic template of piece C, marking the matching dot at the point with a $\frac{1}{16}''$ punch. Using strip C, mark and cut four pieces.

3. Cut one $2\frac{1}{2}''$ square of solid coordinating color for the knot center. On the right side of the fabric, lightly mark the four matching dots on the corners by measuring in $\frac{1}{4}''$ from all the edges.

4. Sew the strips B-A-B together, in that order. Press seams open.

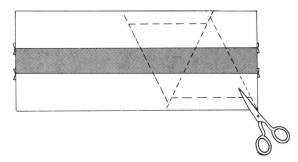

Fig. 4.139 Trace around template B-A-B and hand cut

5. Make a plastic template of piece B-A-B, marking all lines on the template. Place template B-A-B on the reverse side of strip B-A-B. Trace around the template to make four sections. Hand cut.

6. Make a plastic template of piece B^2-A^2-B^2. Mark all lines on the template. Re-press strip B-A-B, pressing seams toward center piece. Place the template $B^2A^2B^2$ on the reverse side of strip B-A-B. Trace around the template to make four sections. Hand cut.

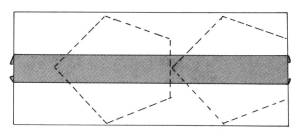

Fig. 4.140 Trace around template B^2-A^2-B^2 and hand cut

Piecing

7. Lay all the pieces together to form the block. This will serve as a reference point when stitching the block together.

8. Stitch a piece C to piece D, with piece C on top. Start stitching at the matching dot and knot securely. Stitch to the other edge. The edges will not line up. Starting at the dot will ensure correct placement on one edge. On the other edge, the intersection where the two pieces overlap should be at the $\frac{1}{4}''$ seam line.

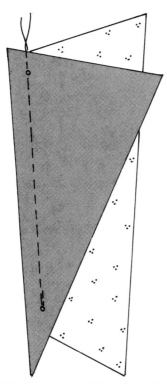

Fig. 4.141 Stitch a piece C to piece D from matching dot

9. Stitch a mirror-image piece D to the D-C unit. Stitch with piece C on the top. Be careful not to catch the first D piece in the second seam. Start stitching at the matching dot. Match as in the previous step. Press the seam toward piece D. Piece E will be inset at this dot.

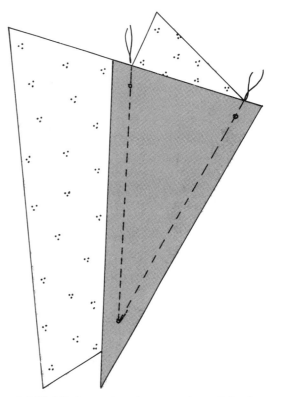

Fig. 4.142 Stitch a mirror-image piece D to the D-C unit, matching dots

10. Stitch unit D-C-D to piece B^2-A^2-B^2. Press open seams.

11. Stitch pieces B-A-B to the D-C-D/B^2-A^2-B^2 unit. If you've done everything correctly, there will be a square hole in the middle of the block.

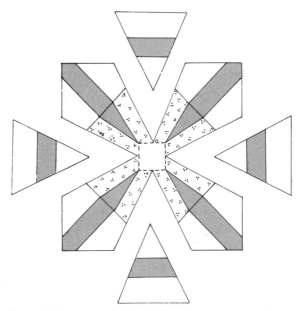

Fig. 4.143 Lay out pieces to complete block. There will be a square hole in the center

12. The center block is an inset piece. It isn't difficult to sew but is unique in that it is sewn in on all four sides. Use one pin along one side to hold the block in place temporarily. Stitching is easier if it is not entirely pinned in place. Pin one side at a time as you work around the piece. Sew with the small square on the bottom and the pieced block on top. Start stitching at the midpoint of one edge—not in a corner. The inset will be easier if you do not catch piece C in the seam. Tip the very point of piece C out of the way as you turn the corners.

Quilting

The design of Lover's Knot is best suited to modified continuous curve quilting. Stitch both the colored and background pieces. A cotton or cotton/polyester blend batting will reinforce the 1930s look of the quilt. For more loft use a low-loft polyester batting. For high-contrast colors use invisible thread.

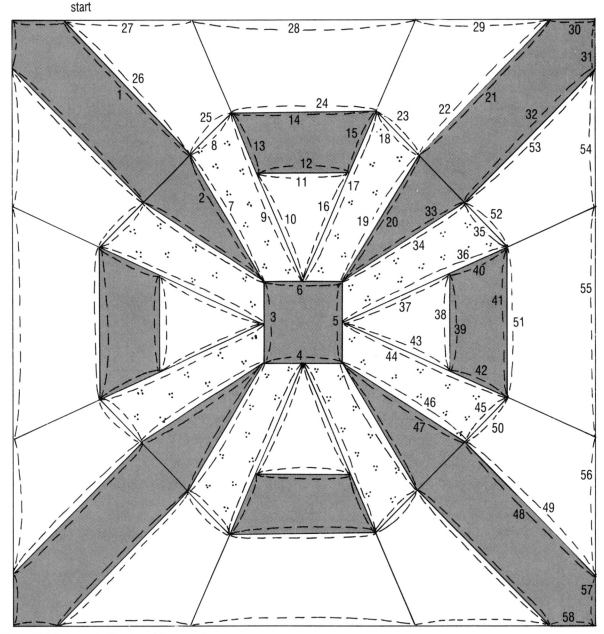

Fig. 4.144 Lover's Knot quilting pattern

Companion Blocks and Sets

Plain Blocks or sashing can be used with Lover's Knot. With this set, the quilt looks like a collection of beribboned gifts waiting to be opened. The block can also be set side-by-side, but it has a strong diagonal line that make the quilt look woven. The matches for a side-by-side set are not difficult.

Alternate Colors

This block is a wonderful scrap quilt. The look of gaily wrapped gifts is unmistakable. In pastels it would be a charming baby quilt. For a holiday quilt use traditional red and green or metallic fabrics. Metallic bows against a black background would be stunning and elegant. The bows are well suited to stripes and plaids. Piece D can be cut in any direction to obtain bias plaids and stripes. High contrast between the background and bows accentuates the three-dimensional look of the block.

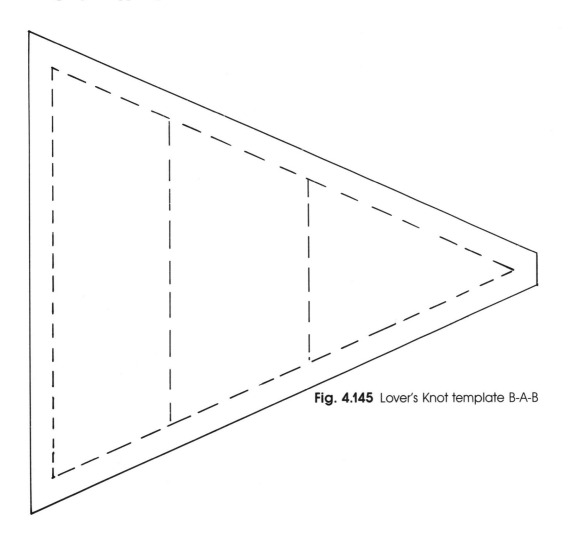

Fig. 4.145 Lover's Knot template B-A-B

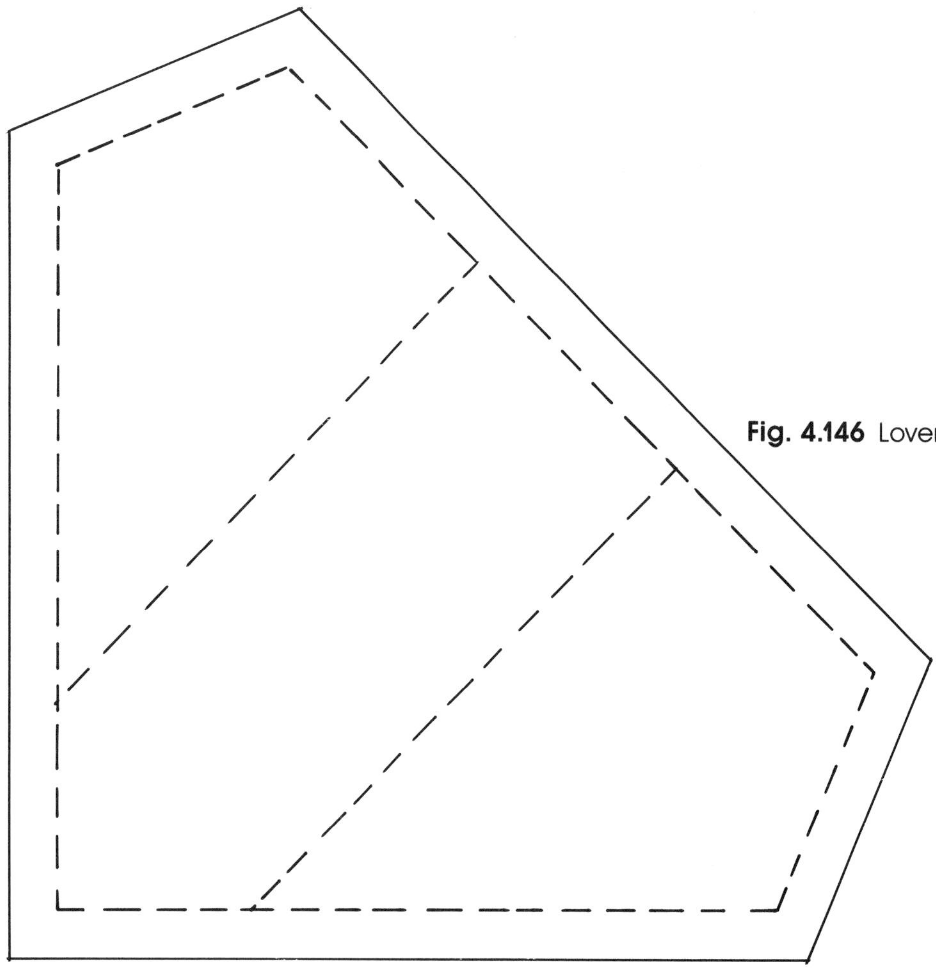

Fig. 4.146 Lover's Knot template B^2-A^2-B^2

LOVER'S KNOT

Number of strips needed to make the blocks:

		Number of Blocks										
		1	**4**	**6**	**9**	**12**	**30**	**35**	**48**	**56**	**64**	**81**
Piece/Width		Number of Strips										
A	2″	1	2	2	3	4	9	10	14	16	19	24
B	2¾″	1	2	4	6	7	18	20	28	32	38	47
A^2	2″	1	2	3	4	6	14	16	22	25	29	36
B^2	2¾″	1	4	6	8	11	27	32	43	50	57	72
C	3¾″	1	1	1	1	2	4	4	6	6	7	9
D	2″	1	4	6	8	11	27	2	4	50	57	72
E	2½″	1	1	1	1	1	2	3	3	4	4	5

Yardages needed to make the blocks:

Piece/Color		Yardages										
A, A^2, C, E	Dark	⅜	½	½	¾	1	1⅞	2⅛	2⅞	3¼	3¾	4⅝
B, B^2	Background	¼	½	⅞	1¼	1½	3½	4	5½	6⅜	7⅜	9¼
D	Print	⅛	¼	⅜	½	⅝	1⅝	1⅞	2½	3	3¼	4

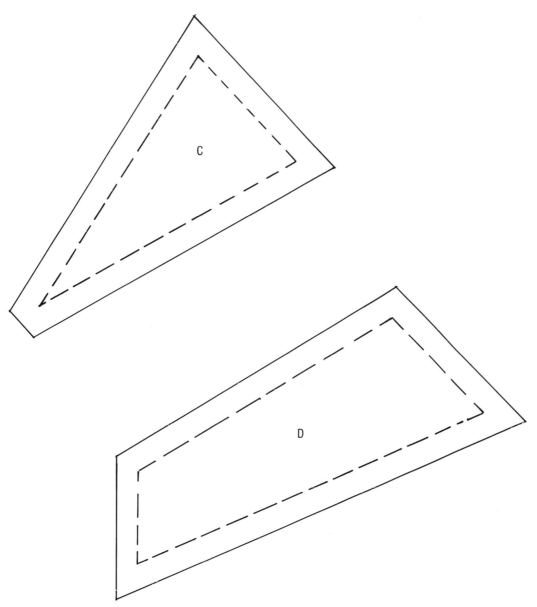

Fig. 4.147 Lover's Knot templates C and D

12. Plain Block

Plain Block is designed to combine with other blocks rather than to be used on its own. The free-motion Feathered Wreath motif can have a stippled or echo background. Plain Block can be an excellent way to reduce the number of pieced blocks required for a quilt top, or the space can emphasize an adjoining complex block. In solid light colors, the block emphasizes your quilting stitch. Dark-colored or printed fabric conceals the stitching. When using Plain Block, consider colors other than the obvious match to the block background. Try the unexpected—use a coordinating print or high-contrast color. In scrap quilts use a mix of solids and prints, rather than one single color.

Another alternative is combining Plain Block with sashing. For solid blocks, use light colors with high-contrast sashing or multicolored pastel blocks with cream sashing. Border prints or striped sashing add unexpected interest to solid or print blocks.

Fabrics

For one 12″ block:

Cut a square $12\frac{1}{2}″ \times 12\frac{1}{2}″$

Quilting

Stitch the vein of the wreath first, following the numbered sequence. The lines between the feathers are stitched twice. Try to follow the same line, but don't be obsessive. The loft of the batting conceals small errors. Work the outer ring of feathers, then the inner. The entire design can be stitched without breaking thread. Upon completion of the wreath, stipple or echo the background (see cover).

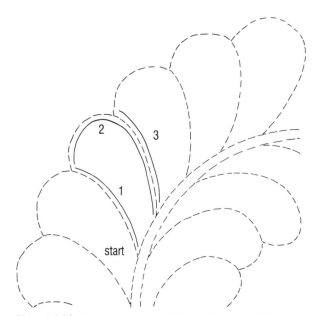

Fig. 4.148 One-quarter of Plain Block quilting pattern; enlarge to fit 12″ square

---

PLAIN BLOCK

Number of strips needed to make the blocks:

					Number of Blocks						
	1	4	6	9	12	30	35	48	56	64	81
Piece					Number of Strips						
A	1	2	2	3	4	10	12	16	19	22	27

Yardages needed to make the blocks:

Piece					Yardages						
A	$\frac{3}{8}$	$\frac{3}{4}$	$\frac{3}{4}$	$1\frac{1}{8}$	$1\frac{1}{2}$	$3\frac{1}{2}$	$4\frac{1}{4}$	$5\frac{5}{8}$	$6\frac{3}{4}$	$7\frac{3}{4}$	$9\frac{1}{2}$

CHAPTER 5

13 Projects

Here are 13 basic project directions, presented in order of style and size. Projects range from a single-block pillow to an 81-block king-size quilt. Seven of the projects are set block-to-block with two borders. This set can be used for alternating plain and pieced blocks. Five of the projects are set with sashing and have three borders. The sashing divides the blocks and forms the first border.

General Instructions

One-quarter-inch seam allowances are used throughout, unless the directions specifically state a different size seam.

Yardages are based on 44"–45" cotton fabric, but assume only 42" usable.

Instructions and yardages for the sashing and borders are for simple, nonmitered corners.

Sashings, borders, and bindings are crosswise cut and pieced. Press open all piecing seams. When cutting the sashing, borders, or binding, any pieced seams should be at least 6" from the corners. The pieced seams can be placed randomly or balanced.

Pin the borders when stitching. On long strips, mark the half and quarters on the quilt and border edges. Match halves and quarters to ensure straight seams and 90-degree joins.

All binding is a straight cut, $\frac{1}{2}$" wide French binding.

Alternative directions are provided to inspire creativity. They assume you have basic sewing skills and are not meant to be step-by-step instructions.

MAKING A SAMPLER QUILT

The blocks and projects in this book make perfect sampler quilts. A sampler usually has a different pattern for every block. It is an excellent way to practice piecing and quilting techniques. Far from a collection of unrelated blocks, a well-planned sampler is a tribute to the quilter's skill.

When making your own sampler, choose your fabrics carefully. To unify the blocks use a limited color range or a distinct print or stripe.

On quilts with more than six blocks, set the blocks with sashing or alternating Plain Block to highlight each block. Side-by-side sets tend to be confusing.

Small quilts, like the four-block wall hanging, are wonderful sampler quilts. The fewer the blocks, the more charming the results. On large quilts limit the variety of pieced blocks by repeating blocks in alternative colors. The color change maintains the sampler look, while repeating blocks gives cohesiveness to the quilt.

CHOOSING BORDERS, SASHING, AND BACKING

The borders and sashing act as frames for your quilt blocks. Well-chosen colors for sashing or borders enhance the quilt and set off the piecing. It is also important to consider the quilting pattern you will use when making your color and fabric selections. There are no pat answers when it comes to making fabric choices, but here are some hints to make the selection easier.

The simplest arrangement uses the same fabrics in both the blocks and border/sashing. On the opposite end of the scale, completely different fabrics are used for each. Here is a compromise: repeat one major color from the blocks and introduce one or two new fabrics.

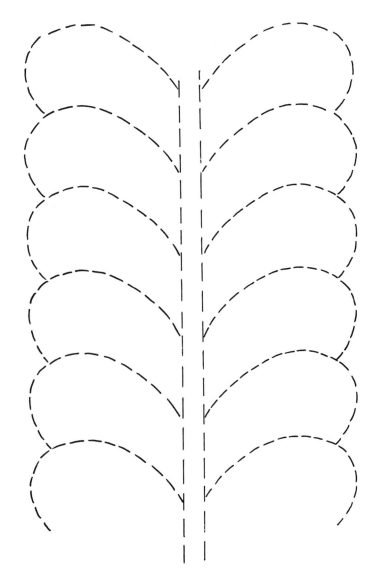

Fig. 5.1 Feather design for outer borders

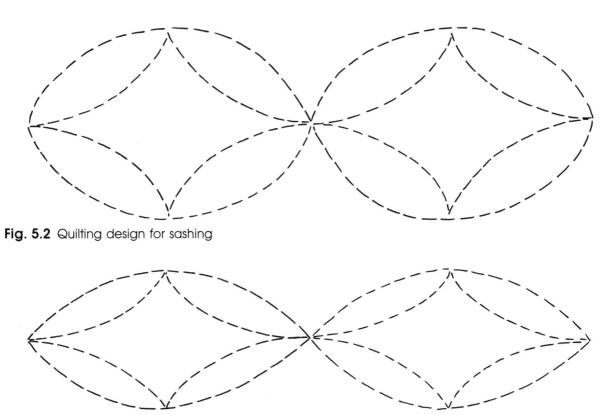

Fig. 5.2 Quilting design for sashing

Fig. 5.3 Quilting design for inner borders

In general, the color of the borders or sashing determines the color scheme of the quilt. For example, a predominately green border emphasizes the green in the blocks.

Consider using large-scale prints or plaids. The large strips of the border or sashing pieces enhance the large prints. By choosing the large print first, you can use it as a guide to selecting the block fabrics.

Striped fabrics are the perfect choice for borders or sashing. Stripes give the quilt a coordinated look unequaled by other fabric designs. The drawback to using striped fabric is the waste. The larger the stripe, the greater the waste. Depending on the repeat, a 9″ stripe may double or triple the fabric requirement. Because every stripe is different, a pattern cannot give a standardized yardage requirement. The border yardages given in the project directions don't apply to striped fabric.

The best way to determine the correct amount of striped fabric needed is to draw the fabric layout on paper. Find your calculator and brush off your basic math skills. Most large stripes are printed lengthwise. Count the number of usable stripes in a width of fabric. (Remember to allow for seams. It is not uncommon to waste every other stripe because of seams.)

Figuring borders is relatively easy. If the number of stripes per width is four or greater, buy the measurement of the longest border. If the number of stripes per width is less than four, add the short and long border measurements together to calculate the yardage.

Determining the sashing yardage is more difficult. Use the quilt illustration at the beginning of the project directions and the number of stripes you can cut from your fabric as the basis. Count the longest strips of sashing first. Note the number and length. Next note the length of the top and bottom sashing. Finally, count the number of crosswise sashing pieces. All of them are 12½″ long because I designed 12″ blocks. Do a rough sketch, laying out the required sashing on the available stripes.

Considering the hassle involved, would anyone use stripes? Let me explain how I buy striped fabric. I never buy less than twice the length of the quilt, usually between five and seven yards. I cut the striped pieces immediately so that if I'm short of fabric, I can return to the store and buy what I need before the bolt is gone. When all else fails, I use the quilter's rule of thumb: "If you like it, buy five yards; if you love it buy ten yards." Great stripes fall in the ten-yard category!

Choosing your backing fabric can be as much fun as choosing the fabrics for the quilt top. Backings do not have to be plain! Use a coordinating print, or piece the backing using scraps from the blocks and borders. It doesn't have to be intricate to be interesting. A center square bordered with wide strips of fabric, or four large blocks of fabric, can give the backing excitement. Consider using a pieced block, like those on the quilt top, in a corner or in the center. The best quilts have that little something extra hidden on the back.

CALCULATING YARDAGES

1. Begin by choosing the block and project you wish to make. Choose the fabric placement for your project. Refer to the section Choosing Borders, Sashing, and Backing when deciding what colors and prints to use in the borders and bindings.

2. Refer to the project directions to find out how many blocks are required. Each project clearly states the number of blocks needed. For projects that allow alternating plain and pieced blocks, the directions state how many of each type of block is required. Only projects with an odd number of blocks, both across and down, are listed as suitable for alternating blocks. Other quilts can use alternating blocks, but odd rows balance the quilt design.

3. Turn to the yardage charts for the block patterns you have chosen. Look across the top of the chart for the number of blocks needed, and read down the chart for the amount of fabric necessary for each color or print.

4. Return to the project directions. Add together the project and block yardages for each color for the total yardage for each color or print in your quilt.

I usually copy the yardage page from the project and blocks. I write all my color choices and do my additions on the copies. The copies are kept with my fabrics during construction of the quilt. That way, if I store the unfinished quilt, the cutting information is with the project. Completing unfinished projects is the bane of all quilters. I hate to admit the number of times I've shelved an unfinished project, to pick it up again six months later without a clue as to what I had been doing. The enclosed pattern information helps me pick up where I left off.

As an example, let's determine the yardage for a four-block wall hanging of the Snowflake block (Fig. 5.4).

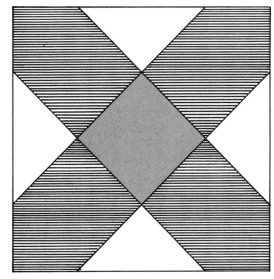

Fig. 5.4 Snowflake

Looking at the yardage chart for the block, I see that Snowflake requires three colors of fabric: light (A), accent (B), and dark (C). To make four blocks I need:

A light: $\frac{1}{4}$ yard
B accent: $\frac{1}{4}$ yard
C dark: $\frac{5}{8}$ yard

Referring to the project directions for the wall hanging, I look up the fabrics I will need. I note the color choices beside each yardage:

Inner border: $\frac{1}{3}$ yard of B accent
Outer border: $\frac{5}{8}$ yard of C dark
Binding: $\frac{1}{2}$ yard of C dark
Rod pocket: $\frac{3}{8}$ yard of unbleached muslin
Backing: $1\frac{1}{8}$ yards unbleached muslin

Add together the yardages for the matching fabrics from the blocks and project to find the total fabric required.

A light: $\frac{1}{4}$ yard total
B accent: $\frac{1}{4}$ yard for the blocks; $\frac{1}{3}$ yard for the border ($\frac{5}{8}$ yard total)
C dark: $\frac{5}{8}$ yard for the blocks; $\frac{5}{8}$ yard for the border; $\frac{1}{2}$ yard for the binding ($1\frac{3}{4}$ yards total)
Unbleached muslin: $\frac{3}{8}$ yard for the pocket; $1\frac{1}{8}$ yards for the backing ($1\frac{1}{2}$ yards total)

When adding thirds and eighths, it is easier to just add the inches and increase the yardage to the next closest number. For help, refer to this chart showing the number of inches in fractions of a yard. I've given the inches in decimals for easy use with the calculator.

$\frac{1}{8}$ yard	4.5 inches
$\frac{1}{4}$ yard	9 inches
$\frac{1}{3}$ yard	12 inches
$\frac{3}{8}$ yard	13.5 inches
$\frac{1}{2}$ yard	18 inches
$\frac{5}{8}$ yard	23 inches
$\frac{2}{3}$ yard	24 inches
$\frac{3}{4}$ yard	27 inches
$\frac{7}{8}$ yard	32.5 inches
1 yard	36 inches

If you are as calculator dependent as I am, you may want to know the decimal equivalents to the fractions of a yard.

$\frac{1}{8}$ yard	.125
$\frac{1}{4}$ yard	.25
$\frac{1}{3}$ yard	.333
$\frac{3}{8}$ yard	.375
$\frac{1}{2}$ yard	.5
$\frac{5}{8}$ yard	.625
$\frac{2}{3}$ yard	.666
$\frac{3}{4}$ yard	.75
$\frac{7}{8}$ yard	.875

SASHED QUILTS

In sashed quilts (see projects 9 through 13 this chapter) the blocks are separated by bands of plain fabric. The sashing acts as a frame around the individual blocks and prevents the secondary patterns that form when blocks are set side-by-side. Sashing also adds visual interest and reduces the number of pieced blocks needed to complete a full-size quilt. Sashing requires only simple matches.

Vertical sashing strips run the full length of the quilt body. I refer to the sashing between the horizontal rows of blocks as cross-sashing. This gives the illusion of a single strip of fabric across the width of the quilt. In reality this sashing strip is composed of 12" lengths stitched between the blocks.

This illusion of a single strip depends on careful matching. To match, begin by joining the blocks and cross-sashing in a vertical row. Stitch one strip of lengthwise sashing to a block and cross-sashing unit. Press the seam toward the sashing. From the wrong side, using a ruler and fabric marker, extend the cross-sashing lines through the lengthwise sashing. Use the marks to match and stitch the next block and cross-sashing unit in place. Continue stitching and marking until the body of the quilt is completed.

1. One-Block Pillow

Yardages
For one 16" × 16" pillow with ruffle:

Sashing: $\frac{1}{4}$ yard
Backing: $\frac{1}{2}$ yard
Ruffle: $\frac{5}{8}$ yard
Batting: 18" square

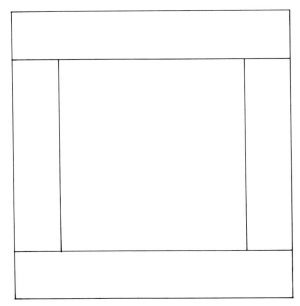

Fig. 5.5 One-Block Pillow

Construction

To make the sashing:

1. Cut two strips $2\frac{1}{2}''$ wide. From these two strips, cut two pieces $12\frac{1}{2}''$ long and two pieces $16\frac{1}{2}''$ long.

2. Stitch the two short strips to opposite sides of the block. Stitch the long strips to the other sides of the block.

To quilt:

3. Cut a backing piece 17″ square.

4. Layer, baste, and quilt the project.

To make the ruffle:

5. Cut three strips $6\frac{1}{2}''$ wide. Stitch the strips together lengthwise to form a single strip approximately $126'' \times 6\frac{1}{2}''$. Join the ends to form a circle. Fold and press the strip in half lengthwise. The circle measures approximately 126″ by $3\frac{1}{4}''$. Stitch a gathering thread $\frac{1}{4}''$ in from the raw edges of the strip.

The best gathering thread is dental floss with a casing of zigzag. Since the floss is a heavy waxed thread, it can't break, and it slides easily through the zigzag casing. Set the machine for a medium-width zigzag. Stitch length can vary but set it slightly shorter than an average stitch length. Do

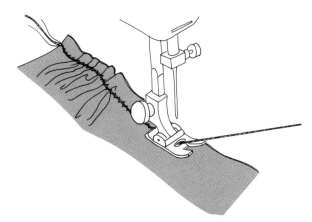

Fig. 5.6 Encase dental floss in zigzag

not cut the dental floss; use it straight from the dispenser to keep it untangled. Place the end of the floss in the needle hole of the presser foot. Thread it from the top, through the hole and under the foot. This way the floss is laying on top of the bridge of the presser foot, where it is easy to see and can't get caught by the needle or stitched to the fabric.

Hold the floss tail with the other thread tails as you start to stitch. Clear the floss with the first few stitches. Unwind the floss as it is needed. Hold it slightly taut and raised above the bridge of the foot. The needle will jump over the floss, no matter how fast you sew. After stitching around the ruffle cut generous thread tails.

Divide the ruffle into four equal sections and mark each with a small safety pin. Match the pins to the four corners. Pin to the right side of the block, raw edges together. Gather the ruffle to fit the sashed block. Arrange the gathers to put a small amount more fabric in the corners. The excess fabric stops the ruffle from cupping around the corner. Machine baste the ruffle in place.

To make the backing:

6. Cut a square $16\frac{1}{2}''$. Pin it to the pillow front, right sides together. The ruffle is encased inside the two pieces. Stitch around the pillow. Leave a 2″ opening to turn the pillow right sides out. Turn the pillow right side out and stuff with polyester fiberfill. Hand stitch the opening.

ALTERNATIVES

Omit the ruffle or substitute piping.

Make double ruffles, combining lace and fabric.

Use a two-color ruffle: from one color cut three $2\frac{1}{2}''$ strips, and from a coordinating color cut three $4\frac{1}{2}''$ strips. Seam to make the $6\frac{1}{2}''$ strips. When folded in half and pressed, this gives the appearance of a double ruffle without the bulk.

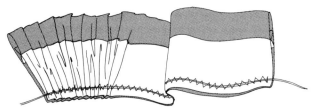

Fig. 5.7 A two-color ruffle gives the appearance of a double ruffle without the bulk

Advanced sewers may wish to put a zipper opening in the center back of the pillow. Substitute two pieces, $16\frac{1}{2}'' \times 9\frac{1}{4}''$, for the single $16\frac{1}{2}''$ square in the preceding directions. Baste the two pieces together on the long edges with a $1''$ seam allowance, resulting in a $16\frac{1}{2}''$ square. Press open seam. Stitch a $12''$ zipper in the seam. Use slot or lap application. Remove the basting.

A wall hanging can be made from the single block and sashing. Follow the piecing, sashing, and quilting directions. Omit the pillow back and substitute binding for the ruffle. The binding will require two $3'' \times 42''$ strips of fabric. Refer to Bindings in Chapter 7 for complete binding instructions.

2. Four-Block Wall Hanging

Yardages

For a $36'' \times 36''$ hanging with four pieced blocks, or two pieced and two plain blocks:

Inner border: $\frac{1}{3}$ yard
Outer border: $\frac{5}{8}$ yard

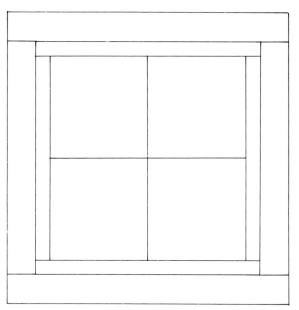

Fig. 5.8 Four-block wall hanging

Binding: $\frac{1}{2}$ yard
Rod pocket: $\frac{3}{8}$ yard
Backing: $1\frac{1}{8}$ yards
Batting: $40''$ square

Construction

1. Sew together the four blocks set two-by-two.

To make the inner border:

2. Cut four strips $2\frac{1}{2}''$ wide.

3. From two of the strips, cut two borders $24\frac{1}{2}'' \times 2\frac{1}{2}''$. From the remaining two strips, cut two borders $28\frac{1}{2}'' \times 2\frac{1}{2}''$.

4. Stitch the two short borders to opposite sides of the quilt. Stitch the long borders to the other sides of the quilt.

To make the outer border:

5. Cut four strips $4\frac{1}{2}''$ wide. From the four strips, cut two borders $28\frac{1}{2}'' \times 4\frac{1}{2}''$ and two borders $36\frac{1}{2}'' \times 4\frac{1}{2}''$.

6. Stitch the two short borders to opposite sides of the inner border, as in the preceding step. Stitch the long borders to the other sides of the inner border.

To make the backing:

7. Cut a $38''$ square of backing fabric.

8. Layer, baste, and quilt the project.

To cut rod pocket and binding:

9. For the rod pocket, cut one strip 12″ wide × 35½″ long. Refer to Chapter 7 on making the rod pocket.

10. For the binding, cut four strips 3″ wide. Stitch them together to form a unit approximately 170″ × 3″.

11. Refer to Bindings in Chapter 7 for complete binding directions.

3. Nine-Block Wall Hanging

Yardages

For 48″ × 48″ hanging with five pieced and four plain blocks:

Inner border: ⅓ yard
Outer border: ⅔ yard
Binding: ½ yard
Rod pocket: ¾ yard
Backing: 2⅞ yards (excess fabric from the backing is sufficient to make the first border, *or* the second border, *or* the binding)
Batting: 50″ square cut from a twin-size batting or yardage

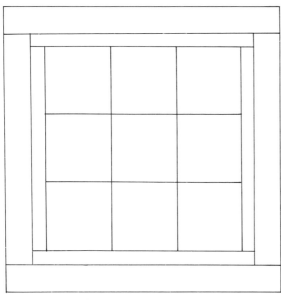

Fig. 5.9 Nine-block wall hanging

Construction

1. Sew together the nine blocks, set three-by-three.

To cut the backing:

2. Cut the backing fabric in half for two pieces approximately 52″ × 42″. Cut one piece lengthwise, 9″ × 52″. The excess fabric will be approximately 33″ × 52″. If you plan to use the excess fabric for a border or binding, cut the strips lengthwise instead of the usual crosswise. Modified instructions using the excess fabric are in parentheses.

To make the inner border:

3. Cut four strips 2½″ wide. From the four strips, cut two borders 36½″ × 2½″ and two borders 40½″ × 2½″. (Backing excess: cut as in preceding instructions.)

4. Stitch the two short borders to the opposite sides of the quilt. Stitch the long borders to the other sides of the quilt.

To make the outer border:

5. Cut five strips 4½″ wide.

6. Using two strips, cut two borders 40½″ × 4½″.

7. Stitch the remaining three strips together to form a single unit approximately 126″ × 2½″. From that unit cut two borders 48½″ × 4½″. (Backing excess: cut four strips 52″ × 4½″.) (From the four strips cut two borders 40½″ × 4½″ and two borders 48½″ × 48½″.)

8. Stitch the two short borders to opposite sides of the inner border. Stitch the long borders to the other sides of the inner border.

To make the backing:

9. Join the backing fabric to form a square approximately 52″ × 52″.

10. Layer, baste, and quilt the project.

To cut rod pocket and binding:

11. For the rod pocket, cut two 12″-wide strips across the fabric. Join the short ends. Trim to 12″ × 48″.

12. For the binding, cut five strips 3″ wide. Join to form a unit approximately 3″ × 210″. (Backing excess: Cut four strips 3″ × 52″. Join the strips to form a unit approximately 208″ × 3″.)

13. Refer to Bindings in Chapter 7 for complete binding instructions.

4. Baby Quilt

Yardages

For a 48″ × 60″, 12-block quilt:

Inner border: $\frac{1}{2}$ yard
Outer border: $\frac{7}{8}$ yard
Binding: $\frac{5}{8}$ yard
Rod pocket: $\frac{3}{4}$ yard
Backing: $2\frac{7}{8}$ yard (excess fabric from the backing is sufficient to make the first border *or* the binding)
Batting: 49″ × 61″ cut from a twin-size batt

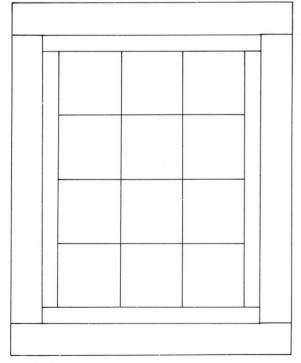

Fig. 5.10 Baby quilt

Construction

1. Sew together the 12 blocks, set three-by-four.

To cut the backing:

2. Cut the backing fabric in half for two pieces approximately 52″ × 42″. Cut one piece lengthwise 52″ × 20″. The excess fabric will be approximately 52″ × 22″. If you plan to use the excess fabric for the border or binding, cut the strips lengthwise instead of the usual crosswise. Modified instructions using the excess fabric are in parentheses.

To make the inner border:

3. Cut five strips $2\frac{1}{2}$″ wide.

4. Using two strips, cut two borders $40\frac{1}{2}$″ × $2\frac{1}{2}$″.

5. Stitch the remaining three strips together to form a single unit approximately 126″ × $2\frac{1}{2}$″. From that unit cut two borders $48\frac{1}{2}$″ × $2\frac{1}{2}$″. (Backing excess: Cut four strips $2\frac{1}{2}$″ × 52″. From the four strips cut two borders $40\frac{1}{2}$″ × $2\frac{1}{2}$″ and two borders $48\frac{1}{2}$″ × $48\frac{1}{2}$″.)

6. Stitch the two long borders to the long sides of the quilt. Stitch the short borders to the short sides of the quilt.

To make the outer border:

7. Cut six strips $4\frac{1}{2}$″ wide.

8. Make two units of three strips each, measuring approximately 126″ × $4\frac{1}{2}$″.

9. From one unit cut two borders $48\frac{1}{2}$ × $4\frac{1}{2}$″. Using the remaining unit, cut two borders $52\frac{1}{2}$″ × $4\frac{1}{2}$″.

10. Stitch the long borders to the long side of the inner border, as in the preceding step. Stitch the short borders to the other sides of the inner border.

To make the backing:

11. Join the backing fabric to form a rectangle approximately 52″ × 62″.

12. Layer, baste, and quilt the project.

To cut rod pocket and binding:

13. For the rod pocket, cut two strips 12″ × 42″. Join to make a unit approximately 12″ × 80″. Cut to 12″ × 48″.

14. For the binding, cut six strips 3″ wide. Join to form a unit approximately 3″ × 252″. (Backing excess: Cut five strips 3″ wide. Join the strips to form a unit 260″ × 3″.)

15. Refer to Bindings in Chapter 7 for complete binding instructions.

5. Twin-Size Quilt

Yardages

For a 72″ × 96″ quilt with 35 blocks (18 pieced, 17 plain blocks):

Inner border: $\frac{5}{8}$ yard
Outer border: $1\frac{1}{4}$ yards
Binding: $\frac{7}{8}$ yard
Rod pocket: $\frac{1}{2}$ yard
Backing: $5\frac{1}{2}$ yards (excess fabric from the backing is sufficient to make the first border)
Batting: 73″ × 97″ cut from a regular-size batt

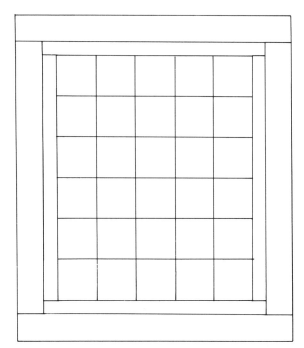

Fig. 5.11 Twin-size quilt

Construction

1. Sew together the 35 blocks, set five-by-seven.

To cut the backing:

2. Cut the backing fabric in half for two pieces approximately 43″ × 98″. Cut one piece lengthwise, 32″ × 98″. The excess fabric will be approximately 10″ × 98″. If you plan to use the excess fabric for the border, cut the strips lengthwise instead of the usual crosswise. Modified instructions using the excess fabric are in parentheses.

To make the inner border:

3. Cut eight strips $2\frac{1}{2}″$ wide.

4. Make four units of two strips each, measuring approximately 85″ × $2\frac{1}{2}″$.

5. Using two of the two-strip units, cut two borders $64\frac{1}{2}″$ × $2\frac{1}{2}″$.

6. Using the remaining two-strip units, cut two borders, $84\frac{1}{2}″$ × $2\frac{1}{2}″$. (Backing excess: Cut four strips $2\frac{1}{2}″$ wide. From the strips cut two borders $64\frac{1}{2}″$ × $2\frac{1}{2}″$ and two borders $84\frac{1}{2}″$ × $2\frac{1}{2}″$.)

7. Stitch the two long borders to the long sides of the quilt. Stitch the short borders to the opposite sides.

To make the outer border:

8. Cut nine strips $4\frac{1}{2}″$ wide.

9. Make two units of two strips approximately 85″ × $4\frac{1}{2}″$. From those units cut two borders $72\frac{1}{2}″$ × $4\frac{1}{2}″$.

10. Join the remaining five strips in one unit, approximately 210″ × $4\frac{1}{2}″$. From that unit cut two borders $88\frac{1}{2}″$ × $4\frac{1}{2}″$.

11. Stitch the two long borders to the long side of the quilt. Stitch the short borders to the opposite sides.

To make the backing:

12. Join the backing fabric to form a rectangle approximately 74″ × 97″.

13. Layer, baste, and quilt the project.

To cut rod pocket and binding:

14. For the rod pocket, cut two strips 12″ × 42″. Join to a make a unit approximately 12″ × 80″. Cut to 12″ × 71″.

15. For the binding, cut nine strips 3″ wide. Join to form a unit approximately 3″ × 378″.

16. Refer to Bindings in Chapter 7 for complete binding instructions.

6. Full-Size Quilt

Yardages

For a 84″ × 96″, 48-block quilt:

Inner border: $\frac{5}{8}$ yard
Outer border: $1\frac{1}{8}$ yards
Binding: $\frac{7}{8}$ yard
Rod pocket: $\frac{1}{2}$ yard
Backing: $5\frac{1}{2}$ yards
Batting: 85″ × 97″ cut from a queen-size batt

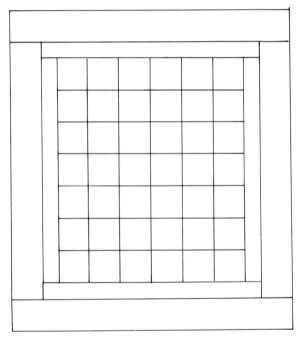

Fig. 5.12 Full-size quilt

Construction

1. Sew together the 48 blocks, set six-by-seven.

To make the inner border:

2. Cut eight strips $2\frac{1}{2}$″ wide.

3. Make four units of two strips each, each strip measuring approximately 85″ × $2\frac{1}{2}$″.

Using two units, cut two borders, $76\frac{1}{2}$″ × $2\frac{1}{2}$″. Use the remaining two units to make two borders, $84\frac{1}{2}$″ × $2\frac{1}{2}$″.

4. Stitch the two long borders to the long sides of the quilt. Stitch the short borders to the opposite sides.

To make the outer border:

5. Cut nine strips $4\frac{1}{2}$″ wide.

6. Make two units of two strips approximately 85″ × $4\frac{1}{2}$″. From those units cut two borders $84\frac{1}{2}$″ × $4\frac{1}{2}$″.

7. Join the remaining five strips in one unit approximately 210″ × $4\frac{1}{2}$″. From that unit cut two borders, $88\frac{1}{2}$″ × $4\frac{1}{2}$″.

8. Stitch the two long borders to the long side of the quilt. Stitch the short borders to the opposite sides.

To make the backing:

9. Cut the backing fabric in half, resulting in two pieces approximately 42″ × 98″.

10. Join the backing to form a rectangle approximately $85\frac{1}{2}$″ × 98″.

11. Layer, baste, and quilt the project.

To cut rod pocket and binding:

12. For the rod pocket, cut two strips 12″ × 42″. Join to make a unit approximately 12″ × $85\frac{1}{2}$″. Cut to 12″ × 83″.

13. For the binding, cut nine strips 3″ wide. Join to form a unit approximately 3″ × 378″.

14. Refer to Bindings in Chapter 7 for complete binding instructions.

7. Queen-Size Quilt

Yardages

For a 96″ × 108″, 56-block quilt:

Inner border: $\frac{3}{4}$ yard
Outer border: $1\frac{3}{8}$ yards
Binding: $\frac{7}{8}$ yard
Rod pocket: $\frac{3}{4}$ yard

Backing: 8¼ yards (excess fabric from the backing is sufficient to make the first border)

Batting: 97″ × 109″ cut from a king-size batt

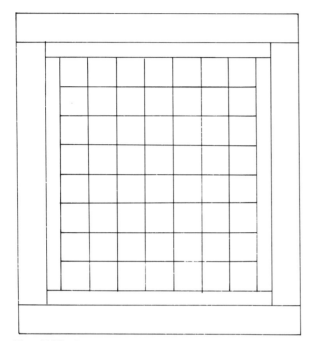

Fig. 5.13 Queen-size quilt

Construction

1. Sew together the 56 blocks, set seven-by-eight.

To cut the backing:

2. Cut the backing fabric into three equal pieces, approximately 43″ × 98″. Cut one piece lengthwise, 27″ × 98″. The excess fabric will be approximately 16″ × 98″. If you plan to use the excess fabric for the border, cut the strips lengthwise instead of the usual crosswise. Modified instructions using the excess fabric are in parentheses.

To make the inner border:

3. Cut ten strips 2½″ wide.

4. Make two units of five strips each, each strip measuring approximately 215″ × 2½″. From one unit cut two borders, 88½″ × 2½″. From the other unit cut two borders, 96½″ × 2½″. (Backing excess: Cut four strips 2½″

× 98″. Cut two borders 88½″ × 2½″ and two borders 96½″ × 2½″.)

5. Stitch the two long borders to the long sides of the quilt. Stitch the short borders on the opposite sides.

To make the outer border:

6. Cut ten strips 4½″ wide.

7. Make two units of five strips each, each strip measuring approximately 215″ × 4½″. From one unit cut two borders 100½″ × 4½″. From the other unit cut two borders 96½″ × 4½″.

8. Stitch the two long borders to the long sides of the quilt. Stitch the short borders to the opposite sides.

To make the backing:

9. Join the three pieces of backing fabric to form a rectangle approximately 98″ × 110″.

10. Layer, baste, and quilt the project.

To cut rod pocket and binding:

11. For the rod pocket, cut three strips 12″ × 43″. Join to make a unit approximately 12″ × 129″. Cut to 12″ × 95″.

12. For the binding, cut ten strips 3″ wide. Join to form a unit approximately 3″ × 430″.

13. Refer to Bindings in Chapter 7 for complete binding instructions.

8. King-Size Quilt

Yardages

For a 120″ × 120″, 81-block quilt, with 41 pieced and 40 plain blocks:

Inner border: ⅞ yard
Outer border: 1⅝ yards
Binding 1⅛ yards
Rod pocket: ¾ yard
Backing: 10¼ yards
Batting: 120″ × 120″, one king-size batt

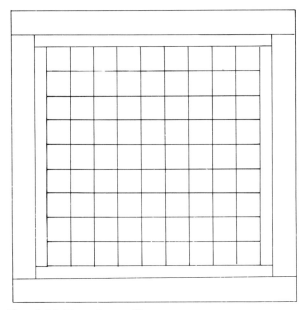

Fig. 5.14 King-size quilt

Construction

1. Sew together the 81 blocks, set nine-by-nine.

To make the inner border:

2. Cut 11 strips $2\frac{1}{2}''$ wide.

3. Join to make a single unit approximately $473'' \times 2\frac{1}{2}''$. From that unit cut two borders $108\frac{1}{2}'' \times 2\frac{1}{2}''$ and two borders $112\frac{1}{2}'' \times 2\frac{1}{2}''$.

4. Stitch the two short borders to opposite sides of the quilt. Stitch the long borders to the remaining sides.

To make the outer border:

5. Cut 12 strips $4\frac{1}{2}''$ wide.

6. Join to make a single unit, $516'' \times 4\frac{1}{2}''$. From that unit cut two borders $112\frac{1}{2}'' \times 4\frac{1}{2}''$ and two borders $120\frac{1}{2}'' \times 4\frac{1}{2}''$.

7. Stitch the two short borders to opposite sides of the quilt. Stitch the long borders to the remaining sides.

To make the backing:

8. Cut the backing fabric into three equal pieces approximately $43'' \times 122''$. Cut one piece lengthwise, $37'' \times 122''$. Discard the excess $5'' \times 122''$.

9. Join the backing fabric to form a square approximately $121'' \times 121''$.

10. Layer, baste, and quilt the project.

To cut rod pocket and binding:

11. For the rod pocket, cut three strips $12''$ wide. Join to make a single unit approximately $12'' \times 129''$. Cut to $12'' \times 119''$.

12. For the binding, cut 12 strips $3''$ wide. Join to form a single unit approximately $12'' \times 516''$.

13. Refer to Bindings in Chapter 7 for complete binding instructions.

9. Sashed Four-Block Wall Hanging

Yardages

For a $43'' \times 43''$ hanging:

Sashing and first border: $\frac{1}{2}$ yard
Second border: $\frac{3}{8}$ yard
Outer border: $\frac{5}{8}$ yard
Binding: $\frac{1}{2}$ yard
Rod pocket: $\frac{1}{2}$ yard

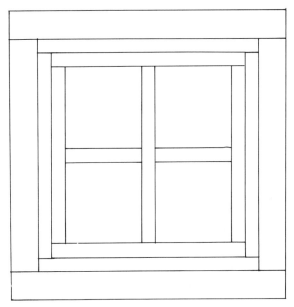

Fig. 5.15 Sashed four-block wall hanging

Backing: 2⅔ yards (excess fabric from the backing is sufficient to make the sashing and first border, *or* the second border, *or* the outer border, *or* the binding, *or* the rod pocket; the other option is to use 1⅓ yards of backing if the fabric is 45″ wide including selvages)

Batting: 44″ square cut from a crib-size batt

Construction

To cut the backing:

1. Cut the 2⅔ yards of backing fabric in half for two pieces approximately 45″ × 43″. Cut one piece lengthwise, 45″ × 4″. The excess fabric will be approximately 45″ × 39″. If you plan to use the excess fabric for the border, cut the strips lengthwise instead of the usual crosswise. Modified instructions using the excess fabric are in parentheses.

To make the sashing and first border:

2. Cut five strips 3″ wide.

3. From two strips, cut two borders 32″ × 2½″.

4. From three strips, cut three sashings 27″ × 2½″.

5. From the strip remnants cut two cross-sashings 12½″ × 2½″. (Backing excess: repeat preceding instructions.)

To join the blocks and sashing:

6. Make two units of block-sashing-block. Press all seams toward the sashing.

7. Join one block and cross-sashing unit and one strip of lengthwise sashing. Mark the matches. Join the second block and cross-sashing unit, completing the quilt body.

8. Stitch the lengthwise sashing to the sides of the block and sashing units. Sew the sashing borders to the opposite sides.

To make the second border:

9. Cut four strips 2½″ wide. Cut two borders 36″ × 2½″ and two borders 32″ × 2½″. (Backing excess: repeat preceding instructions.)

10. Join the short borders to the lengthwise side of the quilt. Stitch the long borders to the opposite sides.

To make the outer border:

11. Cut four strips 4½″ wide. Cut two borders 36″ × 4½″ and two borders 44″ × 4½″. (Backing excess: repeat preceding instructions.)

12. Join the short border to the lengthwise side of the quilt. Stitch the long border to the opposite sides.

To make the backing:

13. Join the backing fabric to form a square 45″ × 45″.

14. Layer, baste, and quilt the project.

To cut the rod pocket and binding:

15. For the rod pocket, cut one strip 12″ wide. (Backing excess: repeat preceding instructions.)

16. For the binding, cut five strips 3″ wide. Join to form a unit 215″ × 3″. (Backing excess: repeat preceding instructions.)

17. Refer to Bindings in Chapter 7 for complete binding instructions.

10. Sashed Six-Block Baby Quilt

Yardages

For a 44″ × 58″ quilt:

Sashing and first border: ⅝ yard
Second border: ⅜ yard
Outer border: ⅞ yard
Binding: ½ yard
Rod pocket: ½ yard
Backing: 2⅔ yards (excess fabric from the backing is sufficient to make the sashing and first border, *or* the second border, *or* the outer border, *or* the binding *or* the rod pocket; the other option is to use 1¾ yards of backing if the fabric measures 45″ wide including selvages)
Batting: 45″ × 59″ one crib-size batt

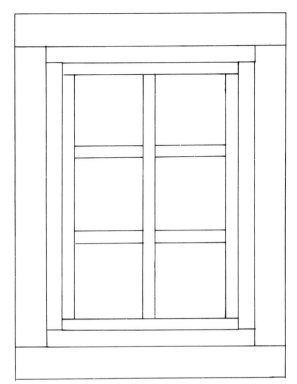

Fig. 5.16 Sashed six-block baby quilt

Construction

To cut the backing:

1. Cut the $2\frac{2}{3}$ yards of backing fabric in half, resulting in two pieces approximately 45″ × 43″. Cut one piece lengthwise 45″ × 17″. The excess fabric will be approximately 45″ × 25″. If you plan to use the excess fabric for the border, cut the strips lengthwise instead of the usual crosswise. Modified instructions using the excess fabric are in parentheses.

To make sashing and first border:

2. Cut seven strips 3″ wide.

3. Using two strips, cut two borders 32″ × 3″. Using the three strips, cut three sashings $41\frac{1}{2}$″ × 3″.

4. From the remaining strips, cut four cross-sashings $12\frac{1}{2}$″ × 3″. (Backing excess: repeat preceding instructions.)

To join the blocks and sashing:

5. Join the blocks and the cross-sashing. Make two units of three blocks and two cross-sashings.

6. Join one block and cross sashing unit and one strip of lengthwise sashing. Mark the matches. Join the second block and cross-sashing unit, completing the quilt body.

7. Stitch the lengthwise sashing to the sides of the block and sashing units. Sew the borders to the opposite sides.

To make second and outer border:

8. For the second border, cut five strips $2\frac{1}{2}$″ wide.

9. Using two strips, cut two borders 36″ × $2\frac{1}{2}$″.

10. With the remaining strips, make one unit of three strips, each strip measuring approximately 129″ × $2\frac{1}{2}$″. From that unit cut two borders $46\frac{1}{2}$″ × $2\frac{1}{2}$″. (Backing excess: repeat preceding instructions.)

11. Join the long borders to the long sides of the quilt. Stitch the short borders to the opposite sides.

To make the outer border:

12. Cut six strips $4\frac{1}{2}$″ wide.

13. Make two units of three strips approximately 129″ × $4\frac{1}{2}$″. From one unit cut two borders $50\frac{1}{2}$″ × $4\frac{1}{2}$″. From the other unit cut two borders 44″ × $4\frac{1}{2}$″. Locate seams at least 6″ from the end of the borders. (Backing excess: Repeat preceding instructions.)

14. Join the long borders to the long sides of the quilt. Stitch the short borders to the opposite sides.

To make the backing:

15. Join the backing fabric to form a rectangle approximately 45″ × 59″.

16. Layer, baste, and quilt the project.

To cut the rod pocket and binding:

17. For the rod pocket, cut one strip 12″ wide. (Backing excess: repeat preceding instructions.)

18. For the binding, cut five strips 3″ wide. Join to form a unit 215″ × 3″. (Backing excess: repeat preceding instructions.)

19. Refer to Bindings in Chapter 7 for complete binding instructions.

11. Sashed Twin-Size Quilt

Yardages

For a 73" × 87", 30-block quilt:

Sashing and first border: 1½ yards
Second border: ⅝ yard
Outer border: 1⅛ yards
Binding: ¾ yard
Rod pocket: ¾ yard
Backing: 5 yards (excess fabric from the backing is sufficient to make the second border)
Batting: 74" × 88" cut from one regular-size batt

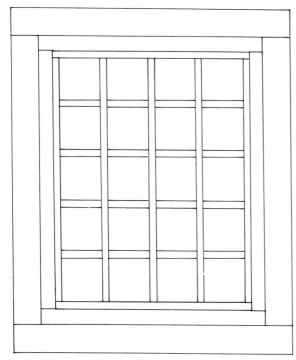

Fig. 5.17 Sashed twin-size quilt

Construction

To cut the backing:

1. Cut the backing fabric in half for two pieces approximately 43" × 88". Cut one piece lengthwise 33" × 88". The excess fabric will be approximately 10" × 88". If you plan to use the excess fabric for the border, cut the strips lengthwise instead of the usual crosswise. Modified instructions using the excess fabric are in parentheses.

To make sashing and first border:

2. Cut 16 strips 3" wide.

3. Make seven units of two strips each, each strip measuring approximately 86" × 3".

4. Using five units, cut five sashings 70½" × 3".

5. Using two units, cut two borders 61" × 3".

6. From the remaining strips and strip remnants cut 16 cross-sashings 12½" × 3".

To join blocks and sashing:

7. Join the blocks and cross-sashing. Make four units of five blocks and four cross-sashings.

8. Join one block and cross-sashing unit and one strip of lengthwise sashing, 70½" × 3". Repeat three times. Mark the matches and join the units to complete the quilt body.

9. Stitch the remaining lengthwise sashings to the quilt. Sew the borders to the opposite sides.

To make second border:

10. Cut eight strips 2½" wide.

11. Make four units of two strips each, each strip measuring approximately 86" × 3".

12. Using two units, cut two borders 64½" × 2½".

13. Using the remaining two units, cut two borders 75½" × 2½". (Backing excess: Cut four strips 2½" × 88". Cut two borders 64½" × 2½" and two borders 75½" × 2½".)

14. Join the long borders to the long sides of the quilt. Join the short borders to the opposite sides.

To make the outer borders:

15. Cut eight strips $4\frac{1}{2}''$ wide.

16. Make four units of two strips approximately $86'' \times 4\frac{1}{2}''$. Using two units, cut two borders $73'' \times 4\frac{1}{2}''$. Use the remaining two units to cut two borders $79\frac{1}{2}'' \times 4\frac{1}{2}''$.

17. Join the long borders to the long sides of the quilt. Join the short borders to the opposite sides.

To make the backing:

18. Join the backing fabric to form a rectangle approximately $75'' \times 89''$.

19. Layer, baste, and quilt the project.

To cut the rod pocket and binding:

20. For the rod pocket, cut two strips $12''$ wide. Join to form a unit $86'' \times 12''$. Cut to $71'' \times 12''$.

21. For the binding, cut eight strips $3''$ wide. Join to form a unit $344'' \times 3''$.

22. Refer to Bindings in Chapter 7 for complete binding instructions.

12. Sashed Full/ Queen-Size Quilt

Yardages
For a $87'' \times 102''$, 42-block quilt:

Sashing and first border: $1\frac{1}{8}$ yards
Second border: $\frac{3}{4}$ yard
Outer border: $1\frac{3}{8}$ yards
Binding: $\frac{7}{8}$ yard
Rod pocket: $\frac{3}{4}$ yard
Backing: $7\frac{1}{2}$ yards (excess fabric from the backing is sufficient to make the second border *or* the outer border, *or* the binding)
Batting: $88'' \times 103''$ cut from queen-size batt

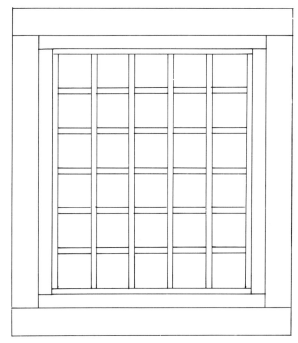

Fig. 5.18 Sashed full/queen-size quilt

Construction
To cut the backing:

1. Cut the backing fabric into three equal pieces, each $43'' \times 89''$. Cut one piece lengthwise $19'' \times 89''$. The excess will be approximately $23'' \times 89''$. If you plan to use the excess fabric for the border, cut the strips lengthwise instead of the usual crosswise. Modified instructions using the excess fabric are in parentheses.

To make sashing and first border:

2. Cut 24 strips $3''$ wide.

3. Make eight units of two strips each, each strip measuring approximately $86'' \times 3''$.

4. Using six units, cut six sashings $85'' \times 3''$.

5. Using two units, cut two borders $76'' \times 3''$.

6. Use the remaining strips and strip remnants to cut 25 cross-sashings, $12\frac{1}{2}'' \times 3''$.

To join the blocks and sashing:

7. Join the blocks and cross sashing. Make five units of six blocks and five cross-sashings.

8. Join one block and sashing unit and one strip of lengthwise sashing 85″ × 3″. Repeat four times. Mark the matches and join the units to complete the quilt body.

9. Stitch the remaining lengthwise sashing to the quilt. Sew the borders to the opposite sides.

To make the second border:

10. Cut nine strips 2½″ wide.

11. Make two units of two strips each, each strip measuring approximately 86″ × 2½″. Using the two units, cut two borders 79½″ × 2½″.

12. Join the remaining five strips to form a unit 215″ × 2½″. Cut two borders 90″ × 2½″. (Backing excess: Cut five strips 2½″ × 89″. Cut two borders 86″ × 2½″. Join three strips to form a unit 267″ × 2½″. From that unit cut two borders 90″ × 2½″.)

13. Join the long borders to the long sides of the quilt. Join the short borders to the opposite sides.

To make the outer borders:

14. Cut ten strips 4½″ wide.

15. Make two units of five strips approximately 215″ × 2½″. From one unit cut two borders 88″ × 4½″. From the other unit cut two borders 94″ × 4½″. (Backing excess: Cut five strips 4½″ wide. Join the five strips to form one unit 445″ × 4½″. From this unit cut two borders 88″ × 4½″ and two borders 94″ × 4½″.)

16. Join the long borders to the long sides of the quilt. Join the short borders to the opposite sides.

To make the backing:

17. Join the backing fabric to form a rectangle approximately 89″ × 104″.

18. Layer, baste, and quilt the project.

To cut rod pocket and binding:

19. For the rod pocket, cut two strips 12″ wide. Join to form a unit 86″ × 12″.

20. For the binding, cut nine strips 3″ wide. Join to form a unit 387″ × 3″. (Backing excess: cut five strips 3″ wide. Join to form a single unit 445″ × 3″.)

21. Refer to Bindings in Chapter 7 for complete binding instructions.

13. Sashed King-Size Quilt

Yardages
For a 116″ × 116″, 64-block quilt:

Sashing and first border: 3½ yards
Second border: ⅞ yard
Outer border: 1¾ yards
Binding: 1⅛ yards
Rod pocket: 1 yard
Backing: 10 yards
Batting: one king-size batt

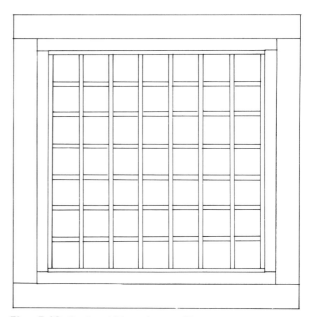

Fig. 5.19 Sashed king-size quilt

Construction
To make the sashing and first border:

1. Cut 39 strips 3″ wide.

2. Using 20 strips, make four units of five strips each, each strip measuring approximately $210'' \times 3''$. From each five-strip unit, cut two sashings measuring $99\frac{1}{2}'' \times 3''$.

3. Using five strips, make one unit of five strips, each measuring approximately $210'' \times 3''$. From this five-strip unit cut two end borders $104\frac{1}{2}'' \times 3''$.

4. From the remaining 14 strips cut 42 cross-sashing pieces measuring $12\frac{1}{2}'' \times 3''$ each.

To join blocks and sashing:

5. Join the blocks and cross-sashings. Make seven units of seven blocks and six cross-sashings.

6. Join one block and sashing unit and one strip of lengthwise sashing $99\frac{1}{2}'' \times 3''$. Repeat six times. Mark the matches and join the units to complete the quilt body.

7. Stitch the remaining lengthwise sashings to the outer edge of the quilt. Sew the borders to the opposite ends.

To make the second border:

8. Cut 11 strips $2\frac{1}{2}''$ wide.

9. Make one unit of five strips measuring approximately $210'' \times 3''$. From this unit cut two borders $104\frac{1}{2}'' \times 2\frac{1}{2}''$.

10. Using the remaining six strips, make two units of three strips, each strip measuring approximately $126'' \times 3''$. From each of the units cut one border $108\frac{1}{2}'' \times 3''$.

11. Join the short borders to opposite sides of the quilt body. Join the long borders to the other sides of the quilt.

To make the outer border:

12. Cut 12 strips $4\frac{1}{2}''$ wide.

13. Make four units of three strips, each strip measuring approximately $126'' \times 4\frac{1}{2}''$.

14. Using two of the three strip units, cut two borders $108\frac{1}{2}'' \times 4\frac{1}{2}''$.

15. Using the remaining three-strip units, cut two borders $116\frac{1}{2}'' \times 4\frac{1}{2}''$.

16. Join the short borders to opposite sides of the quilt body. Join the long borders to the other sides of the quilt.

To make the backing:

17. Cut the backing fabric into three equal pieces approximately $43'' \times 120''$ each. Join the pieces to form a rectangle approximately $120'' \times 126''$.

18. Layer, baste, and quilt the project.

To cut the rod pocket and binding:

19. For the rod pocket, cut three strips $12''$ wide. Join to form a unit $126'' \times 12''$.

20. For the binding, cut 12 strips $3''$ wide. Join to form a unit $504'' \times 3''$.

21. Refer to Bindings in Chapter 7 for complete binding instructions.

CHAPTER 6

Set Options

The fun of quilting is in personalizing the pattern. Fabric and color placement are two ways to make the quilt your own. Another way is to change how the quilt is put together. This chapter offers suggestions on how you can alter your quilt. It is impossible to give yardages and directions for every possible change, so you will have to do some math to determine the patterns and fabric requirements.

Set is the way the blocks are put together to make the quilt top. There are hundreds of quilt sets, but most are variations of four basic types, which can be either straight set or diagonally set. On *straight sets* the blocks run parallel to the edges of the quilt and the rows run vertically and horizontally. In *diagonal sets* the rows of blocks run diagonally across the quilt top. Diagonal sets always require triangle pieces to make the edge of the quilt straight. Here are the four types of set:

Side-by-side. The blocks are stitched together, one next to the other.

Fig. 6.1 Side-by-side blocks

Sashed. The blocks are separated with strips of fabric.

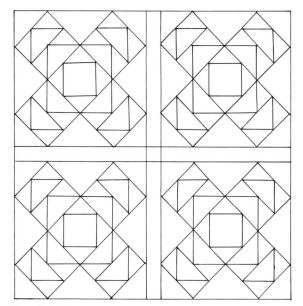

Fig. 6.2 Sashed blocks

Medallion. There is a large central block or group of blocks surrounded with borders that may incorporate blocks.

Fig. 6.3 Medallion layout

Strip set. The blocks are sewn in vertical strips and are either offset one half-block or separated by strips of sashing. Think of it as sashing in only one direction.

Fig. 6.4 Strip set blocks

Using the basic sets as a starting point, you can make dozens of easy variations. The simplest variation is to alternate blocks. The project directions feature two basic sets: side-by-side straight set and sashed straight set. The two basic sets are modified by alternating two pieced blocks or by alternating plain and pieced blocks (see color section for examples of both).

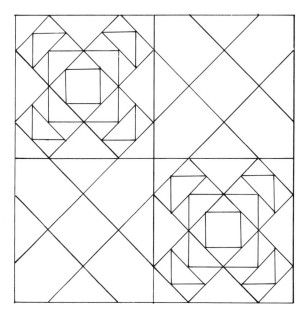

Fig. 6.5 Alternating blocks: Wild Goose Chase and Snowflake

You can change the set by changing the sashing. The projects use simple single-piece sashing, but sashing can be pieced just as blocks are pieced. In a complex quilt the sashing may contain hundreds or thousands of pieces. An excellent example is the quilt pattern New York Beauty, where the sashing has more pieces than the blocks. For the beginner, the simplest pieced sashing has separate squares sewn at the sashing intersections. The squares can be a single square of fabric or they can be pieced. You might choose a pattern like Square in Square or a small LeMoyne Star (similar to Dutch Rose). Sashing can be of any width, and the wider the sashing, the larger the sashing square.

Another simple modification is to piece the sashing lengthwise, just as the borders are pieced with two or three different fabrics. My personal favorite is the three-strip sashing combined with a sashing square (Fig. 6.6). Three equal strips of fabric are used in the sashing, and the sashing square is a single nine-patch block.

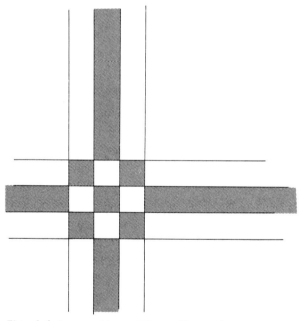

Fig. 6.6 Three-strip sashing with sashing square

Borders can also be altered. They can be omitted or made larger. You can piece one of the borders with sawteeth or Flying Geese. Pieced borders and sashings require planning to fit the piecing to the quilt length. A beginner would do best to add or subtract plain borders or change their width.

Strip set is one of my favorites. The blocks are sewn in vertical strips and offset one-half block (Fig. 6.7) The second row of blocks starts with a half-block. To straighten the edges of the quilt, cut off the extending portion of the blocks. Another way to strip set is to divide the rows of blocks with pieced sashing.

Fig. 6.7 Strip set Wild Goose Chase; blocks offset by one-half block

The same modifications apply to diagonal sets. To help you design your own diagonally set quilt, I've given in the next section quilt sizes and block requirements, along with additional information on side and corner triangles, for standard-size quilts.

Quilt sizes are for the quilt body only; they do not include borders.

Diagonally Set Quilts without Sashing

Based on a 12″ block, the side triangles need to be cut from a square measuring 12⅞″. Cut the square diagonally to make two triangles. The corner squares need to be cut from a square measuring 13¼″. Cut that square diagonally to make four triangles.

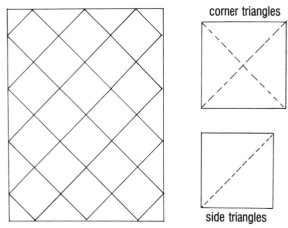

Fig. 6.8 Diagonally set quilt without sashing

Wall hanging: Set two-by-two, using five full blocks, four side triangles, and four corner triangles, the hanging will measure 35″ square.

Baby quilt: Set two-by-three, eight full blocks, six side triangles, and four corner triangles, quilt will measure 35″ × 50″.

Twin-size quilt: Set four-by-five, using 32 full blocks, 14 side triangles, and four corner triangles, quilt will measure 67″ × 85″.

Double/queen-size quilt: Set five-by-six, using 50 full blocks, 18 side triangles, and four corner blocks, quilt will measure 85″ × 101″.

King-size quilt: Set seven-by-seven, using 85 full blocks, 24 side triangles, and four corner blocks, quilt will measure 120″ × 120″.

Diagonally Set Quilts with Sashing

Based on a 12″ block with 2½″ sashing, the side triangles need to be cut from a square measuring 15½″. Cut the square diagonally to make two triangles. The corner squares need to be cut from a square measuring 15¾″. Cut that square diagonally to make four triangles.

Fig. 6.9 Diagonally set quilt with sashing

Wall hanging: Set two-by-two, using five full blocks, four side triangles, and four corner triangles, hanging will measure 43″ × 43″.

Baby quilt: Set two-by-three, using eight full blocks, six side triangles, and four corner triangles, quilt will measure 43″ × 60″.

Twin-size quilt: Set four-by-five, using 32 full blocks, 14 side triangles, and four corner triangles, quilt will measure 72″ × 103″.

Double/queen-size quilt: Set five-by-six, quilt using 50 full blocks, 18 side triangles, and four corner triangles, quilt will measure 93″ × 120″.

King-size quilt: Set six-by-six, using 61 full blocks, 20 side triangles, and four corner triangles, quilt will measure 120″ × 120″.

CHAPTER 7

Finishing and Binding

This chapter covers the finishing touches that give a quilt a polished, professional look: rod pockets, bindings, and ruffles.

Rod Pockets

The rod pocket is a 5″-wide tube of fabric stitched to the back of the quilt. It is used to hang the quilt for display with a decorative rod or wooden lathe. The rod or lathe slips into the pocket so that it doesn't touch the quilt backing. The pocket supports the weight of the quilt and protects it from damage by the rod. Rod pockets can be stitched in with the binding or added after the quilt is completed.

The pockets stitched into the binding are very strong and require only a single line of hand stitching. They are used on quilts and wall hangings that will be permanently displayed by hanging. The rod pocket cannot be removed from the quilt without damage to the binding.

When a quilt is designed to be used as a bed covering, the rod pocket is added to the completed quilt. This type of pocket is used on antique quilts or quilts displayed at quilt shows. The rod pocket is stitched on with two rows of hand stitching and can be removed from the quilt without removing the binding.

Usually the pocket is made from the same fabric as the quilt backing, but plain unbleached muslin can be used in place of a matching fabric. If you are adding a rod pocket to an antique quilt, prewash the pocket fabric. Chemicals used to manufacture new fabrics can have an adverse effect on antique textiles.

Making a Pocket Stitched into Binding

1. Prepare the quilt for binding. Refer to Bindings in this chapter for complete binding instructions.

2. The pocket is cut 12″ wide, and the length is determined by the width of the quilt. The pocket should run from binding to binding. Cut the pocket the finished width of the quilt. For quilts under 43″ use one strip of fabric. For quilts 43″ to 86″ use two strips of fabric. For quilts over 86″ use three strips of fabric.

3. Cut the required strips and seam them together with ¼″ seam allowances. Measure the finished size of your quilt and cut the pocket at that measurement.

4. You will hem the two 12″ side edges of the pocket with a double-turned ¼″ hem. To make the hem, fold in ¼″ and press. Turn again, encasing the raw edge. Straight stitch along the top edge of the hem. Repeat for the other side.

5. Fold the pocket in half lengthwise, right side out. Line up the raw edges and press.

Fig. 7.1 Fold rod pocket in half lengthwise, lining up raw edges

6. Center the pocket and pin it to the back of the quilt, lining up the raw edges of the rod pocket and quilt.

7. Machine baste in place with a ¼″ seam.

8. Hand blind stitch lower edge of pocket to the quilt back. Stitch into the backing and batting; do not stitch into the quilt top. Use hand-quilting thread, which is strong and doesn't knot or tear while hand stitching.

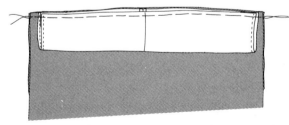

Fig. 7.2 Hand blind-stitch lower edge of pocket to quilt back

9. Bind the quilt as usual.

Adding a Pocket to a Completed Quilt

1. The pocket is cut 12″ wide, and the length is determined by the width of the quilt. The pocket should run from binding to binding. Cut the pocket the finished width of the quilt. For quilts under 43″ use one strip of fabric. For quilts 43″ to 86″ use two strips of fabric. For quilts over 86″ use three strips of fabric.

2. Cut the required strips, and seam them together with ¼″ seam allowances. Measure the finished size of your quilt and cut the pocket at that measurement.

3. You will hem the two 12″ side edges of the pocket with a double turned ¼″ hem. To make the hem, fold in ¼″ and press. Turn again, encasing the raw edge. Straight stitch along the top edge of the hem. Repeat for the other side.

4. Fold the pocket in half lengthwise, wrong sides together. Line up raw edges and stitch with a ½″ seam allowance (see Fig. 7.1).

5. Press seam allowance open.

6. Press the pocket flat, centering the seam on one side of the tube.

7. Center the pocket and pin it to the quilt back. Place the seamed side against the quilt back (Fig. 7.3). Line up a folded edge of the pocket along join of the binding and quilt. Do not stitch the pocket to the binding. Hand blind stitch both edges of the pocket to the quilt back. Stitch only into the backing and batting, not into the quilt top. Use hand-quilting thread, which is strong and doesn't knot or tear while hand stitching.

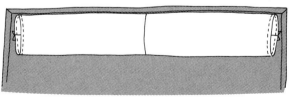

Fig. 7.3 Place seamed side of pocket against quilt back

Bindings

Binding is a strip of fabric that finishes and protects the edge of the quilt. It is used as much for strength and durability as it is for beauty. Bindings vary from a tiny $\frac{3}{16}''$ wide to substantial 1″ wide. They can be an extra strip of fabric or simply the backing turned to the quilt top. Good binding indicates a good quilter. More quilt contests have been won or lost by the quality of the bindings. Knowing how to bind is as important as knowing how to piece or quilt. Of the dozens of ways to finish the edges of a quilt, I've chosen three methods that are very versatile and require the least amount of hand stitching. The three methods are traditional French binding, mock binding, and binding with the backing.

FRENCH BINDING

French binding with mitered corners is my personal favorite. It is extremely neat and durable. Mitered corners are not difficult to do and look fantastic. This binding will impress your quilting friends.

French binding can be made with bias or straight strips of fabric—either way is acceptable. Bias is considered the longest-wearing binding. It turns curved edges and corners equally well. Bias does require more fabric, but the seams and joins tend to be less obvious than with straight cuts. Its one drawback is, that it stretches. When bias is stretched, it becomes narrower. As a consequence the binding may not be a uniform width throughout the quilt.

Straight-cut binding is more susceptible to abrasion and may tear along the outer fold. It corners as well as a bias cut but will not go around curves. It is a very stable binding and can be used to ease the quilt edges if there is a slight discrepancy in the length of opposite sides of the quilt. Straight cut doesn't stretch and makes a uniform-width binding throughout the quilt. It requires less fabric than a bias cut, and it is easy to determine the yardages.

The project yardages are based on $\frac{1}{2}''$ straight-cut French binding. There will be a $\frac{1}{2}''$ of binding showing on both the front and the back of the quilt.

Preparing the Quilt

Before binding, the quilt edges and corners must be checked for accuracy. Do opposite sides of the quilt measure the same length? Are the edges perfectly straight, or is there a slight bow here and there? Are all the corners a true 90-degree angle? Some of the first things checked in quilt contests are the edges and corners. Of course the quilt top was perfectly straight when you started quilting, but machine quilting can distort a quilt. The distortion happens to every quilter, so don't think that because you are a beginner, you are having more than your share of problems. In fact, the more complex the quilt, the more likely the problem will occur. When I learned to sew I was taught that the difference between a great seamstress and a novice is not the number of mistakes made, but knowing how to repair them. The same holds true for quilters. This is the place to do some repair.

Lay the quilt on a large flat surface, like a floor, to get an accurate measurement of the quilt edges. Measure the edges and compare opposite sides to determine if they are the same length. Anything under $\frac{1}{4}''$ can be trimmed off as you cut away the excess batting and backing. Trimming more than $\frac{1}{4}''$ can affect the width of the borders. Another alternative is to ease the slightly longer edge into the binding, but don't be fooled into thinking you can ease more than 1″. Anything more will make the quilt appear gathered to the binding.

For large discrepancies, combine trimming and easing to even the quilt edges. Use a square to check the corners. Mark the correct cutting lines on the quilt top. The line indicates the finished size of the quilt, including the binding. Trim on the line, cutting away excess batting and backing, plus making the edges and corners true.

Preparing the Binding

1. Follow the instructions in the project directions for cutting the binding.

2. The seams joining the strips should be on the bias. A simple seam is made by overlapping the ends of the strips, right sides together, to make a 90-degree corner. Stitch diagonally across the strip, as if you were stitching off the corner (Fig. 7.4). Open the strips to check the join, then trim away the excess fabric and press open the seam. Make sure all the seams are on the same side of the binding. Check every seam before cutting. On plain colors, determining which side to sew can be confusing.

Fig. 7.5 Bias fold start of binding

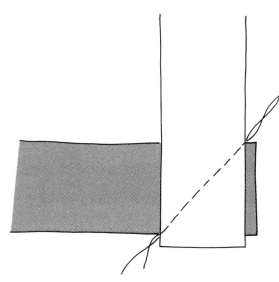

Fig. 7.4 Stitch diagonally across the corner

3. Press the strip in half lengthwise, wrong sides together.

4. The start of the binding needs to be a bias fold. To fold, open the end of the strip, wrong side up. Place the strip on the ironing board with the short edge up. Grasp the left corner and cross it to the right edge of the binding. Line up the raw edges and press in the diagonal fold. Re-press the strip in half.

5. The binding is pinned to the right side of the quilt, one side at a time. Lay the quilt right side up on a large flat surface as you pin the binding in place.

6. Start the binding on any edge, except the edge with the rod pocket. To make the join inconspicuous, do not start at a corner or at the middle of a side.

7. Line up the raw edges of the binding and quilt. Pin the section of binding from the start to the first corner.

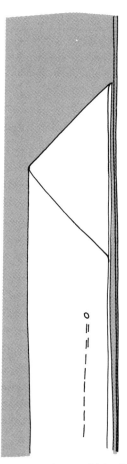

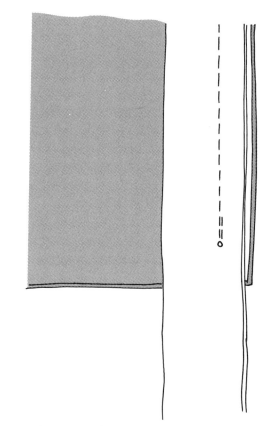

Fig. 7.7 Stitch to ½″ from second side

Fig. 7.6 Line up raw edges of binding and quilt, then stitch

8. Stitch with a scant ½″ seam allowance. Start stitching about 1″ from the bias fold. As you approach the corner, measure ½″ in from the second side and mark with a pin. Sew to the pin, back stitch, and remove the quilt from the machine.

To miter the corner:

9. A mitered corner is a simple twofold step. First, fold the free end of the binding over the stitched binding to form a 90-degree corner. At this point it should look like you've turned the corner the wrong way, since the free end of the binding is off the quilt. Notice the diagonal fold in the corner of the binding; this will be the miter. Place one pin in the binding to hold the miter in place while you make the next fold.

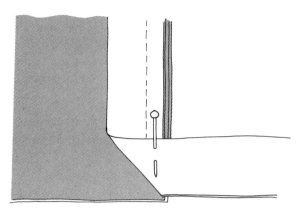

Fig. 7.8 Fold binding to form 90-degree corner

10. Next, fold the free end of binding back onto the quilt. The second fold should line up with the first edge of the quilt (Fig. 7.9). Line up the raw edge of the binding and the second side of the quilt.

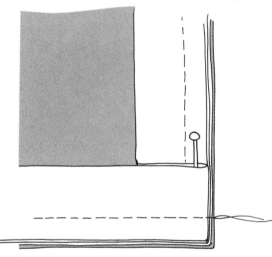

Fig. 7.9 Fold again, lining up fold with first edge of quilt

11. Pin the binding along the entire edge of the quilt.

12. Start sewing on the folded edge and stitch to within $\frac{1}{2}''$ of the corner.

13. Repeat for remaining corners and sides.

To end the binding:

14. Sew to within $1''$ of the bias fold. Back stitch and remove the quilt from the machine.

15. Trim the free end of the binding to fit into the bias fold. Overlap the ends by at least $\frac{1}{4}''$.

16. Pin the join in place. Stitch to secure the remaining part of the seam.

To complete the binding:

17. To make a neat binding, overcast the raw edges of the binding and quilt. Set the machine for a wide and long zigzag. The exact setting is not important, as long as the stitches stay within the seam allowance. Guide the quilt so that the needle in the right-hand swing falls off the edge of the fabric. Only the left-hand stitch should be in the quilt and binding. Overcast all the straight edges; omit the corners.

To fold and hand stitch the binding:

18. Start on any edge except the edge with the join. Tip the binding back over the raw edges of the quilt. Match up the fold in the binding with the straight stitch line on the quilt back. This will be a tight fit; pin securely.

19. On the first edge, hand stitch the entire length of the edge (Fig. 7.10). Stitch to the very edge of the quilt and knot the thread. Clip it. Use a hand blind stitch and hand-

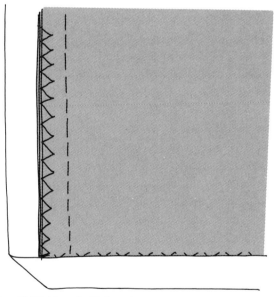

Fig. 7.10 Hand stitch edge

quilting thread. Stitch into the batting and backing, not the quilt top.

20. To turn a mitered corner, simply fold the second section of binding over the first (Fig. 7.11). The miter happens automatically. Stitch to the very edge of the quilt and repeat the process.

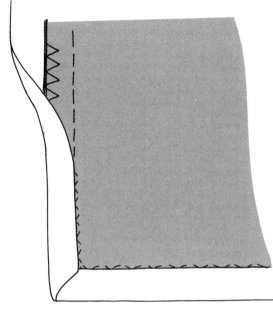

Fig. 7.11 Fold second section of binding over the first

21. Hand stitch the join closed.

22. If you want the mitered corners closed, go back and hand stitch them.

Options

French binding can be made any width, from $\frac{3}{16}$ to 1″. The secret to French binding is in the seam allowance, which must match the finished width of the binding. Half-inch seams result in $\frac{1}{2}$″ binding, $\frac{1}{4}$″ seams in $\frac{1}{4}$″ binding. *The binding is always cut six times the finished width.* To finish at $\frac{1}{2}$″ wide the binding is cut 3″ wide. To finish 1″ wide, the binding is cut 6″ wide. On narrow binding you need to add at least an extra $\frac{1}{4}$″ for the thickness of the quilt. To make a finished binding a $\frac{1}{4}$″ wide, you will cut the binding $1\frac{3}{4}$″ wide. For narrow binding or thick batting, always run a test

binding before cutting yards of binding incorrectly.

I recommend that you stitch your sample binding with wash-away basting thread. You can use this water-soluable thread on your machine as you would any thread. Stitch up a short length of sample binding to your quilt. To remove the sample, simply press with a steam iron. The thread will dissolve and the sample binding can be pulled away.

Fabrics

Bindings don't have to be plain. They can be mismatched colors or stripes, or even pieced from the block scraps.

Stripes work well when cut on the bias. One of my favorite holiday quilts has a red-and-white striped bias binding. The edges appear to be bound in candy canes. Stripes cut on the straight of grain can look like a frame and mat around the quilt or be blocks of multicolors. You can even make your own striped fabric using the block scraps. Strip piece narrow widths of fabrics, using enough pieces to total at least 18″ × 45″. Treat the piece as a single width of fabric. Find the true bias and cut the binding.

MOCK BINDING

Mock binding is like facing the quilt edge. It can look like a traditional French binding when it is turned to the right side of the quilt, or it can be inconspicuously turned to the quilt back. The real purpose of mock binding is to attach ruffles or prairie points without having to hand sew the edges together. Mock binding is an unsuitable edge finish by itself and is always combined with another edge trim.

Like French binding, mock binding can be cut on the bias or the straight of grain. The binding is usually cut $1\frac{1}{2}$″ wide and will finish $\frac{1}{2}$″ wide.

Preparing the Quilt

Prepare the quilt edges as for French binding. The edges and corners of the quilt must be checked for accuracy. Opposite sides of the quilt must measure the same length. The edges should be straight and flat and all the corners a true 90-degree angle. Lay the quilt on a large flat surface, like the floor, to obtain an accurate measure of the quilt edges. Small discrepancies in the length of opposite edges can be corrected when the excess batting and backing are trimmed away.

Another alternative is to ease the slightly longer edge into the binding. Mark the correct cutting line on the quilt. The line indicates the finished size of the quilt *plus* a $\frac{1}{4}''$ seam allowance. Trim on the line, cutting away the excess fabric and batting. On some quilts, especially quilts that are pieced to the outer edges, the cutting line may be in the batting and backing only, just missing the quilt top.

Preparing the Binding

1. Using project directions as a guide, substitute $1\frac{1}{2}''$ strips for $3''$ strips. Cut the required number of strips.

2. The seams joining the strips should be on the bias. A simple seam is made by overlapping the ends of the strips, right sides together, to make a 90 degree corner. Stitch diagonally across the strip, as if you are stitching off the corner. Open the strips to check the join and then trim away the excess fabric and press open the seam. Make sure all the seams are on the same side of the binding. Check every seam before cutting. On solid colors, determining which side to sew can be confusing.

3. Press the strip in half lengthwise, wrong sides together.

4. The start of the binding needs to be a bias fold. To fold, open the end of the strip, wrong side up. Place the strip on the ironing board with the short edge up. Grasp the left corner and cross it to the right edge of the binding (see Fig. 7.5). Line up the raw edges and press in the diagonal fold. Re-press the strip in half.

5. Baste the ruffle (Fig. 7.12) or prairie points to the quilt at this step. For complete instructions on making ruffles and prairie points, refer to the directions later in this chapter.

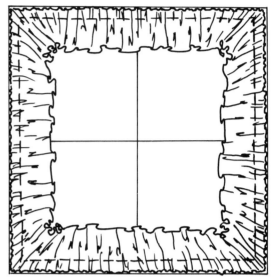

Fig. 7.12 Baste the ruffle to the quilt

6. Start the binding on any edge, except the edge with the rod pocket. To make the join inconspicuous, do not start at a corner or the middle of a side.

7. Line up the raw edges of the binding and quilt (see Fig. 7.6). Pin the section of binding from the start to the first corner.

8. Stitch with a scant $\frac{1}{4}''$ seam allowance. Start stitching about $1''$ from the bias fold. As you approach the corner, measure $\frac{1}{4}''$ in for the second side and mark with a pin (Fig. 7.13). Sew to the pin, back stitch, and remove the quilt from the machine.

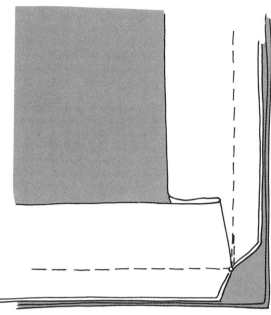

Fig. 7.13 Mark $\frac{1}{4}''$ in from corner with a pin and stitch to pin

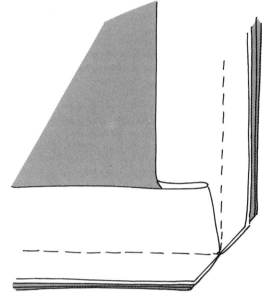

Fig. 7.14 Trim seam allowance at corner

9. Clip the seam allowance of the binding to the last stitch. Turn the corner with the binding, pin in place and continue stitching the remaining edges of the quilt.

To end the binding:

10. Sew to within 1″ of the bias fold. Back stitch and remove the quilt from the machine.

11. Trim the free end of the binding to fit into the bias fold. Overlap the ends by at least $\frac{1}{4}''$.

12. Pin the join in place. Stitch to secure.

To fold and stitch the binding:

13. Trim away the seam allowances at the corners of the quilt and binding.

14. Start on any edge except the edge with the join. Tip the binding to the other side of the quilt. Pressing the edge of the quilt helps the binding turn neatly.

15. Pin a 6″ section of the binding to the quilt. Hand blind stitch or straight stitch by machine along the edge of the binding. Pin new sections as you sew.

To miter the corners:

16. As you approach the corner, stop stitching about 1″ from the corner.

17. Pin the binding to the quilt, up to the very edge of the quilt. Do not stitch.

18. Tip the second side of binding over the first. The miter will happen automatically.

19. Stitch until you reach the second side of the binding. Take one stitch into the second binding and turn the corner. Continue around the quilt.

20. Hand stitch the join closed, if desired.

BINDING WITH THE BACKING

Finishing the quilt using excess backing fabric does not really make a binding, but it is a fast and easy way to finish the quilt. Plus, it doesn't require any extra fabric. The finished width of the edge is determined by the amount of backing fabric that extends beyond the finished width of the quilt. Usually it is stitched to give the appearance of a $\frac{1}{2}''$ binding.

Preparing the Quilt

Before finishing, the edges and corners of the quilt must be checked for accuracy. Opposite sides of the quilt must measure the same length. The edges should be straight and flat and all the corners a true 90-degree angle. Lay the quilt, right side up, on a large flat surface, like a floor, to obtain an accurate measure of the quilt edges. Small discrepancies in the length of opposite edges can be corrected when the excess batting is trimmed away. Mark the correct cutting line on the quilt. The line indicates the finished size of the quilt. Trim on the line cutting away the the excess batting and quilt top. *Do not* cut the backing at this step.

Preparing the Backing

To cut and fold the backing:

1. Measure the backing to 1″ beyond the edge of the quilt top and batting. Mark the line and cut.

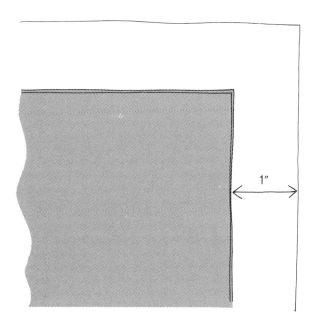

Fig. 7.15 Measure backing to 1″ beyond quilt top

2. Mark and press up a $\frac{1}{2}''$ seam allowance.

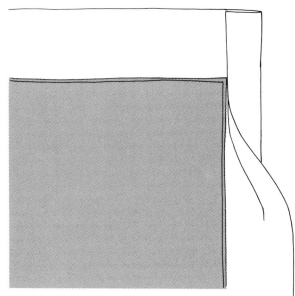

Fig. 7.16 Press up a $\frac{1}{2}''$ seam allowance

To stitch the backing:

3. Begin by mitering all four corners. To miter, fold the corner of the backing diagonally across the quilt top. Press in place. Pin to secure.

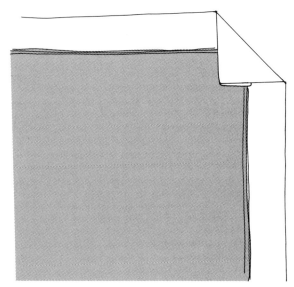

Fig. 7.17 Fold in corner of backing to miter

4. Fold the sides of the backing over the quilt top. The miter will happen automatically. If a small triangle of fabric peeks out from under the corner, undo the pins, trim the point of the corner, and re-pin.

5. I recommend pinning and stitching one edge at a time. The walking foot or even-feed foot helps keep the binding flat and smooth.

6. The binding can be stitched with a straight stitch or the machine's blind hem stitch.

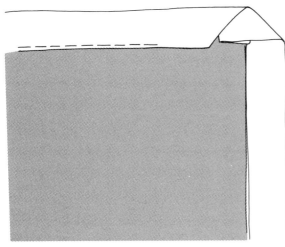

Fig. 7.18 Stitch binding with straight stitch

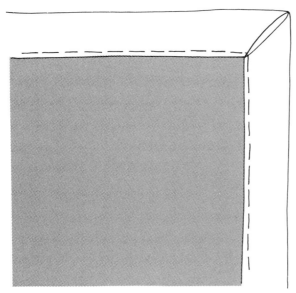

Fig. 7.19 Stitch binding around corner

7. If you want to close the miter, hand stitch it shut.

Using the Blind Hem

Your machine's blind hem can take the place of blind hand stitching (Fig. 7.20). Use invisible thread or a thread that matches the quilt top. Set your machine to

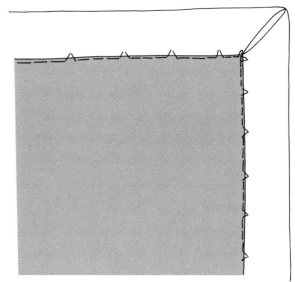

Fig. 7.20 Use machine's blind hem stitch

the blind hem stitch—three to five straight stitches separated with a single zigzag. Set the machine to a narrow stitch width and length. The exact setting isn't crucial, as long as the stitches are short and narrow. The tinier the zigzag width, the less conspicuous the stitch.

Line up the folded edge of the backing so that the straight stitching is right along the fold. The bulk of the quilt is to the right of the needle. Only the straight stitches are on the quilt top. The zigzag stitch hops onto the fold in the backing and secures it in place, just like a hand stitch. If you have a mirror-image feature on your machine, use it so the needle zigzags to the right. Then the bulk of the quilt will be to the left.

Options

The width of the backing strip is determined by the desired width of the binding. Cut the desired width plus a $\frac{1}{2}''$ seam allowance. If you want the binding to finish at $1''$ wide, cut the backing $1\frac{1}{2}''$ wide. Piping or prairie points can be slipped under the binding before it is stitched in place. You can even use a flat lace edging or rickrack.

Ruffles

Ruffles add a soft, feminine touch to a quilt. They can be made a variety of ways: single ruffles, double ruffles, mock double ruffles. Or you can use a pre-gathered trim. It is impossible to give specific instruction for every type and width of ruffle. Instead I've chosen my favorite ruffle, a 3″ mock double ruffle, to use as basic instructions. Check the Single and Double Ruffles section for other ideas.

MOCK DOUBLE RUFFLE

This two-color 3″ ruffle gives the illusion of two ruffles without the work or bulky seams of a traditional double ruffle.

Yardages

Measure the distance around the quilt. Multiply that number by two. For a baby quilt 45″ × 60″, the ruffle totals 420″. Divide the total by 43″, the width of your fabric. In this case, 420 divided by 43 equals 9.7, the number of strips needed to make the ruffle. I usually round the number up to the next full digit. In this case I will cut ten strips of my ruffle fabrics.

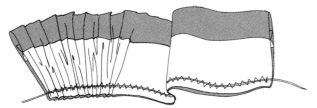

Fig. 7.21 A two-color ruffle gives the appearance of a double ruffle without the bulk

Construction

To cut and stitch the strips:

1. For the inner ruffle the strips are cut 2½″ wide. For my baby quilt I would cut ten strips 2½″ wide. Seam the strips together to make a strip 430″ × 2½″. Press open seams.

2. For the outside ruffle the strips are cut 4½″ wide. For the baby quilt, I would cut ten

strips 4½″. Seam the five strips together to make a strip 430″ × 4½″. Press open seams.

3. Seam the two long strips to make a single strip 6½″ × 430″. Press seam open.

4. Join the ends to make a circle. Press seam open.

5. Fold the strip in half lengthwise, wrong sides together, and press. The lengthwise seam will be on the front of the ruffle.

To gather the ruffle:

6. Stitch a gathering thread ¼″ in from the raw edges of the ruffle.

The best gathering thread is made by zigzagging over dental floss (see One-Block Pillow in Chapter 5). The zigzag acts like a casing for the floss (see Fig. 5.6). Set the machine for a medium width zigzag. Place the end of the floss in the needle hole of the presser foot. Thread it from the top, through the hole, and under the foot so that the floss lays on the top of the bridge of the foot. Hold the floss tail with the other thread tails as you start to stitch. Watch the first few stitches clear the floss. Unwind the floss as needed. Holding it slightly taut and raised above the bridge of the foot. After stitching around the ruffle, cut generous thread tails.

7. Gather the ruffle to measure 210″. Evenly arrange the gathers around the quilt. Line up the raw edges and pin in place.

8. If you want the mock binding to show on the right side of the quilt, pin the ruffle to the quilt backing, with the unseamed side of the ruffle against the quilt backing. Baste to the quilt with a ¼″ seam allowance. Stitch the mock binding onto the wrong side of the quilt and tip it to the quilt top to complete.

9. If you want the mock binding on the back of the quilt, pin the ruffle to the quilt top with the seamed side of the ruffle against the quilt top. Baste together with a ¼″ seam allowance. Stitch the mock binding to the right side of the quilt and tip it to the quilt back to complete.

SINGLE AND DOUBLE RUFFLES

A single ruffle is a strip of fabric folded in half and gathered along the raw edges.

Double ruffles are two single ruffles of different widths. They are usually gathered with the same thread to help reduce the bulky seam allowance. Double ruffles can be made with two fabric ruffles or with a single fabric ruffle and a lace or eyelet ruffle.

The ruffles can be straight-cut or bias-cut. Bias-cut is especially effective on plaids or stripes.

The mock double ruffle can be combined with a traditional double ruffle to make a triple ruffle.

Prairie Points

Prairie points are folded squares of fabric that make a row of triangles along the edges of the quilt (see color section). They remind me of the chains of gum wrappers I made as a child. Prairie points require careful planning to successfully turn the corners. Like ruffles there are many different sizes and styles. I have chosen a standard 4″ prairie point.

Yardages

Measure the distance around the quilt. A 45″ × 60″ baby quilt measures 210″ around the edge, and each 4″ prairie point covers about 2″ of the edge. Divide 210 by 2 for a total of 105 points.

Each point is made from a 4″ square, and there are ten squares across a 43″ width of fabric. Dividing 105 points by ten squares equals 10.5 strips. I usually round the digit up to the next whole number, in this case 11. It will take 11 4″ strips for this quilt.

Construction

To cut and fold the points:

1. Cut all the 4″ squares you can from the strips. Usually it takes a few extra squares to balance the points and turn the corners, so be generous.

2. To make one prairie point, fold the square in half diagonally (Fig. 7.22). Press. Fold the resulting triangle in half again (Fig. 7.23), lining up the four raw edges (Fig 7.24). Press. This is a lot of pressing when you multiply it by the 111 blocks needed for the baby quilt. I suggest that you lower your ironing board, find a chair, and sit down while pressing.

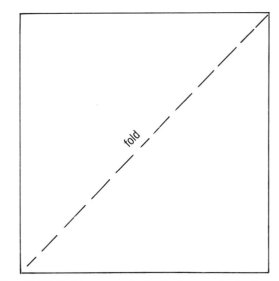

Fig. 7.22 Fold square in half diagonally to form triangle

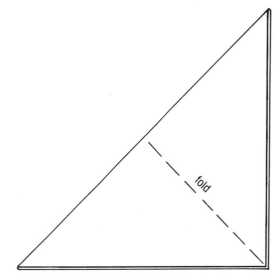

Fig. 7.23 Fold triangle in half

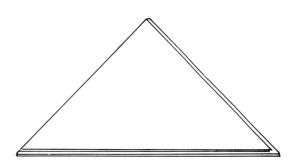

Fig. 7.24 Line up four raw edges and press

To stitch the points to the quilt:

3. Notice that the points have an opening on one side and a single fold on the other. When they are stitched they slip together, the single fold into the opening. For that reason the openings must all face in the same direction around the quilt.

4. Do one edge at a time. Begin by placing two points in each corner (Fig. 7.25). These two points turn the corner. They do not overlap, but merely touch. Line up the raw edges of the points and the quilt. Pin in place.

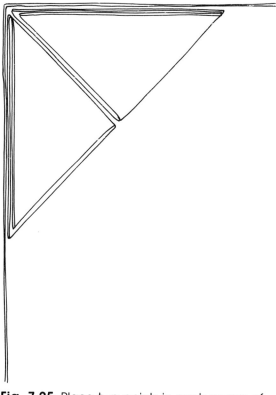

Fig. 7.25 Place two points in each corner of quilt

5. Next, center a prairie point in the middle of the edge. Count out the appropriate number of points for the edge. For the baby quilt, the 45″ edge requires 23 points. Subtract one for each corner and one for the center mark, leaving a total of 20.

6. With the center point as a guide arrange the 20 points equally along the quilt edge. Pin in place.

7. Baste the points to the first edge. Use a ¼″ seam allowance.

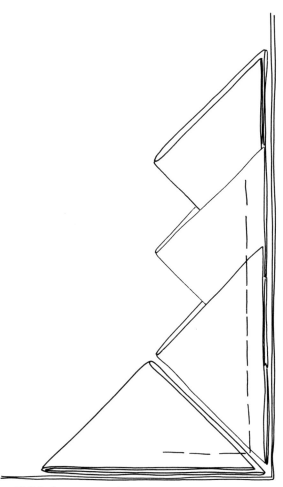

Fig. 7.26 Arrange points along quilt edge and baste

8. Repeat for the other edges.

To add the mock binding:

9. If you want the mock binding to show on the quilt top, stitch the prairie points and binding to the back of the quilt. Tip to the front side to complete.

If you want the mock binding on the back of the quilt, stitch the prairie points and binding to the front of the quilt. Tip to the back side to complete.

Options

Prairie points are wonderful. They can be delicate or bold. Points can overlap a lot or not even touch. There are no rules to using prairie points. Any look you like is right. Prairie points don't have to extend beyond the edge of the quilt. They can be combined with French binding and point to the interior of the quilt. They can even be stitched in along a border or sashing. Prairie points can be made all of one color or of alternating colors. They can even be made of multicolored scraps. Another look can be achieved by alternating 4″ points with 3″ points, or by combining prairie points with a ruffle.

Signing Your Quilt

Every quilt should be signed and dated. This information can be printed or embroidered directly onto the quilt, or it can be on a separate label that is hand stitched to the quilt. The signature can be on the front or back. You may also want to add a quote, a poem, or a few lines of the quilt's history. There are as many ways to sign a quilt as there are quilters. Here are a few ideas:

A separate label is ideal. The label can be remade if there are mistakes in spelling or if the ink blotches. The single drawback is that the label can be removed.

Writing directly on the quilt back is an option, although embroidering or writing on a finished quilt can be difficult. The advantage is that the signature and date are permanently part of the quilt. I usually sign the quilt back in an inconspicuous place and use a label as well. That way, if the label should be separated from the quilt, the quilt is still signed.

To write the label or sign the quilt you can:

♥ Hand embroider the signature using cross-stitch or outline stitch
♥ Make the label using the writing capabilities of a computerized sewing machine
♥ Quilt in the signature and date with contrasting color of quilting thread
♥ Ink in the signature with a fine-line permanent marker (test for color fastness first!)
♥ Use fabric crayons and paints to make bold, colorful labels
♥ Type the label on solid, light-colored cottons; letters are small, neat, and easy to read
♥ Combine calligraphy and typing on a label: signature and date are inked, while a poem or quote is typed

Signatures on a quilt can be a special way to remember friends and family. Many antique quilts are friendship quilts. The quilt served as an album, its blocks bearing the names, signatures, and well wishes of friends and family. Often the signed quilt was a presentation quilt, given in memory of a special event or as a going-away present.

We can carry on that tradition. Recently a quilting friend of mine made a quilt top for her parents' fiftieth wedding anniversary. The unquilted top was used in place of the guest book. It was spread out on a large table with a selection of permanent pens, fabric markers, and fabric crayons. The guests, including the children, were encouraged to sign the top, write a short note, or draw a picture. The top was then quilted and bound. The quilt is a wonderful keepsake of an exceptional day.

For more information about signing quilts and suitable quotes and poems, see the Bibliography.

CHAPTER 8

Care and Display of Your Quilt

Proper care will ensure that your quilt has a long life. Dirt, chemicals, and light—not age—are the enemies of fabric. How you handle the quilt today will affect its survival.

The information presented in this chapter is for new quilts, not antiques. Pre-1950 quilts require special care to prevent the fabrics from fading or disintegrating. Check with your local quilt store or historical society for help in caring for your old quilt. If you're lucky enough to have an old unquilted top, treat it with respect. A pet peeve of mine is the modernization of old quilts. Don't add new fabric to increase the size of the quilt or cut off part of the quilt because it's the wrong color for your decor. Check with your local quilt store for help in locating antique fabrics to repair or complete the quilt. Use only low-loft batting, preferably cotton or cotton blends, to maintain the antique look. Chose a quilting pattern and style in vogue when the quilt top was made. Don't use machine quilting—older fabrics are weak and may tear from the stitching. "Less is best" when caring for antique textiles. If you are interested in learning more about caring for antique quilts, refer to the Bibliography.

WASHING

Many machine quilters make a habit of washing the quilt when it is completed. The quilt isn't really dirty, but it is soiled from the spray starch, markers, frequent handling, and dirt and oil from the machine. Washing the quilt is not difficult, just a little frightening. I advocate washing the quilt by machine. I wouldn't dream of washing a new quilt in the bath tub. The fabrics were all prewashed by machine; the quilt was all pieced and quilted by machine. Why should I wash it by hand?

Use a large-capacity washer for gentle wash, slow spin, and the highest water level. I use the special fabrics setting on my machine.

For the first wash use tepid water and *no* soap or detergent, which can set markers. I run a single rinse cycle for the first wash.

After the first rinse, wash the quilt using a mild soap, like dishwashing soap, or one of the special soaps designed for quilts. "Mild soap" is the key phrase. *Do not use detergent!* I recommend that you purchase the soap for washing your quilt from your local quilting store or quilting catalog.

After washing the quilt, rinse it in cool water. Chemicals, even the chemicals in soap, can harm the fabric, so it is important to rinse the quilt thoroughly.

Remove the quilt from the machine. Handle it with care. Water adds excess weight to the quilt that can break the piecing or quilting threads.

Lay the quilt on a large flat surface to dry. Do not expose the quilt to direct sunlight or place it on the grass or clothesline. I recommend that you place the quilt on a bedsheet and lay it on a carpeted floor. The sheet and carpeting act like a wick to disperse the moisture and help dry the quilt. To speed things up, use an oscillating fan to keep the air moving. On average it takes about an hour for my quilts to dry.

Never dry clean a quilt. The dye may not be colorfast in dry cleaning.

STORAGE

There is a popular saying about storing quilts: "The best storage is on the bed." That is a great idea, as long as you have only few quilts or an extra bed. But as your quilt collection grows, you are sure to run out of bed space. You will need another way to store your quilts.

Quilts should be stored away from light, especially sunlight. They need to be kept away from extremes in heat and humidity. Do not store quilts in cedar chests or closets, and keep the quilt from touching wooden surfaces.

Fold the quilt right side in. Fold in loose folds, or, if possible, roll the quilt onto a tube. Refold the quilt at least once a year, to prevent permanent creases along the fold

lines. Do not stack the quilts: the weight of three or four can permanently crease the bottom quilt.

There should be at least one layer of washed fabric between the quilt and any wood or cardboard surface. The chemicals used to manufacture wood products can discolor the fabrics.

Never store a quilt in a plastic bag, which restricts the air circulation and dries out the fabrics. A friend of mine placed her cotton lace wedding dress in a plastic bag for safekeeping. On her twenty-fifth anniversary, she opened the plastic bag and found that her dress and veil were disintegrating.

One of the most creative ways I've heard of for storing a quilt came from Kathy Tollefson of Willmar, Minnesota. She makes large pillow cases to match the quilt. The quilts are stored in the matching case, and she can tell the quilts apart at a glance. She also has the best-looking linen closet in town!

At least once a year, treat your quilts to a few weeks of laying flat on a bed. If possible, lay your quilts on an unused bed in a darkened room.

DISPLAY

Quilts have become an art form. Half the fun of owning quilts is displaying them. The problem is that displaying quilts exposes them to light and dirt. Following a few simple rules can ensure that your quilts survive for future generations.

Hanging the Quilt

Use a rod pocket to hang quilts on the wall. Never pin or tack a quilt to the wall. Use a metal or wooden rod or lathe. Finish wooden rods with polyurethane to seal the wood.

Hang the quilt away from direct sunlight or bright spotlights. Most cotton fabrics fade when exposed to natural or artificial light.

Do not hang the quilt near radiators or heat ducts.

Hang the quilt in low-traffic areas, or where it cannot be reached or touched. The oil and perspiration on our hands wreak havoc on textiles. That's why helpers at quilt shows wear white gloves.

Consider sewing two rod pockets at opposite ends of the quilt. The quilt can be rotated 180 degrees to reduce the strain on the edges.

To remove dust from the quilt, use a vacuum cleaner and a fine window screen. Place the screen over the area of the quilt to be cleaned. Vacuum through the screen. The screen protects the fabrics, while the vacuum removes the dust.

Displaying Quilts on Furniture

Quilt racks are a popular method for displaying and storing quilts. The wood should be sealed with polyurethane. Do not display quilts on wood finished with oil or varnish.

Antique cupboards and trunks make excellent showcases for quilts. Antiques and quilts look great together. A few precau-
tions will protect your quilts. The wood and wood finishes in antiques may spot the quilts, so always line any surface that will touch the quilt with washed, natural muslin. Be especially cautious about metal hinges, closures, and nails that can rust or tear the quilt. Fold the quilts loosely and do not stack them over two deep. Refold frequently to prevent fading and permanent creasing.

Draping quilts on tables is charming, but quilts are not good tablecloths. Consider this a temporary display. The part of the quilt on the table top is exposed to dust, dirt, and light. The weight of the quilt falling over the edges of the table can break the stitches or tear the fabrics. The quilt can stretch on the bias and distort the edges. When displaying quilts this way, choose small quilts with low-loft batting. Use circular tables, or place the quilt diagonally on the table top so that the quilt does not hang over a corner. If possible, cover the table top with a clear Plexiglas sheet.

Glossary

Ankle or shank. The part of the sewing machine presser foot that is attached to the machine. Presser feet come in three basic shank types: high, low, or clamp-on. The feet are purchased by shank type.

Appliqué. (verb) To layer and stitch pieces of fabric to a background fabric. Appliqué is used for complex designs requiring intricately shaped pieces.

Backing. The underside of the quilt.

Batting. A layer of fibers between the top and back. Used to give the quilt warmth and loft.

Beard. (verb) The tendency of the batting fiber to slip between the seams or fabric threads of the quilt top. The symptom of bearding is white fibers working through the quilt top or backing. Bearding can ruin a quilt and cannot be corrected. It is caused by a number of factors, including abrasion on the quilt surface and the use of low-thread count fabrics or cotton/polyester blend fabrics in combination with certain synthetic fiber battings.

Bedspread. A bed covering with a drop to the floor. It does not require a dust ruffle. It is often made to cover the pillows, with an allowance for the pillow tuck. Bedspreads should have rounded corners to keep the quilt off the floor and to prevent accidents.

Bias. Refers to a 45-degree angle on fabric. Bias strips are used for binding and some piecing.

Binding. The edge finish on the quilt.

Bleed. (verb) The characteristic of some fabrics and threads to release excess dye when washed. Bleeding may color the wash water or surrounding fabrics. Can also be referred to as "running."

Block. An appliquéd, pieced, or plain square that is repeated throughout the quilt. The block size can vary from a fraction of an inch to 30″ or 40″.

Border. Strips of fabric surrounding the quilt. Can be appliquéd, pieced, or plain, in any width.

Bridge. Part of a sewing machine presser foot, it is the small section of foot in front of the needle.

Comforter. A bed covering with a drop that extends just past the mattress, not over the box springs. Requires a dust ruffle.

Counterpane. Usually refers to a woven blanket, but can mean a quilt. Often refers to a whole-cloth quilt rather than a pieced quilt.

Coverlet. A bed covering with a drop that extends past the box spring but does not touch the floor. Doesn't require a dust ruffle, but having one improves the appearance.

Drop. (noun) The part of the quilt that hangs on the sides of the bed.

Dust Ruffle. A gathered or pleated skirt that fits the box spring of the bed. It extends from the top of the box spring to the floor.

Feed dogs. A sewing machine part, they are the metal or plastic teeth that move the fabric. The presser foot rests on the feed dogs.

Grainline. Refers to the direction of the threads that make fabric. The grainline runs either from selvage to selvage across the fabric (crosswise grain) or along the length of the fabric (lengthwise grain).

Lap robe. A small quilt approximately $45'' \times 60''$ used in much the same way as an afghan, for additional warmth when sitting or napping.

Lattice. See sashing.

Loft. The thickness of the batting.

Medallion. A quilt set: a large central block surrounded by borders. Can be appliquéd, pieced, or put together using a combination of techniques.

Piece. (verb) To stitch fabrics together to make a quilt top or back. Pieced blocks tend to be geometric designs made of straight lines and gentle curves.

Pillow sham. A pillow cover usually made to match a quilt or bed covering.

Pillow tuck. The allowance for tucking a small portion of the quilt under the pillows. Used when the quilt rather than a pillow sham is to cover the pillows. The tuck allowance is usually $10''$.

Quilt. (noun) A minimum of two layers of fabric stitched together. It can also refer to two layers of fabric with batting between them. (verb) To stitch the layers of the quilt together.

Quilt-as-you-go. A method of quilting a block at a time. The quilted blocks are joined to form the complete quilt. Often used with machine quilting because it reduces the amount of fabric on the machine.

Sashing. Also called lattice. Sashings are the strips of fabric separating the blocks. Sashings can be pieced, plain, or appliquéd, and can vary in size from a fraction of an inch to $12''$ or $18''$.

Set. (noun) The way the blocks, sashing, and borders are arranged to make the quilt top. Common sets include side-by-side, alternating with plain or companion block, or set with sashing. The blocks can be straight-set or diagonally-set.

Selvage. The tightly woven edge on fabrics, usually about $\frac{1}{4}''$ wide. It should be cut off prior to using the fabric.

Sheering. The movement of warp and weft thread when the fabric is pulled on the bias. On the positive side, sheering makes it possible to straighten skewed grainlines. The disadvantage is that it can cause diagonal folds between quilting lines.

Sole. The part of a sewing machine presser foot that rests on the feed dogs. On some machines the ankle or shank is fixed to the machine, and only the sole is changed.

Stencil. A paper or plastic pattern used for tracing the quilting pattern. Stencils also can be made from metal or cardboard.

Template. A paper or plastic pattern used for piecing.

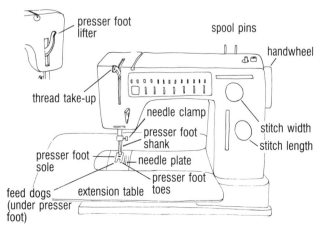

Tie. A knot or bow used to hold the layers of the quilt together. It replaces quilting.

Toes. The curved ends on the front of the presser foot.

Top. The right side of the quilt.

Trapunto. Extra stuffing is forced into small sections of the quilting design, giving a raised or relief effect. Popular in the first half of the 1800s, trapunto is frequently done in feathered designs and floral motifs. Well-done trapunto has evenly stuffed spaces, without any scarring from the entry of the excess stuffing.

Trapunto now is being done with a technique called "yarning." A special needle threaded with white or colored yarn pulls the yarn into the space between the top and backing of the quilt. The yarn is cut close to the fabric and the raw ends worked into the space. This method leaves no scars on the fabric and can be worked from the top or back side of the quilt.

Whole-cloth quilt. A quilt top made from a single piece of fabric. It may have seams but should appear to be a single unseamed piece of material. Quilting is the only stitching on this quilt. Often the quilts were trapuntoed.

Resource List

This list of businesses is by no means a complete list of all the reputable quilting stores or mail-order businesses. It is a list of those businesses I have dealt with and found to be courteous and helpful. I have listed the specialties of each, along with the mailing address and the most recent catalog price.

Access to Recreation, Inc.
2509 E, Thousand Oaks Blvd., Suite 430
Thousand Oaks, CA 91362
1-800-634-4351

Source for the spring-band scissor.

Anderson's Wheelchair, Inc.
1117 Second Street S.W.
Rochester, Minnesota 55902

Source for the spring-band scissor.

Cabin Fever Calicoes
P.O. Box 550106
Atlanta, GA 05538

Send $2.50 for catalog. Cabin Fever Calicoes carries fabrics, including specialty fabrics for Baltimore album quilts. They also have fabric packs that take the work out of matching fabrics. They handle battings, books, patterns, and a large selection of notions and rotary tools.

The Cloth Cupboard
(Home of The Cotton Club)
P.O. Box 2263
Boise, ID 83701
(208) 345-5567 Tues–Fri
    10:30 A.M.–4:30 P.M.

Send SASE with 50¢ postage for current product list. Carries many quilting notions, including threads, fabrics, and batting. This is my source for the $\frac{1}{16}''$ punch.

Clotilde Inc.
1909 S.W. First Ave.
Fort Lauderdale, FL 33315-2100

Send $2 for catalog. Clotilde specializes in sewing notions for all types of sewing—markers, scissors, cutters, patterns, rulers, and pressing aids.

Come Quilt with Me
P.O. Box 021063
Brooklyn, NY 11202-0023

Wide selection of quilting supplies and books, but not fabrics. Supplies include markers, rulers, batts, scissors, patterns, and videos.

Enrichments
145 Tower Drive
P.O. Box 579
Hinsdale, IL 60521
1-800-323-5547

A source for the spring band scissor

G Street Fabrics Mail Order Service
12240 Wilkins Ave.
Rockville, MD 20852
Phone (301) 231-8960

Not only does G Street carry quilting fabric, they also have a large selection of other fabrics, like 100 colors of Ultrasuede and 80 colors of Facile.

Keepsake Quilting
32 Dover Street
P.O. Box 1459
Meredith, NH 03252

Send $1 for the catalog. Keepsake carries a large selection of quilting supplies, including books, patterns, fabrics, rulers, and cutting tools. They offer fabric medleys (the fabrics are matched for you).

Nancy's Notions
P.O. Box 63
Beaver Dam, WI 53916-0683
Phone (800) 765-0690.

Call for a free catalog. Nancy's carries a large selection of sewing notions, including threads, cutting tools, rulers, pressing aids, markers, and other sewing notions.

Quilting Books Unlimited
1158 Prairie
Aurora, IL 60506
Phone (708) 406-0237

Send $1 for book list. Specializes in books, books, and more books. Its ad states it has every quilting book currently in print, and after dealing with them, I believe it. It is a book buyer's dream.

Quilts and Other Comforts
PO Box 94-231
Wheatridge, CO 80034

Wide selection of quilting supplies, including books, patterns, and fabrics, also markers, rulers, and cutting tools.

The Sewing Emporium
1079 Third Ave.
Chula Vista, CA 92010

The Sewing Emporium specializes in hard-to-find presser feet. They also handle a large selection of machine accessories, parts, even cabinets and commercial machines.

Thimbleberries Inc.
205 Jefferson St
Hutchinson, MN 55350
612-587-3944

This pattern company has two of my quilt patterns, Fairfield Stars, and Atlanta Garden.

Treadle Art
258334 Narbonne Ave, Suite I
Lomita, CA 90717
Phone (213) 534-5122

Send $1 for catalog. Treadle Art is a supplier of threads and notions for machine-embroidery enthusiasts. They carry a wide selection of machine threads, along with other notions, patterns, and books.

Bibliography

Beyer, Jinny. *Patchwork Portfolio*. McLean, Va.: EPM Publications, 1989.

———. *The Quilter's Album of Blocks and Borders*. McLean, Va.: EPM Publications, 1986.

Clawson, Eileen. *Simply Elegant Machine Quilts*. Huntsville, Utah: Elegant Design, 1984.

Dietrich, Mimi. *Happy Endings: Finishing the Edges of Your Quilt*. Bothell, Wash.: That Patchwork Place, 1987.

Dodson, Jackie. *Know Your Sewing Machine*. Radnor, Pa.: Chilton Book Company, 1988.

Fanning, Robbie, and Tony Fanning. *The Complete Book of Machine Quilting*. Radnor, Pa.: Chilton Book Company, 1980.

———. *The Complete Book of Machine Embroidery*. Radnor, Pa.: Chilton Book Company, 1986.

Fons, Marianne. *Fine Feathers: A Quilter's Guide to Customizing Traditional Feather Quilting Designs*. Lafayette, Calif.: C & T Publishing, 1988.

Hargrave, Harriet. *Heirloom Machine Quilting*. Lafayette, Calif.: C & T Publishing, 1990.

Hughes, Trudie. *Template-Free Quiltmaking*. Bothell, Wash.: That Patchwork Place, 1986.

James, Michael. *The Quiltmaker's Handbook: A Guide to Design and Construction*. Englewood Cliffs, N.J.: Prentice-Hall, 1978.

Johannah, Barbara. *Continuous Curve Quilting: Machine Quilting the Pieced Quilt*. Menlo Park, Calif.: Pride of the Forest, 1980.

Lehman, Bonnie, and Judy Martin. *Taking the Math Out of Making Patchwork Quilts*. Wheatridge, Colo.: Moon Over the Mountain Publishing, 1981.

McCloskey, Marsha, and Nancy Martin. *A Dozen Variables*. Bothell, Wash.: That Patchwork Place, 1987.

McKelvey, Susan. *Friendship's Offering Techniques and Inspiration for Writing on Quilts*. Lafayette, Calif.: C & T Publishing, 1990.

Martin, Nancy J. *Back to Square One*. Bothell, Wash.: That Patchwork Place, 1988.

Miles, Elaine. *Guiding Stars: A Sampler of Quilters' Favorite Quotations*. San Pedro, Calif.: R. and E. Miles, 1989.

O'Bryant Puentes, Nancy. *First Aid for Family Quilts*. Wheatridge, Colo.: Moon Over the Mountain Publishing, 1986.

Rodgers, Sue H. *Trapunto: The Handbook of Stuffed Quilting*. Wheatridge, Colo.: Leman Publications, 1990.

Saunders, Jan. *Teach Yourself to Sew Better: A Step-by-Step Guide to Your Sewing Machine*. Radnor, Pa.: Chilton Book Company, 1990.

Shirer, Marie. *Quilt Settings*. Wheatridge, Colo.: Moon Over the Mountain Publishing, 1989.

Index